The Future of Children

PRINCETON-BROOKINGS

VOLUME 20   NUMBER 1   Spring 2010

Transition to Adulthood

Introducing the Issue

Gordon Berlin, Frank F. Furstenberg Jr., and Mary C. Waters

That the schedule for coming of age has been rather sharply revised both in the United States and more broadly throughout the industrialized world is by now widely recognized. Over the past decade, especially, the mass media have trumpeted the findings of a growing body of research showing that young people are taking longer to leave home, attain economic independence, and form families of their own than did their peers half a century ago. The forces behind this new timetable have been evident for several decades, but social science researchers, much less policy makers, were slow to recognize just how profound the change has been. A trickle of studies during the 1980s about the prolongation of young adulthood grew to a steady stream during the 1990s and then to a torrent during the first decade of the new millennium.[1] Now that researchers have shown how and why the timetable for becoming an adult has altered, policy makers must rethink whether the social institutions that once successfully educated, trained, and supported young adults are up to the task today.

Changes in the coming-of-age schedule are, in fact, nothing new. A century or more ago, the transition to adulthood was also a protracted affair. In an agriculture-based economy, it took many young adults some time to gain the wherewithal to leave home and form a family. Formal education was typically brief because most jobs were still related to farming, the trades, or the growing manufacturing sector. By their teens, most youth were gainfully employed, but they frequently remained at home for a time, contributing income to their families and building resources to enter marriage and form a family.

By contrast, after World War II, with opportunities for good jobs abundant, young Americans transitioned to adult roles quickly. In 1950, fewer than half of all Americans completed high school, much less attended college. Well-paying, often unionized jobs with benefits were widely available to males. The marriage rush and baby boom era at mid-century was stimulated not only by a longing to settle down after the war years but also by generous new government programs to help integrate veterans back into society.

Today young adults take far longer to reach economic and social maturity than their contemporaries did five or six decades ago. In large part, this shift is attributable to the expansion of higher education beginning in the late 1960s. Employers have become

Gordon Berlin is president of MDRC. Frank F. Furstenberg Jr. is the Zellerbach Family Professor of Sociology at the University of Pennsylvania. Mary C. Waters is the M. E. Zukerman Professor of Sociology at Harvard University.

increasingly reluctant to hire young people without educational credentials. Failing to complete high school all but relegates individuals to a life of permanent penury; even completing high school is hardly enough to ensure reasonable prospects. Like it or not, at least some postsecondary education is increasingly necessary. In short, education has become an ever more potent source of social stratification, dividing the haves and the have-nots, a theme in this volume to which we will return.

Many observers, especially in the mass media, worry that this new timetable for adulthood has created a growing sense of entitlement and a lingering pattern of dependency.

The boom in higher education is not the only reason why young adults are taking more time to gain independence from their families and establish themselves in adult roles. The schedule for growing up, no doubt, has been affected by the lengthening of the life span over the past century. Most young adults today can expect to live into their late seventies, a decade longer than their counterparts even fifty years ago. It makes sense to continue investing into the third and even fourth decades of life when one can expect to live another fifty years or more.

Cultural changes, such as the post-1960s shift in sexual attitudes and practices, have also slowed what was once a rush into adult roles. Fifty years ago, premarital sex was still highly

stigmatized. Although the stigma did not deter many young couples from breaching the norms, marriage served as a safety net in the event of a premarital pregnancy. Today, most young people expect to have sex before marriage and have the means to prevent unwanted childbearing. Their contraceptive efforts are still imperfect, but the point is that they need not marry to have sex, and they will not necessarily become pregnant when they do.

The past several decades, then, have witnessed a big change in how and when youth take on adult roles—to put it another way, another notable shift in the "normal" pattern of moving from adolescence to adulthood. Although today's delayed schedule is reminiscent of the pattern a century ago, however, the two are fundamentally different. Today, young people (unless they are the children of recent immigrants) rarely contribute earnings to the household; by and large, they are either fully or partially beholden to their parents for support while they complete their schooling and find a foothold in the labor force. Typically, they defer marriage in favor of cohabitation even when they do leave the natal household.

Although today's young adults and their parents value independence highly, both tolerate and even endorse a slower schedule for attaining economic and social maturity. In effect, what is becoming normal, if not normative, is that the age of eighteen, or even twenty-one, has lost its significance as a marker of adult status. The transition to adulthood is drawn out over a span of nearly a decade and consists of a series of smaller steps rather than a single swift and coordinated one. Moreover, the social construction of adulthood seems to rely much less on the traditional demographic markers—home

leaving, full-time work, and family formation—and more on personal psychological
self-assessments of "maturity." At any rate,
the traditional markers do not any longer
stand for attaining adulthood.

Many observers, especially in the mass media,
worry that this new timetable for adulthood
has created a growing sense of entitlement
and a lingering pattern of dependency. Much
of the evidence, however, points to a different conclusion: attaining adult roles (as
measured by independence from the natal
family, union formation, and parenthood) is
simply more difficult than it was, especially
three or four decades ago. In fact, the vast
majority of young adults in their late teens
and early twenties are not at leisure—they are
working, going to school, or doing both at the
same time. Many unemployed and underedu-
cated young people are desperate to work but
cannot secure stable employment or make
enough money to live on their own. Although
they probably do receive support from their
families during this period of semi-autonomy,
most do not exhibit the signs of entitlement
that are frequently ascribed to them.

The nation's young adults are highly unlikely
to return any time soon to the schedule for
growing up that was normative among their
parents and grandparents. The conditions
driving the shift in the schedule are likely to
be long-lasting. Policy makers must therefore
begin to rethink and renovate the social institutions that were suited to the past, a time
when the age of eighteen or twenty-one signi-
fied something different than it does today.

Understanding the New Schedule
Concern about the mismatch between the
new realities of coming of age and the social
institutions that once successfully supported
young people moving toward adulthood gave

rise, in 1999, to the MacArthur Network on
Adult Transitions and Public Policy. The
Network, a team of twelve researchers from
diverse social science disciplines, began its
work by assessing the demographic, economic,
sociological, and psychological evidence on
adult transitions to learn what had changed
and why. In a series of recent publications, the
Network has documented that the changes in
the timing, sequencing, and even attainment
of adult roles have indeed been substantial and
that they are affecting young adults in varying
socioeconomic circumstances quite differently.[2] Drawing on both quantitative and qualitative data in the initial phase of its work, the
Network reported that young adults between
the ages of eighteen and thirty-four are
employing some familiar and some different
strategies than those that their parents and
grandparents used to make a successful
transition to adult work and family roles. In
particular, young adults and their families are
much more skeptical about the wisdom of
early transitions to work and marriage, even
taking into account geographical, religious,
and socioeconomic differences. The Network
also discovered that gender differences in the
timing of adult transitions had virtually
disappeared.[3] By contrast, differences by
social class have, if anything, become more
pronounced.

These changes coincided with and were
reinforced by a wave of immigration during
the 1980s that attracted many young adult
immigrants as well as immigrant families to
the United States. These immigrants have
imported traditional family practices while
simultaneously demonstrating a high level of
adaptation to American ways. First-generation
immigrants often arrive as young adults—the
peak age period for immigration. Social-
ized in their sending society, they enter the
United States seeking work and are often cut

off from their parents and extended family. They achieve independence very young and are more likely to be in the labor force than native-born Americans of the same age and educational background. Second-generation immigrants—native-born children of immigrants—are more likely to live at home as young adults than are comparable natives, and they achieve higher levels of education than natives of similar socioeconomic backgrounds. As a result they have more extended transitions to adulthood than both their parents and comparable native-born Americans.

Network researchers then turned to the challenging task of examining some of the institutions that house and serve young adults—the family, higher education, the workplace, the community, and, for a group of especially vulnerable youth, the juvenile justice, foster care, and related systems. The aim of the second phase of the research program was to assess the ability of each of these institutions to support young adults in their quest for economic independence, intimacy, and civic responsibility—goals widely shared among both young adults and their parents. This volume of *The Future of Children* provides a summary of research findings to date and suggests policy steps that could make these institutions more effective.

How Well Do Traditional Supports Work?

One important if not unexpected finding of the Network was that existing institutions work much better for affluent young adults than they do for most others. Family resources and the opportunities they afford have become more central to educational attainment. And, with educational attainment an increasingly potent predictor of economic success and stable family life, growing levels of inequality have created an ever larger

chasm between the affluent third (roughly corresponding to college graduates) and the rest of the population. The economic burden on families, particularly those in the bottom two-thirds of the income distribution, has been growing far more rapidly than their capacity to undertake a longer and more expensive period of investment in their children's futures. Increasingly, parents are being asked to take on the costs of education, health care, and, often, support of children in their early twenties (and often later).

Although parents of all social strata seem to understand and accept the new schedule for growing up, middle- and lower-income parents are ill-equipped to handle the costs entailed, and the result is a sharply tilted playing field for young adult development. The new demands of supporting young adults for longer periods create impossible burdens for lower-income households and pose serious problems for all parents who must balance the need to make increased financial (and emotional) investments in their adult children against the need to ensure their own retirements. This privatized approach to investment in the nation's young is quite different from the accepted public approach to education for children below the age of eighteen.

Health care represents a glaring example of how the nation's public arrangements simply do not work for young adults who follow the new schedule for coming of age. Today's health care system more or less protects low-income children up to age eighteen, or in some instances twenty-one, but it does nothing for older youth who lack work-based or school-based health insurance. All but the most affluent parents are frustrated in their efforts to fill the health insurance gap. The pending health care bill, if passed by

Congress and signed by the president, will go a long way toward correcting the problem.

The new public-private approach to supporting higher education is equally problematic. Parents of modest means are hard-pressed to help their children obtain a college education. Although, as described in several articles in this volume, the nation makes both grants and loans available to low-income students, the process for applying for that money—and for finding out how large the grant or loan would be—is complex, intimidating, and cumbersome. As a result, many low-income students simply do not apply. Others end up borrowing and eventually owe considerable amounts of money or try to put themselves through school by working. These two options may not represent a problem for low- and moderate-income families whose children are well-prepared for college. But many youth from these families grow up in areas with poorly functioning school systems and are ill-prepared to make the transition to college. Without adequate economic and social support, they may flounder in the transition to college, creating a nightmare scenario where they fail to get a degree that enables them to repay their educational debts. Although the educational burdens on upper-income families are considerable, these parents are better equipped to help meet the costs of higher education, and their children are better prepared to succeed in college. Here too recent efforts to amend the student financial aid system and to increase Pell Grants and other sources of support could help to address these challenges for low- and moderate-income families.

Once students arrive at college, they tend to receive strikingly different levels of support depending on their economic background. Most four-year residential institutions, which are largely populated by relatively affluent youth, are extremely well-suited to assist young adults in transition. They provide orientations for incoming students and their families, an array of services and counseling should students encounter problems, mentoring delivered by older students, recreational and extracurricular programs, health and mental health services, and, of course, residences. Students who get off track receive academic and emotional guidance. Many of these colleges and universities even offer career counseling and job placement for graduates. Furthermore, these institutions are conveniently linked to postgraduate education programs that are, generally speaking, similarly well-designed for youth in their mid- and late-twenties.

By contrast, the two-year community colleges that less affluent students are likely to attend are typically bare-bones institutions stretched thin by a myriad of demands and insufficient resources. Although potentially useful portals of entry for students hoping to move on to a four-year college, a skilled job, or a semi-profession that requires an associate's degree or a licensing exam, many two-year colleges lack the most basic amenities offered by a four-year residential college or even a four-year commuter school. Campus life is frequently limited, and the services afforded are meager or nonexistent. Students, often unprepared and overcommitted by outside obligations, pose serious challenges to the sometimes underpaid, overburdened faculty and administrators. Rather than serving as beacons of opportunity, too many of these two-year colleges are revolving doors through which students wander aimlessly in search of future direction. Indeed, research supported by the U.S. Department of Education shows that close to half of students who enter a community college do not earn a degree and are not enrolled in any other postsecondary institution six years later.

In collaboration with MDRC, Network researchers undertook an assessment of how community colleges could realize their mission of providing academic training to allow students to get a degree or secure a job that might be otherwise unattainable without special training. Analysts examined several programs aimed at improving student outcomes, including changes in instructional practices, enhancements to student services, and increases in financial support. Although not all the programs were successful, some led to significant improvements in students' academic performance and persistence. The findings, as presented in the article in this volume by Thomas Brock, suggest that policy makers and educators need not accept high dropout rates as a given. Rather, by making changes in institutional practices— including new forms of flexible financial aid that incentivize and reward students who get good grades and complete courses, as well as innovative "learning community" programs that integrate courses and create study peer groups—they can boost the odds that more young people will earn college degrees and succeed in the labor market.

During the middle decades of the twentieth century and extending through the Vietnam War, military service represented an attractive possibility for youth who were not college bound. It provided, as Ryan Kelty, Meredith Kleykamp, and David R. Segal report in their article in this volume, an effective bridge from high school to work for a large number of young men who lacked vocational direction. Although the military continues today to provide a supportive environment for men and women who want to serve their country, leave home, and get training, it is increasingly

meant to provide a military career rather than a transition to the civilian labor market. Smaller and more select than the draft-era military, today's military is disinclined to afford training to youth who may exhibit educational deficits. Other youth-oriented institutions could learn much from the way the military trains and supports young adults, but the military itself is no longer a significant remedial institution for poorly functioning young adults.

Countless studies have assessed and evaluated the effect of service corps of various types. One rigorous study concluded that they can and often do play a useful role.

From the Depression-era's Civilian Conservation Corps, to the Great Society's Peace Corps and VISTA, to the 1980s state and urban conservation corps, and to the 1990s Corporation for National and Community Service and its dramatic expansion in the Edward M. Kennedy Serve America Act of 2009, policy makers have experimented episodically with institutions that serve the community while providing training and experience for young people who are unemployable or who simply want to gain skills, serve the community, or move on to independent living. Countless studies have assessed and evaluated the effect of service corps of various types. One rigorous study concluded that they can and often do play a useful role in providing time and space for young people to gain experience, acquire useful work skills and direction, and build a sense of commitment to the larger community. If such results can be extended and built on by the Serve America Act, community service programs could begin to reach the scale needed to provide a new "institution" to help meet the needs of youth making the extended transition to adulthood.

Often coming as a year-long experience between high school and college or work, or as a year off during or after college, youth service programs could be a valuable bridging program with double social utility. Through these programs, young people do important work in their local communities—in hospitals, schools, and other public and nonprofit settings— and gain many experiences needed to make a successful transition to adulthood. In the long-standing debate about the pros and cons of mandatory national service for all, the passage of the Serve America Act may signal a commitment to build a voluntary, as opposed to a mandatory, system of opportunities for a diverse group of young people. This signal notwithstanding, unless concrete steps are taken to build the capacity of service models that work, to collect evidence of their ongoing effectiveness, and to build a record of their accomplishments—much as the WPA's accomplishments were documented and remain for all to see in the nation's parks and other structures—history suggests that expansion could be followed by contraction. After all, it was only a few short years ago that the Corporation for National and Community Service survived a near-death experience in Congress. But this time, getting it right may matter more than it has in the past, given the dearth of institutions to help meet the demands of a lengthened transition to adulthood.

Some proportion of young adults—those exiting foster care; youth in special education or with physical, emotional, or cognitive limitations; the homeless; and the many exiting jail or prison—are at much higher risk in the transition to adulthood. Because these populations often overlap, however, it is hard to estimate their number precisely. Most experts believe that the share of youth who are at risk of encountering serious problems is significant. The vast majority come from poor and near-poor families that are disproportionately African American and Latino.

Much of the Network's attention has been focused on the very expensive systems that serve these vulnerable populations as children—foster care, juvenile justice, special education, and social security disability. No easy or cost-free solutions are available to help these youth improve their prospects as young adults. Early detection of youths with problems, better schooling, and better alternatives to foster care and incarceration could reduce the share that enters early adulthood without the requisite skills to take advantage of educational opportunities and eventually find good jobs. But even with the best schooling and most effective preventive and ameliorative services, another challenge would be how to integrate the diverse systems that serve vulnerable youth. In addition, these youth often lack the family supports that other young people have as they age into young adulthood. The failure of existing institutions to adapt to current realities and the dearth of new institutions to serve young people without family supports are huge problems, as many of these young adults at risk will face lifelong problems that must be paid for one way or another.

The Changing Nature of Young Adulthood
The premise of this issue of *The Future of Children* is that the nation's public policy and its social institutions fail to reflect the realities

of the new transition to adulthood—and thus do not adequately serve the needs of young adults. Although each article in the volume opens with a full summary, in this section we briefly highlight some of the findings we think are the most important.

Overview

Richard Settersten of Oregon State University and Barbara Ray of Hired Pen, inc., open the issue by surveying the changes that have taken place over the past few decades in the timing and sequencing of young adulthood. They describe the later age at marriage, the rise in the number of young people living at home with their parents into their twenties, and the longer period of time young people are staying in school. They stress that these changes create strains not only on the families of young adults but also on the institutions—colleges and universities, the military, youth service organizations, and the work setting—that have traditionally supported them. Noting that these institutions are not designed for this new pattern of life choices, Settersten and Ray raise the question of whether the risks and costs newly associated with the early adult years should be borne privately by families or publicly by government. They also point out that despite the problems it creates, the lengthening transition to adulthood creates opportunities for some young people, especially those from more affluent backgrounds, to explore careers and lifestyles before settling into traditional adult roles.

Immigration

One of the most notable changes in American young adulthood is a demographic one. Young adults today are remarkably ethnically and racially diverse, owing in no small part to the enormous volume of immigration during the past four decades that has swelled the ranks of first- and second-generation immigrants and children of immigrants. Rubén Rumbaut and Golnaz Komaie of the University of California–Irvine document these demographic changes and explore the ways in which generation and national origin shape the experience of young adulthood. The first generation of immigrants, having arrived in this country as young adults themselves, are the least likely of all young adults in the United States aged eighteen to thirty-four to live in their parents' households. They are also the least likely to be attending school, but the most likely to be working full time, to be married, and to have children. By contrast, the second generation is the most likely to live in the natal household and to be attending school between eighteen and thirty-four; they are by far the least likely to be married and to have children. In addition to these vast differences between the generations, immigrant groups also experience gaps in social, economic, and legal status that are even greater than the gaps between native whites and blacks. Sizable segments of immigrant youth, especially the undocumented and the less-educated poor, face structural barriers in their transitions to adulthood, and the authors discuss possible policy options to deal with those barriers.

Family Changes

Frank Furstenberg of the University of Pennsylvania surveys the important family changes that characterize the transition to adulthood. He notes that both patterns of family formation and the shape of the family have changed often in American history and that the period often used as a benchmark for measuring family change—that immediately after World War II—was in reality an anomaly in the long sweep of family history, notable for its very early pattern of attaining such markers of adulthood as employment, marriage, and childbearing. It should therefore come as no surprise that U.S. family formation patterns today differ dramatically from those of fifty years ago. Young adults are on average marrying later, and a substantial fraction, not at all. Cohabitation has become increasingly acceptable as an alternative to marriage, and the average age of childbearing has risen. Furstenberg documents two major trends in these family formation patterns. First, gender equality has increased, with men and women growing more alike in the age at which they leave home, marry, and have children. And, second, class inequality has grown substantially, with lower-income young people less likely to follow an orderly and predictable sequence of education, full-time employment, home-leaving, marriage, and parenthood. Higher-income young adults are more likely to follow the traditional sequence, but they take longer to complete it and often must go through an extended period of financial dependence on parents while they complete their education. The share of young adults residing with parents has risen since the 1960s, when adult transitions started at an earlier age. Furstenberg argues that the popular media often portray these changes as objectionable for parents and young adult children, but the few studies to examine this question find that parents and young adults accommodate well to the new schedule.

As a result of delays in establishing themselves financially, young people tend to depend longer on their families of origin. Although all industrialized countries have experienced this same pattern, the U.S. welfare state is relatively undeveloped, meaning that the burden of supporting young adults falls more heavily on American families. Furstenberg calls for further research on how families are managing these new demands and warns that the need for active parenting extending into their children's twenties and even thirties may discourage people from becoming parents in the first place, leading to a trend toward lower fertility, especially among more affluent families.

Second Chances for High School Dropouts

The American labor market has little to offer workers who do not complete high school, and at least some college is increasingly required to attain a well-paying job. Yet somewhere between 9 and 16 percent of young people aged sixteen to twenty-four have not completed high school. Over the past several decades a variety of "second-chance" programs have been developed to help dropouts finish high school or obtain a General Educational Development (GED) credential and get a foothold in the labor market. Dan Bloom of MDRC reviews the types of programs available, as well as their efficacy, and then considers their implications for the transition to adulthood. Although he notes that it is difficult to prove that the collapse of the job market for high school dropouts over the past several decades caused the steep decline in the share of dropouts who marry—from 68 percent of men aged twenty-two to thirty-two in 1970 to only 26 percent in 2007—the two trends certainly reflect each other. Bloom surveys eleven major programs intended for young dropouts, dividing them into three categories—work programs, training and education programs, and mandatory, welfare-based programs for teen mothers. All have been evaluated using rigorous random-assignment techniques. Though the evaluation findings are mixed, they show at least short-term modest effects for many of the programs. Bloom also cites descriptive studies showing that young people who obtain a GED tend to do relatively poorly in the labor market, in part because they are much less likely to pursue postsecondary education than those who get a high school degree. Based on these findings, Bloom proposes three focuses for future research and policy: strengthening programs for youth who voluntarily seek to continue their education or find jobs, including building tighter links between GED preparation programs and postsecondary occupational certificate programs; identifying strategies to engage disconnected youth who are unlikely to volunteer for programs such as the Job Corps; and analyzing local systems to support disconnected youth.

Improving Higher Education Outcomes
Even though the value of a college education has increased markedly over the past forty years, with college graduates earning 1.8 times as much as high school graduates, college graduation rates have not improved in decades, largely because students' rates of persistence to a degree have not improved. The five-year college graduation rate is 60 percent at four-year colleges, but only 32 percent at community colleges. The low community college graduation rate is a growing concern, because more than a third of all college students attend two-year colleges. Meanwhile, access to college has improved substantially, with the share of women on campus catching up to and surpassing that of men and the share of nonwhite college students doubling in the past two decades.

Thomas Brock of MDRC outlines these trends in college attendance and persistence and reviews the research on interventions aimed at improving college outcomes for young adults. The changing nature of young adulthood, with more youth combining work, school, and parenthood, results in a diverse college student population—one that is older, more part time, and more likely to attend episodically than has been conventional until

recently. Indeed, Brock reports that only 27 percent of current undergraduates are "traditional students" who attend full time immediately following high school and who rely on parents for financial support. Of all undergraduates in 1999–2000, 28 percent were highly nontraditional—in their twenties or older, combining work with school, and raising children. And nontraditional students are much less likely than traditional students to persist to a degree. Brock surveys a number of interventions that have been evaluated by rigorous random-assignment design. Among the more promising interventions are remedial education courses that foster more student engagement and belonging on campus, enhanced student services such as counseling and support, and performance-based scholarships that tie financial incentives to successful course completion. Brock concludes that many of the interventions show modest positive effects and that performance-based scholarships show pronounced positive effects. Although many people believe that making federal financial aid more effective will also increase persistence, surprisingly little systematic research has addressed that question. One clear finding is that simplifying the application form for federal financial aid (FAFSA) has a substantial payoff in increasing college enrollment.

The Labor Market
One of the key markers of the transition to adulthood, and arguably one necessary for success, is finding stable and well-paying employment. Dramatic changes in the labor market in recent decades, however, have complicated young people's prospects of finding such employment. In their survey of the labor market and the transition to adulthood, Sheldon Danziger and David Ratner of the University of Michigan contend that young people now must struggle to attain

financial independence—a development with implications in other areas. Although it cannot be proved, for example, that the delay in achieving financial independence has caused delays in leaving home and in marrying, these trends are correlated.

Even though the value of a college education has increased markedly over the past forty years, college graduation rates have not improved in decades, largely because students' rates of persistence to a degree have not improved.

Danziger and Ratner stress that gender plays an important part in the story of the labor market. The prospects of young men, especially less-educated young men, have declined precipitously, while more young women are working and their earnings have increased relative both to inflation and to the earnings of young men. The median annual earnings (in constant 2007 dollars) of men between the ages of twenty-five and thirty-four who worked at some time during the year fell 21 percent between 1973 and 2007, whereas the median earnings of women rose 62 percent. Job turnover—what economists call "churning"—has also increased dramatically. The fraction of individuals in jobs lasting less than one year has risen faster for younger than for older workers. The share of workers in longer-term jobs declined precipitously for men, while

holding steady for women. Employment for men with the least education also fell during the past few decades, with the sharpest declines for African American men with less than a high school education. Because of the increasing labor market returns to education and the importance of postsecondary education for employment, Danziger and Ratner recommend programs that increase educational attainment, including early childhood education and second-chance programs such as those described by Dan Bloom. They also support raising the minimum wage and expanding the earned income tax credit (EITC), both of which could raise the incomes of workers at the lower end of the distribution.

Civic Participation

In their article on civic participation, Constance Flanagan of Penn State University and Peter Levine of Tufts University reinforce a theme running throughout the volume— the ways in which class, race, and immigrant status shape very different patterns in young adulthood. They find that more affluent young people are more likely to be civically engaged than the less affluent, both in terms of political activity such as voting and in terms of volunteering. This civic divide is a consequence both of cumulative disadvantage in the pre-adult years and of a dearth of institutional opportunities for young adults who are not in college. The authors argue that young adulthood is a critical period for forming political beliefs and behaviors, and they trace the ways in which an elongated transition to adulthood might provide opportunities for increased civic engagement among young people. They also trace generational differences in political attitudes and behaviors and suggest that young people in more recent cohorts may be shifting to more active engagement.

The Military

Although only a small fraction of U.S. young adults serve in the nation's all-volunteer military, young adults are very much the focus of the military, because the majority of military personnel fall into this age group. In their article on young adulthood and the military, Ryan Kelty of Washington College, Meredith Kleykamp of the University of Kansas, and David R. Segal of the University of Maryland explain that in periods of mass conscription, such as during World War II, the military is for most people a hiatus between adolescence and adulthood. By contrast, today's all-volunteer military is more likely to be a period of active transition into young adulthood and, often, into a career in the military.

The military's new, more career-oriented system has led it to implement a number of policies to cope with the family needs of young adults. Indeed Kelty, Kleykamp, and Segal document the ample material support the military provides to young adults—reasonable wages, generous in-kind transfers, free medical care, housing, educational benefits, and training designed to promote responsible membership in intimate relationships and the wider community. As a result, the pattern of family formation in the military is earlier and more stable than it is among civilians of the same age. The majority of enlisted personnel are parents, and the racial differences in family formation that exist among civilians do not characterize the military. No black-white gap in marriage exists among military personnel. The transition to adulthood, including economic independence from parents, is thus much more stable and orderly for military personnel.

Kelty, Kleykamp, and Segal note that much about what the military does cannot easily be replicated in the wider society. As an institution, the military has unique control over young adult behavior through its code of conduct. It also restricts who can enlist, barring openly homosexual personnel, restricting the occupations available to women within the military, drawing recruits who have high school diplomas, and refusing to enlist high school dropouts or people with criminal records. The authors also note that the military in a time of war holds dangers for young adults, most especially in the long-run effects of injuries, both psychological and physical, from the war and the long-run effects of the physical and symbolic violence women experience in a male-dominated institution.

Justice System and Social Services

All the articles in this volume stress the varying needs of young adults and the ways in which young people with fewer financial resources, less education, and less support from their families of origin have a harder time than their more affluent peers in making a successful transition to independent adulthood. The point holds particularly true in the case of vulnerable youth—defined by D. Wayne Osgood and E. Michael Foster of Penn State University and Mark E. Courtney of the University of Washington as those involved in the social service, health, and justice systems in childhood and adolescence. The authors survey the special challenges faced by youth involved in the mental health system, the foster care system, the juvenile justice system, the criminal justice system, special education, and the health care system, as well as runaway and homeless youth. Although noting that these populations overlap and that many young people need services from multiple systems, Osgood, Foster, and Courtney show that the categorical ways in which state and federal funding for these systems are designed often keep these issues compartmentalized and prevent service providers from seeing or helping the whole person. The authors explain that at age eighteen or twenty-one, young people age out of more supportive and inclusive systems designed for children to either no services or services with less support designed for adults. Many of these systems still function as if youth become independent adults overnight, and they are at odds with the longer period of semi-autonomy that characterizes young adulthood today. The authors point to the poor outcomes among these vulnerable youth and stress the need to redesign targeted services for them. They also argue that universal programs for all young adults would greatly benefit vulnerable populations. Finally, they highlight recent promising policy developments such as the 2008 Fostering Connections Act, which extends government responsibility for youth in foster care from age eighteen to age twenty-one, and the Shared Youth Vision Initiative, designed to improve and coordinate systems that serve vulnerable youth as they transition to adulthood.

Key Policy Issues

The Network's research has revealed three urgent policy issues. The first is the twin problem of access and persistence in higher education, especially at the nation's community colleges. In response to findings from research, some of it supported by this Network, federal policy makers are moving rapidly and forcefully to strengthen these critical institutions that bridge the gap between a generation ill-prepared for college-level work and a labor market that is demanding ever more complex skills.

The second pressing need is to design and implement effective new programs to identify and prepare at-risk youth for the transition.

Such programs, for example, would help young people to complete their secondary education so that they are better prepared to take the next step, whether directly into the labor force, into military service or alternative forms of service, or into higher education. Although the Network's focus was on the period of adult transitions (age eighteen to thirty-four), one signal research effort was an evaluation of ChalleNGe, a unique program developed by the National Guard to provide an alternative for high school dropouts between the ages of sixteen and eighteen. The program intervenes early to help these young people complete high school or obtain a GED during a five-month military-academy style residential program that emphasizes schooling, service, leadership, and healthy living among other skills needed in adulthood. After youth complete the residential portion of the program, trained mentors work with them in their own communities over the next twelve months to effectuate a successful transition to postsecondary education, work, or military service. As the articles in this volume by Dan Bloom and by Sheldon Danziger and David Ratner demonstrate, the consequences of school dropout are devastating to the long-term transition to adulthood. Early evaluation results from a randomized controlled trial of the ChalleNGe program present encouraging evidence that the program could offer valuable lessons for tackling this difficult set of problems.

The third policy priority is diagnosing and attending to the problems of especially vulnerable youth and the systems that serve them, like foster care and juvenile justice, and rethinking how the nation might build a better integrated system of care. The list of systemic issues is long. One key problem is the failure to coordinate among systems that often define their jurisdiction narrowly, especially when young people are known to more than one system and when needs overlap. Another is conflicting missions and funding sources. Yet another is the age at which services end—a crucial issue at a time of lengthening transitions to adulthood. Although families with means are extending help to their children well into their twenties and beyond, the special education, foster care, juvenile justice after-care, and related systems end service eligibility abruptly, often at age eighteen and only rarely much past age twenty-one. Promising strategies would reward collaboration and coordination, extend the reach of these systems well into adulthood, strengthen existing services and develop new ones to meet the special developmental needs of vulnerable youth at this stage of life, and better integrate services with those from more mainstream systems. Examples include building links to programs like ChalleNGe for foster care youth who drop out of school or facilitating access to community colleges and four-year colleges when skills permit. Here too, policy makers are beginning to recognize the need for change—witness the passage in 2008 of federal legislation extending services in the foster care system from age eighteen to twenty-one. Other efforts to coordinate these systems at the federal level are also under way. But more remains to be done. One way to stimulate change would be to free a few willing states from federally imposed categorical restrictions and ask them to experiment with integrated systems of care geared to making mainstream links and providing supports that extend into adulthood.

In sum, when the Research Network on Transitions to Adulthood and Public Policy began its work more than a decade ago, the lengthening of the transition and the concept of early adulthood as a distinct stage in

human development were only dimly perceived. As a result, the real and tangled implications of young people taking a decade or more after leaving high school to attain the markers commonly associated with adulthood—full-time work, an independent household, a stable relationship with a significant other in marriage or cohabitation, child-rearing, civic engagement, and, increasingly in the twenty-first century, at least some postsecondary education or training—were only poorly understood.

Research uncovered several important consequences of the extended transition. The first was the growing burden placed on the middle- and lower-income families who were providing their children with schooling, housing, health insurance, and income well beyond the age range of eighteen to twenty-one, the traditional age of majority. Instead of saving for retirement, or meeting their own needs, parents found themselves continuing to invest in their children's future. The second consequence was the unexpected strain being imposed on key social institutions. Many young adults found themselves without health insurance and with few viable options to obtain it. Colleges often labeled students who came back to school later in life as "nontraditional," when in fact taking time off to work, see the world, or volunteer was increasingly the norm and not the exception for young adults. And the academic, financial, social, and emotional needs of this new breed of students differed from those of fresh-out-of-high-school students. Third, few new institutional options were available to promote development at this stage of life. Youth corps and other volunteer programs existed, but the total number of slots available was generally small. Possibly most consequential of all, children in the care of the state—foster care, special education, the juvenile justice system—had been particularly hard hit by the new transition. These social systems continued to end their support abruptly at age eighteen, even while low- and middle-income families were increasingly stepping in to help their more advantaged young adult children weather a longer transition. In effect, the most disadvantaged—those least able to adapt and most in need of transitional help well into adulthood—had been left "on their own without a net."

A decade later, as the articles in this volume testify, recognition and change are in the air. While families still bear the brunt of the burden and institutions have not completely made the transition, policy and practice are now both astir. Out of necessity, to attract and hold a volunteer army, the military has made a number of changes to encourage and support the transition to adulthood—paying for higher education, offering more attractive pay, and providing better housing, supports, and work hours for married couples. For vulnerable youth, the Fostering Connections to Success and Increasing Adoptions Act of 2008 extends the definition of a "child" up to age twenty-one and offers federal matching funds to states that opt to allow young people to remain in foster care past age eighteen. It also encourages states to provide that support in more constructive ways that facilitate mastery of the skills needed to become productive adults and lead independent lives. Similarly, the Edward M. Kennedy Serve America Act of 2009, as noted, expands and extends the work of the Corporation for National and Community Service. It more than triples (from 75,000 today to 250,000 by

2017) the number of positions available each year for young people to engage in service learning opportunities in education, health, clean energy, economic opportunity, and other national priorities, thus providing a new rite of passage to adulthood in the way that military service did during the draft era. In the health care area, sweeping new legislation would offer health insurance options for all Americans, including young adults who have not yet connected with employer-based health insurance and who are not covered by college-based plans. Change is stirring in higher education as well. The Obama administration has proposed a bold, potentially transformative set of reforms and expansions in student grant and loan programs including significant increases in Pell Grant amounts, a $12 billion investment in community college facilities, accountability measures, instructional innovation, and programs— investments that would help these strategically placed institutions meet the needs of a twenty-first century student body.

Taken as a whole, these developments signal an unusually bold set of initiatives and, most important, resources that would significantly help to relieve parental burden and drive key institutions to adapt to the changing needs of young adults in transition. But as is the case for all policy changes, the devil will be in the details of on-the-ground practice. The articles in this volume provide a blueprint for harnessing resources to need and policy to practice that could help to put derailed young people back on the pathway to adulthood in the twenty-first century.

Endnotes

1. William S. Aquilino, "Two Views of One Relationship: Comparing Parents' and Young Adult Children's Reports of the Quality of Intergenerational Relations," *Journal of Marriage and the Family* 61 (1999): 858–70; Frances K. Goldscheider and Calvin Goldscheider, "The Effects of Childhood Family Structure on Leaving and Returning Home," *Journal of Marriage and the Family* 60 (1998):745–56; Frances K. Goldscheider and Linda J. Waite, *New Families? No Families? The Transformation of the American Home* (University of California Press, 1991); Michael J. Rosenfeld, *The Age of Independence: Interracial Unions, Same-Sex Unions, and the Changing American Family* (Harvard University Press, 2007); Michael Shanahan, "Pathways to Adulthood in Changing Societies: Variability and Mechanisms in Life Course Perspective," *Annual Review of Sociology* 26 (2000): 667–92.

2. MacArthur Foundation Research Network on Transitions to Adulthood, www.transad.pop.upenn.edu.

3. Richard A. Settersten, Frank F. Furstenberg Jr., and Rubén G. Rumbaut, eds., *On the Frontier of Adulthood: Theory, Research, and Public Policy* (University of Chicago Press, 2005).

What's Going on with Young People Today? The Long and Twisting Path to Adulthood

Richard A. Settersten Jr. and Barbara Ray

Summary

Richard Settersten and Barbara Ray examine the lengthening transition to adulthood over the past several decades, as well as the challenges the new schedule poses for young people, families, and society.

The authors begin with a brief history of becoming an adult, noting that the schedule that youth follow to arrive at adulthood changes to meet the social realities of each era. For youth to leave home at an early age during the 1950s, for example, was "normal" because opportunities for work were plentiful and social expectations of the time reinforced the need to do so. But the prosperity that made it possible for young adults of that era to move quickly into adult roles did not last. The economic and employment uncertainties that arose during the 1970s complicated enormously the decisions that young adults had to make about living arrangements, educational investments, and family formation.

The authors next take a closer look at changes in the core timing shifts in the new transition—the lengthening time it now takes youth to leave home, complete school, enter the workforce, marry, and have children. They stress that today's new schedule for attaining independence leaves many families overburdened as they support their children for an extended period. The continued need to rely on families for financial assistance, the authors say, exacerbates the plight of young people from a variety of vulnerable backgrounds. It also raises complex questions about who is responsible for the welfare of young people and whether the risks and costs newly associated with the early adult years should be absorbed by markets, by families, or by governments.

Settersten and Ray stress that the longer transition to adulthood strains not only families but also the institutions that have traditionally supported young Americans in making that transition—such as residential colleges and universities, community colleges, military service, and national service programs. They emphasize the need to strengthen existing social institutions and create new ones to reflect more accurately the realities of a longer and more complex passage into adult life.

www.futureofchildren.org

Richard A. Settersten Jr. is a professor of human development and family sciences at Oregon State University. Barbara Ray is president of Hired Pen, inc. The authors wish to thank Jeylan Mortimer, the editors (Gordon Berlin, Frank Furstenberg, and Mary Waters), and participants in the authors' conference at Princeton University for their insightful feedback.

Becoming an adult has traditionally been understood as comprising five core transitions—leaving home, completing school, entering the workforce, getting married, and having children. Recent research on how young adults are handling these core transitions has yielded three important findings that contributors to this volume will explore in the pages to come. First, both in the United States and in many European countries, the process of becoming an adult is more gradual and varied today than it was half a century ago.[1] Social timetables that were widely observed in that era no longer seem relevant, and young people are taking longer to achieve economic and psychological autonomy than their counterparts did then. Experiences in early adulthood now also vary greatly by gender, race and ethnicity, and social class.

Second, families are often overburdened in extending support to young adult children as they make their way through this extended process. In the United States, in particular, parents contribute sizable material and emotional support through their children's late twenties and into their early thirties. Such flows are to be expected in more privileged families, but what is now striking are the significant flows—and associated strains— in middle-class families at a time when families themselves have become increasingly stressed or fractured. The heavier reliance on families exacerbates the already precarious plight of young people from a variety of vulnerable backgrounds.[2] It also raises complex questions about who is responsible for the welfare of young people and whether markets, families, or governments should absorb the risks and costs associated with the early adult years.

Third, there is a mismatch between young people making the transition to adulthood today and the existing institutional supports, including residential colleges and universities, community colleges, military and national service programs, work settings, and other environments. The policies, programs, and institutions that served young adults a half-century ago no longer meet the needs of youth today, either in the United States or Europe, and are based on assumptions that do not reflect the realities of the world today.[3]

These findings point to the need to strengthen the skills and capacities of young people on the path to adulthood as well as to improve the effectiveness of the institutions through which they move.

Together, these three findings point to the need to strengthen the skills and capacities of young people on the path to adulthood and to improve the effectiveness of the institutions through which they move. Although some of the broad changes we describe are taking place in Canada and some Western European nations, as well as in the United States, the factors that explain them, the consequences of and responses to them, and the national histories in which they are embedded are often unique. For these reasons, we focus most of our attention on the story at home, in the United States. Because our aim is to provide an overview of changes and challenges in the contour and content of the early adult years, we focus on the larger story at the expense of more nuanced ones, which are told in the topic-focused articles that follow. We begin with a brief history of becoming an adult in the United States. We then take a closer look at a few particularly important shifts—in leaving the family home, in completing schooling, in securing work, in marriage and childbearing, and in the provision of family support. We close by illustrating the need to buttress or reform social institutions in light of a longer and more complex passage to adulthood.

Becoming an Adult: A Brief History

During the first few decades of the twentieth century, the period known as "adolescence" was relatively brief. By their late teens, only a small fraction of the population was still in school, and most men had begun to work. While many left their natal homes early, surprisingly high shares of men and women nonetheless remained at home for a while, as we will later see, and marriage and childbearing did not happen immediately. As the century progressed, however, growing proportions of young people had formed families by their late teens or early twenties. The Great Depression slowed the timing of family formation, but by the end of World War II, marriage and childbearing took place almost in lockstep with the conclusion of schooling. In the postwar boom that followed, high-paying industrial jobs were plentiful, and a prosperous economy enabled workers with high school degrees (or less) and college degrees alike to find secure employment with decent wages and benefits. Between 1949 and 1970, the income of earners in the lower and middle brackets grew 110 percent or more, while the income of those in the top brackets rose between 85 percent and 95 percent.[4]

These stable jobs made it possible for couples to marry and form families at young ages.

By the 1950s and 1960s, most Americans viewed family roles and adult responsibilities as being nearly synonymous. For men, the defining characteristic of adulthood was having the means to marry and support a family. For women, it was getting married and becoming a mother; indeed, most women in that era married before they were twenty-one and had at least one child before they were twenty-three. By their early twenties, then, most young men and women were recognized as adults, both socially and economically.

In some ways, adult transitions today resemble those before industrialization, during the late nineteenth and early twentieth century, when the livelihoods of most families were bound to farms and agricultural jobs rather than the job market. Becoming an adult then, as now, was a gradual process characterized by "semi-autonomy," with youth waiting until they were economically self-sufficient to set up independent households, marry, and have children. There are important differences, however, in the ways young people today and in the recent and more distant past define and achieve adulthood.

How do Americans today define adulthood? To seek an answer, the MacArthur Research Network on Transitions to Adulthood developed a set of questions for the 2002 General Social Survey (GSS), an opinion poll administered to a nationally representative sample of Americans every two years by the National Opinion Research Center.[5] The survey asked nearly 1,400 Americans aged eighteen and older how important it was to reach certain traditional markers to be considered an adult: leaving home, finishing school, getting a full-time job, becoming financially independent from one's parents, being able to support a family, marrying, and becoming a parent.

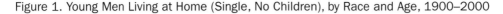

Figure 1. Young Men Living at Home (Single, No Children), by Race and Age, 1900–2000

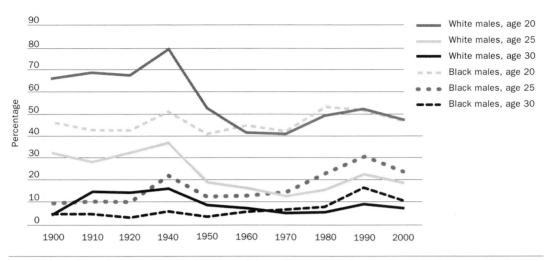

Source: Adapted from data compiled in Elizabeth Fussell and Frank F. Furstenberg Jr., "The Transition to Adulthood during the Twentieth Century," in *On the Frontier of Adulthood: Theory, Research, and Public Policy,* edited by Richard A. Settersten Jr., Frank F. Furstenberg Jr., and Rubén G. Rumbaut (University of Chicago Press, 2005), pp. 29–75.

Today, more than 95 percent of Americans consider the most important markers of adulthood to be completing school, establishing an independent household, and being employed full-time—concrete steps associated with the ability to support a family. But only about half of Americans consider it necessary to marry or to have children to be regarded as an adult. Unlike their parents' and grandparents' generations, for whom marriage and parenthood were prerequisites for adulthood, young people today more often view these markers as life choices rather than requirements, as steps that complete the process of becoming an adult rather than start it.

Definitions of adulthood also differ markedly by social class. For example, Americans who are less educated and less affluent give earlier deadlines for leaving home, completing school, obtaining full-time employment, marrying, and parenting. Around 40 percent of those in the bottom third of the economic distribution said that young adults should

marry before they turn twenty-five, and one-third said they should have children by this age. Far fewer of the better-off respondents pointed to the early twenties, and about one-third of them said that these events could be delayed until the thirties.

Some important new realities underlie these definitions. First, becoming an adult today usually involves a period of living independently before marriage, even though growing shares of young people are staying at home longer or returning home later on. Second, the early adult years often involve the pursuit of higher education, as a decent standard of living today generally requires a college education, if not a professional degree. Third, regardless of whether young people enter college, it takes longer today to secure a full-time job that pays enough to support a family, and young people now have a greater range of employment experiences in getting there. Fourth, as a consequence of these changes, marriage and parenting now come

Figure 2. Young Women Living at Home (Single, No Children), by Race and Age, 1900–2000

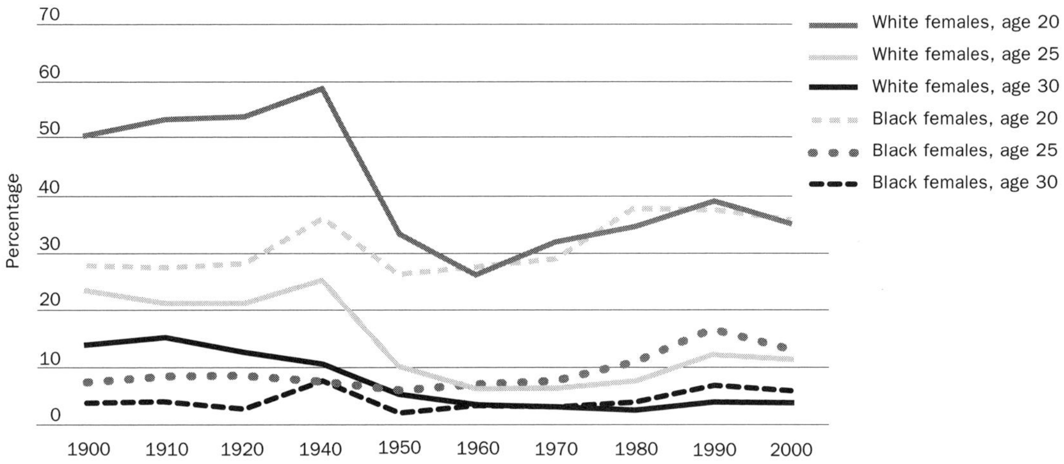

Source: Adapted from data compiled in Elizabeth Fussell and Frank F. Furstenberg Jr., "The Transition to Adulthood during the Twentieth Century," in *On the Frontier of Adulthood: Theory, Research, and Public Policy,* edited by Richard A. Settersten Jr., Frank F. Furstenberg Jr., and Rubén G. Rumbaut (University of Chicago Press, 2005), pp. 29–75.

significantly later in the life course. Finally, on each of these fronts, young adults often have starkly different sets of options and experiences depending on their family backgrounds and resources. Young adults today are also more likely to be black, Hispanic, immigrant, and multi-ethnic than any other of the nation's age groups.[6] They are also more likely to be foreign-born, a characteristic that in past generations was truer of families' oldest members. These shifts, too, have prompted new inequalities in early adult life.

Living Independently

The post-World War II script for life left such an indelible mark that it often remains the benchmark against which individuals judge themselves and others, even today. Yet the postwar model was something of an aberration then as now. Families of the 1950s and 1960s did many things differently from their predecessors, including launching themselves into adulthood at very early ages. This is apparent in figures 1 and 2, which show the proportion of men and women (single and without children) living with their parents at the ages of twenty, twenty-five, and thirty from 1900 to 2000, and table 1, which adds a recent data point, 2007.

In 1900, roughly one-third of white men aged twenty-five were living at home with their parents—two and a half times the share in 1970.[7] By 2000, the share living at home was one-fifth; by 2007, it had increased to one-fourth. Since the 1970s, black men have lived more often with parents than their white peers at both ages twenty-five and thirty. Figures 1 and 2 show that during this period women have tended to leave home earlier than men, and, as we show later, cohabit or marry earlier as well.

It might be tempting to infer from these figures that Americans have now returned to a more "normal" pattern of delayed home-leaving. That inference, however, would miss the important and often unique conditions

Table 1. Percentage of Young Adult Men and Women Living with Parents, 2007, by Race

	Men			Women		
	All	**White**	**Black**	**All**	**White**	**Black**
Age 20–24	43.0	42.9	45.2	38.0	37.0	40.8
25–29	19.8	18.9	24.8	15.9	14.6	20.0
30–34	10.1	9.5	14.6	7.9	7.3	11.4
At age 20	54.0	54.3	54.6	48.1	47.2	51.5
At 25	26.3	25.5	30.2	21.4	20.1	25.1
At 30	12.1	11.4	18.4	9.7	8.8	13.7
At 35	7.5	6.8	12.1	6.1	5.8	9.5
At 40	5.8	5.8	7.5	4.4	4.0	7.7

Source: Authors' computations, *2007 American Community Survey*, U.S. Bureau of the Census.

that every historical era presents. To leave home quickly in the 1950s was "normal" because opportunities were plentiful and social expectations of the time reinforced the need to do so. At the turn of both the twentieth and twenty-first centuries, greater proportions of young people stayed at home longer than those who came of age at mid-century because they faced distinctive social and economic conditions of their own.

Carrying the picture forward to 2007, table 1 shows the proportion of black and white young adults, at different ages, who live with their parents. The trends in co-residence with parents evidenced in figures 1 and 2 have made dramatic leaps.[8] In every age bracket men are more likely than women to live with parents. Black men live with parents more often than white men, and more often than white and black women, at every age. Black women more often live with parents than do white women, again at every age. The share living with parents is particularly high for men and women in their early twenties, spanning 43 to 50 percent depending on the group, although proportions fall as the age rises. At each five-year mark—from age twenty, to twenty-five, to thirty—percentages are cut in half. Yet even at the ages of thirty-five and forty, between 4 and 12 percent of adult children live with their parents, depending on the group.

Comparisons between native-born whites and blacks overlook the very sizable group of young people from other ethnic and immigrant populations who live at home. In 2008, among young men and women aged eighteen to twenty-four across ten distinct immigrant groups, second-generation youth (those born in the United States to foreign-born parents) are consistently more likely to be living at home than first-generation or so-called 1.5-generation youth (those who arrived at age thirteen or older, or age twelve or younger, respectively).[9] Immigrants of the second generation are more likely to live at home than native-born blacks and especially whites, and some groups show very high rates of home-staying (for example, between 64 and 75 percent of young adults from Indian, Dominican, Chinese, Filipino, and Salvadoran/Guatemalan backgrounds live at home).

Figure 3. Share of Men and Women Aged Twenty-Five Living with Parents, 1970 and 2000

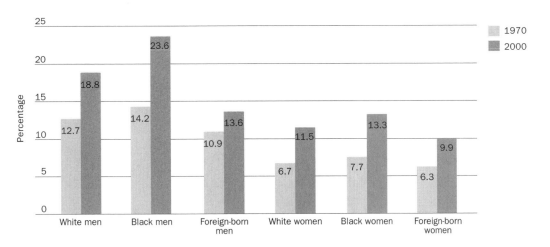

Source: Adapted from data compiled in Elizabeth Fussell and Frank F. Furstenberg Jr., "The Transition to Adulthood during the Twentieth Century," in *On the Frontier of Adulthood: Theory, Research, and Public Policy,* edited by Richard A. Settersten Jr., Frank F. Furstenberg Jr., and Rubén G. Rumbaut (University of Chicago Press, 2005), pp. 29–75.

Although residential independence has been and continues to be one of the markers of attaining adulthood in the United States, particularly among native-born youth, recent downturns in the economy may create pressure on families to house adult children. Growing numbers of young people have also been staying at home while enrolled in school or to make ends meet while working.[10]

For women, it was not until the 1960s that large numbers began to live on their own before marriage, thus creating a critical "hiatus" (as sociologist Frances Goldscheider has called it) that allowed women to become more fully integrated into the paid labor market and college classrooms.[11] By 1970, the share of twenty-year-olds who were living on their own before marrying was more than double that for both white men and women at the turn of the century.[12] As we show later, marriage was becoming less urgent and desirable for a host of reasons, and when young people did not marry, they still considered moving out and living on their own—and

women *en masse* did so for the first time. During this era, housing was also inexpensive, and staying with parents humiliating.

Figures 3 through 6 demonstrate how much has changed in just a generation or so. These snapshots show that in 1970, only 13 percent of white males were living with their parents at age twenty-five, compared with 19 percent in 2000. Only about 10 percent were living on their own or with roommates in 1970, compared with one-third in 2000. Most profoundly, nearly seven in ten were married in 1970, compared with only one-third by 2000. The trend, then, has been for men to move out of their parents' homes, but not into marriages or even cohabitation; by contrast, the proportion living with parents has grown only modestly. Trends are similar for women and for those of other racial and ethnic groups at age twenty-five. Half as many black men, for example, were living at home with parents in 1970 as in 2000. Likewise, the share married at age twenty-five in 1970 was triple that in 2000.

Figure 4. Share of Men and Women Aged Twenty-Five Living Independently, 1970 and 2000

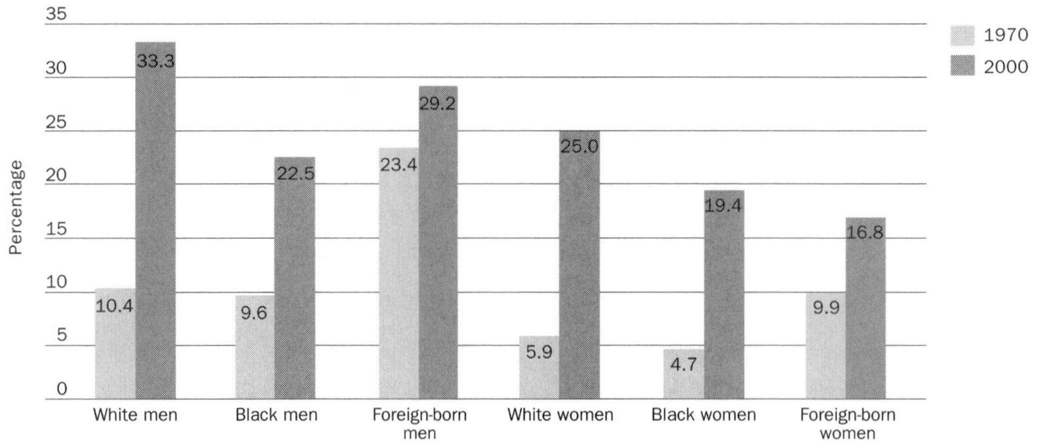

Source: Adapted from data compiled in Elizabeth Fussell and Frank F. Furstenberg Jr., "The Transition to Adulthood during the Twentieth Century," in *On the Frontier of Adulthood: Theory, Research, and Public Policy*, edited by Richard A. Settersten Jr., Frank F. Furstenberg Jr., and Rubén G. Rumbaut (University of Chicago Press, 2005), pp. 29–75.

It is clear that the emergence of a period of independent living—despite more recent social concerns about young people staying at home longer or returning home later—is one of the most profound changes in the experiences of young adults in the past several decades.[13] This significant shift coincides with a few other major transformations in the early adult years, including the rising demand for, and attainment of, advanced education, to which we now turn.

The Rising Demand for Education

Higher education has flourished in all post-industrial and emerging post-industrial societies. Once reserved for the elite, a college education is now a necessity for both men and women who want access to good jobs. Education and training are more valuable than ever because jobs are less secure and work careers have become more fluid. The demand for education and training has increased relentlessly over the past four decades, and the economic returns to education have grown in recent years, even after

the higher costs of getting an education are taken into account.[14]

Young adults have heard the message loud and clear: to get ahead, one needs a college degree. And, in fact, today's young adults are better educated than any previous generation in the nation's history. Yet many youth are also floundering badly. Approximately eight in ten high school seniors plan to attend some form of college or training after high school.[15] But even high school dropout rates are high: among people sixteen to twenty-four years old in 2006, high school dropout rates were 9.3 percent overall and 5.8 percent, 10.7 percent, and 22.1 percent for whites, blacks, and Hispanics, respectively.[16] More disturbing estimates suggest that as many as three in ten ninth graders today will not graduate from high school four years later; for Hispanics, blacks, and Native Americans, the figures hover around a disturbing five in ten.[17]

"College for all" may be a salient cultural message, but only one-quarter of young

Figure 5. Share of Married Couples Aged Twenty-Five Living Independently, 1970 and 2000

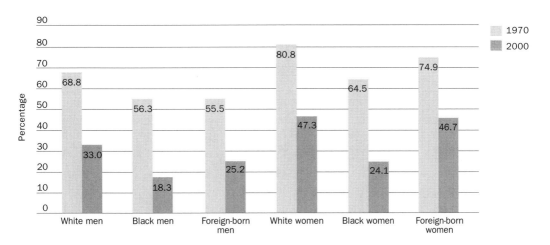

Source: Adapted from data compiled in Elizabeth Fussell and Frank F. Furstenberg Jr., "The Transition to Adulthood during the Twentieth Century," in *On the Frontier of Adulthood: Theory, Research, and Public Policy,* edited by Richard A. Settersten Jr., Frank F. Furstenberg Jr., and Rubén G. Rumbaut (University of Chicago Press, 2005), pp. 29–75.

adults between the ages of twenty-five and thirty-four have a bachelor's degree today, and only 5 percent have graduate degrees.[18] Popular perceptions to the contrary, these shares have not changed significantly in the past three decades. The breakdown of degree holders has changed, however, by gender and by race and ethnicity. Women have now surpassed men in college graduation rates and in educational attainment generally.[19] Asians are most likely to have bachelor's degrees or higher, followed by whites. Hispanics are least likely. Only 9 percent of Hispanics between the ages of twenty-five and thirty-four had a bachelor's degree in 2005. Asians are four times more likely than Hispanics to have a bachelor's degree.[20] Among whites, the share with a bachelor's degree is 27 percent; among blacks, the share is 15 percent.[21]

It is telling that only 40 percent of those who enter four-year institutions earn degrees within six years—and the rest are unlikely ever to earn degrees, as six years is generally understood to be the point of no return.[22]

The children of parents who have themselves graduated from college are far more likely to have both the skills and the resources to enter and complete college. Although six in ten students whose parents have college degrees finish college in four years, only about one in ten students whose parents lack college degrees finishes in four years.[23]

The gap between young adults' high aspirations for college and their low graduation rates sounds an important alarm. Youth who are ill-prepared for the rigors of higher education may start school, but they are also more likely to have unclear plans and inadequate skills, veer off course, cycle in and out, or drop out altogether.[24] The growth of the "nontraditional" student (one who is older, working, or parenting) is also a key reason why it now takes longer to get a "four-year" degree.[25] Youth who have dropped out of four-year colleges or who are not seeking four-year degrees often find their way to community colleges. In his article in this volume, Thomas Brock explores the formidable

Figure 6. Share of Singles With Own Children Aged Twenty-Five Living Independently, 1970 and 2000

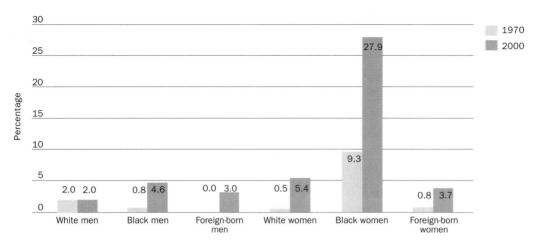

Source: Adapted from data compiled in Elizabeth Fussell and Frank F. Furstenberg Jr., "The Transition to Adulthood during the Twentieth Century," in *On the Frontier of Adulthood: Theory, Research, and Public Policy*, edited by Richard A. Settersten Jr., Frank F. Furstenberg Jr., and Rubén G. Rumbaut (University of Chicago Press, 2005), pp. 29–75.

challenges these students and these institutions now face.

More worrisome is the plight of young adults who have no education beyond high school and who are largely disengaged from social institutions and economic life—schools, the labor market, and the military. In 2005, even before the current recession and during the height of the Iraq war, roughly three in ten white men between ages sixteen and twenty-four with only a high school degree were not in school, in the military, or at work.[26] For young black men, the proportion is staggering: more than half were not in school, in the military, or at work.

Of even more concern is the high probability that poorly educated men, particularly black men, will be imprisoned in early adulthood. Economist Steven Raphael estimates that 90 percent of black male high school dropouts in California aged forty-five to fifty-four have histories of imprisonment.[27] Other studies

using national data have found similar, but lower, probabilities of imprisonment.[28] The most conservative estimates, from the U.S. Department of Justice, though nonetheless startling, are that about one in three black men and one in six Latino men are expected to go to prison during their lifetime—compared with one in seventeen white men—if current incarceration rates remain unchanged.[29] Among all American men in their twenties in 2008, 1.5 percent of whites, 4 percent of Latinos, and fully 10 percent of blacks were incarcerated.[30] These are very high rates of incarceration for all groups, but far higher for blacks than for others. These data highlight just how difficult the adult experiences and circumstances of black and Latino men are, particularly for those with the least education, for whom risks grow in the late adolescent and early adult years.

Getting Ahead Gets Harder
The prosperity that made it possible for young adults to move quickly into adult roles

Figure 7. Earnings of Men Aged Twenty-Five to Thirty-Four, by Education Level, 1975 and 2002

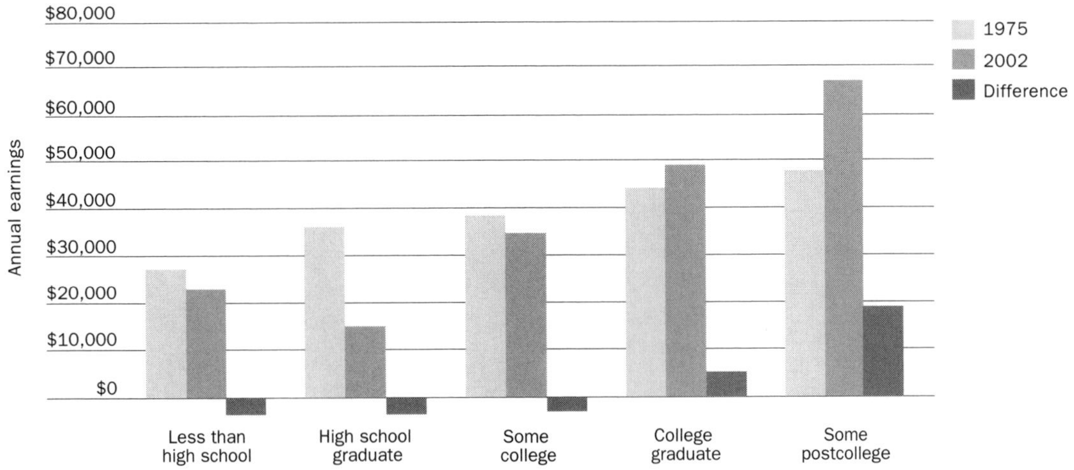

Source: Adapted from data compiled in Sheldon Danziger, "Earning by Education for Young Workers: 1975 and 2002," *Data Brief* 17 (Philadelphia: MacArthur Network on Transitions to Adulthood, 2004). Earnings adjusted for inflation.

continued for several decades after World War II. During the 1970s, however, wages stagnated and inflation rose. The manufacturing sector that had been the backbone of the middle class and had ensured lives of relative security for the working class crumbled. For the next thirty years, wages for workers without college degrees stagnated, and the pensions and benefits that they had once enjoyed began to vanish. Globalization increased competition, markets became internationalized, and new technologies spread networks and knowledge.[31] All these forces gave rise to new economic and employment uncertainties that now complicate young adults' decisions about living arrangements, educational investments, and family formation.

At mid-century a high school degree was enough to establish a solid standard of living; today not even a college degree guarantees success. As shown in figure 7, young men (aged twenty-five to thirty-four) with a high school degree or less earned about $4,000

less in 2002 than in 1975 (with earnings adjusted for inflation).[32] Men with some college also lost ground, earning about $3,500 a year less in 2002 than in 1975. College graduates made gains, but the big winners were men who had completed at least some graduate school, whose earnings grew by about $19,000.[33] And even small gains, of course, have significant effects on lifetime earnings.

Over the past quarter-century, the earnings of women, unlike those of men, have risen (see figure 8). Figures 7 and 8 indicate that women's earnings have grown faster than those of men—although men have continued to outearn women. In part because women's wages were much lower to start, their average earnings have remained well below those of men. In 1975, a female high school graduate earned about 46 percent as much during the year as a male; by 2002, she earned 62 percent as much. As with men, the most educated women saw the largest earnings gains. Finally, for each group (except those with

Figure 8. Earnings of Women Aged Twenty-Five to Thirty-Four, by Education Level, 1975 and 2002

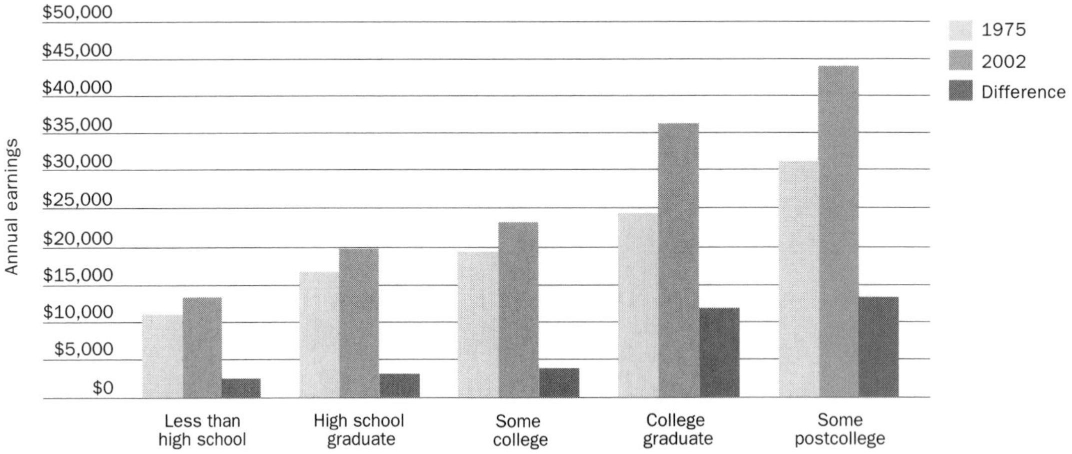

Source: Adapted from data compiled in Sheldon Danziger, "Earning by Education for Young Workers: 1975 and 2002," *Data Brief* 17 (Philadelphia: MacArthur Network on Transitions to Adulthood, 2004). Earnings adjusted for inflation.

some graduate-level education), the share whose earnings were below poverty levels (about $19,000 for a family of four in 2002) was greater in 2002 than in 1975.

Having an income—or at least the ability to earn an income—has always been a precursor to being independent and taking on adult roles, such as marrying and settling down. In 1969, only about 10 percent of men in their early thirties had wages that were below poverty level. By 2004, the share had more than doubled. Women fared a little better over the same time span, but nearly half were still earning poverty-level wages by their mid-thirties.[34] Overall, the share of young adults in 2005 living in poverty was higher than the national average.[35] Given these and a host of other new economic vulnerabilities, it is perhaps not so surprising that by age thirty, only half as many young adults in 2005 as in 1960 had achieved all the traditional markers of adulthood—particularly marriage and parenthood.[36]

Delaying "I Do"

Young adults today take a different view of marriage than their counterparts did in times past.[37] Whereas once couples came together to build a life together, today couples build their own lives separately and then marry. Because acquiring educational credentials and work experience—a key part of the foundation to be built before marriage—takes time, it is no surprise that young adults are delaying marriage. Between 1960 and 1980, the median age at first marriage for young people rose from twenty to twenty-three; by 2000 it had reached twenty-five.[38] Today, median age at first marriage for men is over twenty-seven, and for women, twenty-six.[39] These are extraordinary leaps.

Young adults, however, are hardly celibate while they build that foundation. Advances in contraception and reproduction rights have left women and couples with greater control over fertility and fewer risks associated with premarital sex. Views on the acceptability of living together before marriage have also

Table 2. Percentage of Young Adult Men and Women, Single and Never Married, 2007, by Race

	Men			Women		
	All	**White**	**Black**	**All**	**White**	**Black**
Age 20–24	88.0	87.3	92.5	79.6	78.0	89.9
25–29	58.9	55.8	73.8	47.0	42.2	71.4
30–34	35.8	33.0	52.4	27.3	22.8	52.9
At 20	95.2	95.0	97.0	91.1	90.7	96.2
At 25	70.6	68.0	82.5	58.4	54.6	78.5
At 30	43.8	41.4	49.2	33.3	29.0	50.8
At 35	27.8	25.4	42.5	21.1	16.7	43.0
At 40	21.5	19.2	34.2	16.1	12.5	34.6

Source: Authors' computations, *2007 American Community Survey,* U.S. Bureau of the Census.

become more positive. Fifty years ago, very few couples lived together before marrying; today, more than half of first marriages are preceded by cohabitation, a trend that shows no signs of abating.[40] About half of high school seniors say that they plan to cohabit as couples before they marry.[41]

For young adults with fewer prospects ahead of them—those with the least education and lowest incomes—children often come before marriage. Nearly 40 percent of all first births occur before marriage, and the vast majority of these premarital births are to young adults who have not attended, much less completed, college.[42] The risk of divorce is also consistently highest for couples who marry earliest. Sixty percent of those who marry before age eighteen will be divorced by age thirty-four. Forty percent of those who marry by age twenty will not make it to their tenth wedding anniversary, compared with roughly 25 percent of those who wait until twenty-five.[43]

For those who bemoan the demise of marriage, there is heartening news. Young adults may be postponing marriage, but they are not abandoning it altogether. By age thirty-four, seven in ten have tied the knot.[44] At the same time, the proportions of young people who are single and have never married, by age and race, are striking, as shown in table 2.

In 2007, men in every age bracket through age thirty-four were more likely to be single and never-married than women. Black men and black women were consistently more likely to be single and never-married than whites, with Hispanic men and women falling in between. As the table shows, the proportions of single and never-married people drop by age for all groups, although less dramatically for black men and women than for whites. In their early thirties, more than half of black men and women are single and never-married. Even later, at age forty, sizable proportions of men and women, and especially black men and women, are still single and never-married. The percentages of people who have never married, and who are intentionally childless, are higher now than at any other time in American history—and policy makers have not yet begun to anticipate the future social ramifications of this profound fact.[45]

The Crucial Role of Families and Social Relationships

Both the government and the general public in the United States place a high premium on personal responsibility and self-reliance.[46] The prevailing "sink or swim" philosophy leaves it up to young people and their families to take advantage of the opportunities they encounter or actively create, and to shoulder responsibility for problems that ensue as they navigate markets for education, jobs, and partners using their own knowledge and resources.

Stark inequalities therefore exist in the skills, resources, and opportunities of young people, depending on what parents can provide during their children's third decade and what they provided in the first two decades. To understand these inequalities, one need only look at the financial supports that parents provide to their young adult children. U.S. data from 1988—seemingly outdated but the best available over a long time span—showed that parents spent about one-third of the total cost of raising a child from birth to age eighteen again between eighteen and thirty-four. This support included the provision of material assistance (in the form of housing, food, and educational expenses) and direct cash assistance, although support diminished as adult children grew older.[47] Even more striking, children from families in the top quarter of the income distribution received at least 70 percent more in material assistance than children in the bottom quarter.

One can safely assume that these outlays have only increased dramatically since those data were collected in 1988. A 2005 update of that study, based on parents of youth aged eighteen to twenty-one, shows that, regardless of income, parents are spending 10 percent of their annual incomes to help their young adult children. All families are thus devoting similar proportions of their resources to their young adult children, although the amounts they spend are obviously drastically different (10 percent of $40,000 is considerably different from 10 percent of $200,000). The higher transfers in financially well-positioned families give a further boost to children who are already better off going into adulthood.

This expensive new stage of life is creating some consternation for families that have to adjust to the changing pace of adult transitions. For the most privileged young adults—those who receive ample support from their parents—the new, extended path to adulthood is a time of unparalleled freedom: freedom to proceed directly through college, travel or work for a few years, or perhaps participate in community service, and then enter graduate or professional school. Relatively few Americans, however, have this good fortune. Youth from less well-off families shuttle back and forth between work and school or combine both while they gradually gain their credentials; they wait for jobs that can support the families they wish to start or perhaps have already started; and they feel little control over their lives.

More than at any time in recent history, then, parents are being called on to provide material and other types of assistance to their young adult children. A century ago, it was the other way around: young adults typically helped their parents when they first went to work, particularly if they still lived together. Now, many young adults continue to receive support from their parents even after they begin working. The exceptions seem to be in immigrant families, where young adult children stay in the parental home and feel strong obligations to help support parents.[48]

The challenges of a longer transition to adult-hood pose chronic dilemmas for families with limited means that must find ways to support their children, especially in a course of extended education. Of course, it has always been true that some youth do well and others do not, regardless of resources. Having resources is no guarantee of success, just as the absence of resources is no guarantee of failure. But having additional resources would surely seem to foster positive outcomes in early adulthood. Resources may also soften the consequences of poor judgments and mistakes, which seem more perilous today as the safety nets on which post-World War II generations could rely—pensions and health insurance, steady work with benefits, company loyalty—are fraying.

The weakened position of families in the current volatile economy exacerbates the challenges to populations of young people who are already vulnerable going into adulthood—those whose skills and resources are less than adequate, whose family relationships are absent or fragile, or who have long been in foster care, special education, or juvenile justice systems only to be abruptly cut off from support when they reach the legal ages of adulthood, eighteen or in some cases twenty-one.[49] Most supports for these youth now end at age eighteen—a time when, as noted, their more advantaged peers are continuing to receive sizable assistance from their families of origin. For these populations, maintaining supports is an important priority, even—or especially—in times of economic hardship.

Even middle-class families that once seemed strongly positioned to invest in young adult children may now be experiencing new vulnerabilities amid the "Great Recession" that began in 2008. As the middle class shrinks and family incomes fluctuate from year to year in an uncertain economy, families cannot offer the same set of resources to their children.[50] Families on the low end of middle-income seem especially vulnerable—they have some, but not ample, resources, and their incomes are just high enough to make them ineligible for government support.

Young people who can build stronger and wider connections to adults *other than* parents (for example, teachers and adult mentors) also end up faring better than those who do not. Especially for those young people with limited or absent relationships with their parents, relationships with other adults are invaluable in replacing or compensating for the support that their parents cannot or do not provide. The presence of meaningful relationships with adults significantly bolsters school achievement, success in jobs, emotional maturity, and satisfaction with life, and keeps in check problematic behaviors such as substance abuse.[51] Relationships with adults other than parents are also important in opening opportunities and resources by connecting young people to the larger and loosely connected social networks in which these adults are embedded.[52]

In the United States, the solutions for managing this extended transition are, to a great degree, private ones, made possible by whatever social connections or resources young people and their parents happen to have or can create. But the transition takes place within multiple institutional contexts, and the investments that society makes in the institutions around young people and their parents are also important. These supports are particularly important for families that are unable to extend help because of limited resources or because they lack the knowledge and skills to help their children move forward.

Beyond Personal Solutions: Strengthening Social Institutions

As the transition to adulthood evolves, so too must society's institutions. As young people and their families struggle with the new reality of a longer and more demanding pathway into adult life, existing institutions may need to change and new ones may have to be developed. Which institutions are most important to a successful transition, which will reach the largest share of young adults in meaningful ways, and which are most open to intervention and reform? We highlight three institutions: community colleges, service learning programs, and the military.

As young people and their families struggle with the new reality of a longer and more demanding pathway into adult life, existing institutions may need to change and new ones may have to be developed.

Community colleges are an ideal target for intervention. These two-year colleges touch large numbers and a wide variety of young people, serve many purposes, are flexible, and offer connections to a range of potential career paths. Yet they are seriously in need of support and reform if they are to meet the needs of youth in transition to adulthood. Four-year residential colleges and universities, by contrast, provide a perfect example of how a social institution can successfully address the needs of young adults—by providing shelter, directed activities, adult and peer support,

health care, and entertainment. Explicitly designed as a bridge between a student's family and the wider society, four-year colleges have increasingly been tailored to provide the sort of semi-autonomy that characterizes early adulthood. In his article on community colleges in this issue, Thomas Brock notes the irony that the most selective institutions of higher education take the most capable students and wrap them in support, while community colleges are the least selective institutions and provide the least support.

Community colleges, however, can be restructured to provide these same kinds of services. The Obama administration has already recognized the important role that community colleges can play in strengthening the skills and opportunities of youth who do not or cannot go on to four-year colleges. It has proposed $12 billion in additional funding, with the goal of graduating 5 million more community college students by 2020. It also aims to forge tighter links between community colleges and employers.

The second institution, service learning programs in schools and workplaces, provides important networks and opportunities for young people to "take stock" of themselves and of society, wrestle with social and political attitudes and values, explore their identities, build skills, contribute to their communities, and develop a larger sense of purpose beyond the pursuit of individual gain.[53] For young people, the new Edward M. Kennedy Serve America Act (PL 111-13) increases the numbers of slots in AmeriCorps programs and adds several new corps and fellowships. It also increases the education award and adds flexibility in how young people can get engaged in service and balance service with their other responsibilities. Finally, it targets the needs of low-income communities and prioritizes the inclusion of marginalized youth.[54]

Targeting marginalized youth is especially important because research has consistently shown that youth from disadvantaged backgrounds have few opportunities to gain civic skills and be recruited into civic action. They are much less likely to have parents who participate in community organizations; to have peers who are incorporated into mainstream institutions; to live in neighborhoods that are safe and include opportunities to be involved in civic life; and to attend schools that have strong civic programming, teachers, counselors, and parent participation.[55] National service can serve as an important bridge to jobs, not only in building job-related skills and experience, but also in fostering connections to adult mentors, social networks, and organizations.

The third institution, the military, also serves many young people. For the majority of enlistees, the military is not a second-chance institution, but a first choice—though it too is in need of significant reform.[56] Still, the military, like four-year residential colleges and universities, is designed to shape the futures of young adults by providing a setting in which they can successfully live, work, and learn. By coupling expectations and demands with guidance, mentoring, and other resources, military service helps young adults acquire skills and fosters a sense of competence. Like national service programs, it also provides a bridge from school to higher education or the labor force by providing tuition credits, loan forgiveness, financial stipends, access to jobs, or health insurance and other benefits.

By strengthening community colleges, service learning programs, and military service, the nation can establish clearer and more viable paths into adulthood for those who are not college bound and engage these young people positively in social institutions. College is not the only route to a successful adulthood, but alternatives are few and must be improved. Although youth with a bachelor's degree clearly have multiple advantages, the "college for all" mentality does a disservice to many young adults who simply do not have the intellectual, motivational, and economic resources to complete a four-year (or more) program of higher education.

These are but a few examples of the existing institutions that must be reformed or buttressed in response to the longer and more complex transition to adulthood today. And because this new, lengthened transition is not a passing phenomenon and is likely to grow yet more complicated, it may be necessary to create new institutions, especially ones that can better support middle- and working-class families alongside populations that have traditionally been viewed as socially or economically disadvantaged. The inability to reform existing institutions and create new ones carries significant costs for young people, their families, and our society.

Although many policy makers in Washington are now focused on programs designed for the early years of a child's life (the critical "zero to three" years), it remains important to offer supports as youth make their way into adulthood. Without discounting the importance of services in infancy and early childhood, we stress that young adults make and take exceedingly consequential decisions and actions that carry strong and cumulative effects—on schooling, work, marriage, and parenthood—over the many decades of life ahead. Only by continuing or increasing investments in young people after the age of eighteen can policy makers implement the supports needed to make the road to adulthood less perilous.

The Good with the Bad

Much of the media attention and public debate on the subject of the changing transition to adulthood start from the assumption that something is wrong with young people today as they take longer to "grow up," that the "fault" is of their own doing. To counter that assumption, we have pointed to some of the large cultural, economic, and demographic forces that have altered the landscape of the early adult years and complicated young people's efforts to leave home, finish school, look for jobs, find partners, and start families.

We would be remiss, however, in not acknowledging that we see some benefits to the way this period of life is being shaken up and to the more varied pathways to adulthood that young people are adopting as a consequence. The rigid three-part model of life (education-work-retirement) through which men born in the first half of the past century marched lockstep, has loosened. So, too, have the family constraints known to those same cohorts of women.[57] Educational attainment has expanded dramatically, and a college education is now within reach for many. Many young people now have more time to build their skills and earn credentials, to pursue activities meant for personal growth, to experience multiple jobs, and to experiment in romantic relationships before they settle in.

As we have noted, the story of the changing transition to adulthood is not just one of privileged youth versus underprivileged youth—that is, those who have the luxury to use the early adult years for exploration versus those who have limited opportunities, inadequate personal resources, or fragile family circumstances. It is also a story of the middle class, which is increasingly losing institutional support at precisely the same time as it takes on the heavy burden of supporting young people in the face of dwindling public resources.

Of some things we can be certain. Little about education, work, and family life today comes close to what past generations have known. In some ways life is better, in some ways it is worse, but in most ways it is different. Societies have not yet become fully aware of, or begun fully to address, the ramifications of the longer and more varied transition into adult life. Social institutions, much like young people and their families, are without a clear script for a new era and need to be refashioned to better reflect the times. Finally, for most young people, whether by choice or by circumstance, adulthood no longer begins when adolescence ends.

Endnotes

1. See Hans-Peter Blossfeld and others, eds., *Globalization, Uncertainty, and Youth in Society* (New York: Routledge, 2005); M. Corijn and Erik Klijzing, eds., *Transitions to Adulthood in Europe* (London: Kluwer Academic Publishers, 2001); Frank F. Furstenberg Jr., ed., "Early Adulthood in Cross-National Perspective," *Annals of the American Academy of Political and Social Science* (London: Sage, 2002); Anne H. Gauthier, ed., "Becoming a Young Adult: An International Perspective on the Transitions to Adulthood," *European Journal of Population* 23, nos. 3–4 (October 2007); Cynthia B. Lloyd, ed., *Growing Up Global* (Washington: National Academies Press, 2005); Richard A. Settersten Jr., Frank F. Furstenberg Jr., and Rubén G. Rumbaut, eds., *On the Frontier of Adulthood: Theory, Research, and Public Policy* (University of Chicago Press, 2005).

2. For illustrations, see *On Your Own without a Net: The Transition to Adulthood for Vulnerable Populations,* edited by D. Wayne Osgood and others (University of Chicago Press, 2005).

3. For illustrations, see Richard A. Settersten Jr., "Social Policy and the Transition to Adulthood," in *On the Frontier of Adulthood*, edited by Settersten, Furstenberg, and Rumbaut (see note 1). Richard A. Settersten Jr., "Passages to Adulthood," *European Journal of Population* 23, nos. 3–4: 251–72.

4. Robert Frank, *Falling Behind: How Rising Inequality Harms the Middle Class* (University of California Press, 2007).

5. Information about the MacArthur Research Network on Transitions to Adulthood can be found at: www. transad.pop.upenn.edu.

6. Rubén G. Rumbaut and Golnaz Komaie, "Young Adults in the United States: A Mid-Decade Profile" (Philadelphia: MacArthur Network on Transitions to Adulthood, September 2007).

7. Ibid.

8. It is important to note, however, that the data source for the recent update differs from the continuous data source for the century-long view found in figures 1 and 2. The 2007 data point comes from the American Community Survey of the U.S. Bureau of the Census, available through the Integrated Public Use Microdata Series (IPUMS), whereas the 1900–2000 data points come from the decennial Census, which is also available through IPUMS. Because the data sources are different, and because the leaps from 2000 to 2007 are in some cases rather large, we have not added the 2007 data point directly to the figure. Instead, we use the 2007 data source as a window into the contemporary context until the 2010 decennial Census data are available.

9. Rubén G. Rumbaut and Golnaz Komaie, "Immigration and Adult Transitions," *Future of Children* 20, no. 1 (2010), pp. 43–66.

10. See *On the Frontier of Adulthood*, edited by Settersten, Furstenberg, and Rumbaut (see note 1); see also Sheldon Danziger and Cecelia Rouse, eds., *The Price of Independence: The Economics of Early Adulthood* (New York: Russell Sage Foundation, 2007).

11. Frances K. Goldscheider and Calvin Goldscheider, "Moving Out and Marriage: What Do Young Adults Expect?" *American Sociological Review* 52 (April 1987): 278–85. Women in the 1930s also worked, largely to support their parents during the Depression and later to support the country in the war effort in the

1940s. With prosperity following the war, they would leave the workforce for homemaking. Their absence from the workforce in large numbers was once again a blip on the historical radar. Furthermore, African American women had always worked.

12. These early trends toward greater independence at the cusp of the twenties were similar for black men and women, with one exception. Black men and women were more often becoming parents (married or not).

13. For more information on this topic, see Michael Rosenthal, *The Age of Independence: Interracial Unions, Same-Sex Unions, and the Changing American Family* (Harvard University Press, 2007).

14. Lisa Barrow and Cecilia Rouse, "Does College Still Pay?" *Economist's Voice* 2, no. 4 (2005): 1–8.

15. National data show that between 85 and 93 percent of high school graduates plan to pursue college degrees, and all but 10 percent of them enroll in postsecondary education. See Charles Adelman, "The Toolbox Revisited: Paths to Degree Completion from High School through College" (Washington: U.S. Department of Education, Office of Educational Research and Improvement, 2006); U.S. Department of Education, National Center for Education Statistics, *The Condition of Education 2004,* NCES 98-013 (Washington: U.S. Government Printing Office, 2004). See also Barbara Schneider and David Stevenson, *The Ambitious Generation* (Yale University Press, 1999).

16. "Dropouts" are those who are not enrolled in school and who have not earned a high school diploma or equivalent credential, such as a GED. See the National Center for Education Statistics, *Digest of Education Statistics: 2007* (Washington: National Center for Education Statistics, 2008). Some dropouts will, of course, go on to receive a GED. See Dan Bloom, "Programs and Policies to Assist High School Dropouts in the Transition to Adulthood," *Future of Children* 20, no. 1 (2010): 89–108.

17. Fifty-eight percent of Hispanics, 55 percent of African Americans, and 51 percent of Native Americans graduate from high school. Gates Foundation, "Diplomas Count" (Seattle: Bill and Melinda Gates Foundation, 2008). The Gates method results in higher estimates.

18. Rumbaut and Komaie, "Young Adults in the United States" (see note 6).

19. Claudia Goldin, Lawrence F. Katz, and Ilyana Kuziemko, "The Homecoming of American College Women: The Reversal of the College Gender Gap," *Journal of Economic Perspectives* 20 (Fall 2006): 133–56. For women, gains in education were particularly dramatic in the final few decades of the past century. For example, the share of women completing college by age thirty-five quadrupled for those born between 1940 and 1975; for men, it rose by 50 percent.

20. Rumbaut and Komaie also emphasize that, for most adult transitions, the differences between native-born whites and blacks are often more narrow than the gap between Asians, on the upper end, and Hispanics, and especially Mexicans and Puerto Ricans, on the lower. This is especially true where educational attainment is concerned.

21. Rumbaut and Komaie, "Young Adults in the United States" (see note 6).

22. Sara Goldrick-Rab and Josipa Roksa, "A Federal Agenda for Promoting Student Success and Degree Completion" (Washington: Center for American Progress, 2008). Also, the methods of calculating dropout rates vary across studies, and therefore studies often arrive at slightly different figures.

23. U.S. Department of Education, National Center for Education Statistics, *2001 Baccalaureate and Beyond Longitudinal Study* (Washington: NCES, 2002), table II.11.

24. See Thomas Brock, "Young Adults and Higher Education: Barriers and Breakthroughs to Success," *Future of Children* 20, no. 1 (2010): 109–32.

25. Maria Fitzpatrick and Sarah E. Turner, "Blurring the Boundary: Changes in Collegiate Participation and the Transition to Adulthood," in *The Price of Independence*, edited by Danziger and Rouse (see note 10).

26. The numbers are significantly underestimated because the tallies exclude those who are sent to prison. The reasons for the disparity between black and white young men are many, and include a very different set of advantages and blocked opportunities. While lack of education is a common obstacle for both white and black men who are struggling to get started in life, black men have the added burden of racism, greater social isolation in inner cities, and an all-too-tempting drug and gang trade that quickly fills the void of lost jobs.

27. Steven Raphael, "Early Incarceration Spells and the Transition to Adulthood," in *The Price of Independence*, edited by Danziger and Rouse (see note 10).

28. For example, Becky Pettit and Bruce Western, "Mass Imprisonment and the Life Course: Race and Class Inequality in U.S. Incarceration," *American Sociological Review* 69 (2004): 151–69.

29. Department of Justice, Bureau of Justice Statistics, "Prevalence of Imprisonment in the U.S. Population, 1974–2001," Special Report, August 2003, NCJ 197976 (www.ojp.usdoj.gov/bjs/pub/pdf/piusp01.pdf).

30. Heather C. West and William J. Sabol, "Prison Inmates and Mid-Year 2008," Special Report, NCJ 225619, Department of Justice (Washington: Bureau of Justice Statistics, March 2009).

31. Blossfeld and others, eds., *Globalization, Uncertainty, and Youth in Society* (see note 1).

32. Of course, this difference also reflects the fact that education has also been inflated: a high school graduate was at a lower percentile in the educational distribution of the population in 2002 than in 1975.

33. Sheldon Danziger, "Earnings by Education for Young Workers, 1975 and 2002," Data Brief 17 (Philadelphia: MacArthur Network on Transitions to Adulthood, November 2004).

34. Ibid.

35. Rumbaut and Komaie, "Young Adults in the United States" (see note 6). In 2005, 14.9 percent of young adults aged eighteen to thirty-four were in poverty, by government standards. The national poverty rate in 2005 was 12.6 percent. Women were more likely than men to live in poverty (17.7 percent versus 12.1 percent).

36. Ibid.

37. Andrew Cherlin, "American Marriage in the Early 21st Century," *Future of Children* 15, no. 2 (2005): 33–55. See also Frank Furstenberg, "On a New Schedule: Transitions to Adulthood and Family Change," *Future of Children* 20, no. 1 (2010): 67–87.

38. Ibid.

39. Ibid.

40. Suzanne Bianchi and Lynne Casper, "American Families," *Population Bulletin* (December 2000).

41. Wendy Manning, Monica Longmore, and Peggy Giordano, "The Changing Institution of Marriage: Adolescents' Expectations to Cohabit and Marry," Working Paper 2005-11 (Bowling Green, Ohio: Center for Family and Demographic Research, Bowling Green State University, 2005). These plans vary slightly by religion (far fewer from more religious backgrounds plan to live together), and by education. Among women aged twenty-two to forty-four in 2002, roughly 69 percent with a high school degree or less had ever lived together compared with 46 percent among college-educated women. U.S. Department of Health and Human Services, "Fertility, Family Planning, and the Health of U.S. Women: Data from the 2002 National Survey of Family Growth" (Hyattsville, Md.: National Center for Health Statistics, 2006).

42. See Furstenberg, "On a New Schedule" (see note 37).

43. Centers for Disease Control, "Probability of First Marriage Disruption by Duration of Marriage and Wife's Age at Marriage," Advance Data 323 (Atlanta: CDC, May 31, 2001), table 3.

44. Rumbaut and Komaie, "Young Adults in the United States" (see note 6).

45. See Furstenberg, "On a New Schedule" (see note 37).

46. Jacob Hacker, *The Great Risk Shift* (Oxford University Press, 2006). For a cross-national description of different types of welfare states, see Karl Ulrich Mayer, "Whose Lives? How History, Societies and Institutions Define and Shape Life Courses," *Research in Human Development* 1, no. 3 (2003): 161–87. On welfare states and the transition to adulthood, see Settersten, "Social Policy and the Transition to Adulthood" (see note 3).

47. Robert Schoeni and Karen Ross, "Material Assistance from Families during the Transition to Adulthood," in *On the Frontier of Adulthood*, edited by Settersten, Furstenberg, and Rumbaut (see note 1). Adult children are financially supported by parents through their twenties. The network's study using 1988 data found that amounts drop off after age twenty-two, but even at age thirty, young adults received about $1,600 from their parents in the previous year. Data from the Youth Development Survey at the University of Minnesota also show that even at age twenty-nine to thirty, 13 percent of respondents received at least some economic support (covering living expenses) from their parents, a drop from 20 percent at age twenty-five to twenty-six, and 39 percent at age twenty-three to twenty-four (Jeylan Mortimer, personal communication). This general trend is echoed in new international evidence, which shows significant declines in economic self-sufficiency among youth in Belgium, Canada, Germany, Italy, the United Kingdom, and the United States from the mid-1980s through 2000. See Lisa Bell and others, "A Cross-National Survey of Trends in the Transition to Economic Independence," in *The Price of Independence*, edited by Danziger and Rouse (see note 10).

48. See Rumbaut and Komaie, "Immigration and Adult Transitions" (see note 9).

49. For American illustrations across a wide range of vulnerable populations, see *On Your Own without a Net*, edited by Osgood and others (see note 2). See also D. Wayne Osgood, E. Michael Foster, and Mark E. Courtney, "Vulnerable Populations and the Transition to Adulthood," *Future of Children* 20, no. 1 (2010): 209–29.

50. Peter Gosselin, *Hire Wire: The Precarious Financial Lives of American Families* (New York: Basic Books, 2009).

51. Jean Rhodes and Sarah Lowe, "Mentoring in Adolescence," in *Handbook of Adolescent Psychology,* edited by Richard Lerner and Lawrence Steinberg (Hoboken, N.J.: Wiley), 152–90.

52. Mark Granovetter, "The Strength of Weak Ties," *American Journal of Sociology* 78, no. 6 (1973): 1360–80.

53. See Constance Flanagan and Peter Levine, "Civic Engagement and the Transition to Adulthood," *Future of Children* 20, no. 1 (2010): 159–79. See also Constance Flanagan, Peter Levine, and Richard A. Settersten Jr., "Civic Engagement and the Changing Transition to Adulthood," Working Paper (Boston: Tufts University Center for Information and Research on Civic Learning and Engagement, 2009).

54. Ibid.

55. Ibid.

56. See Ryan Kelty, Meredith Kleykamp, and David Segal, "The Military and the Transition to Adulthood," *Future of Children* 20, no. 1 (2010): 181–207.

57. Richard A. Settersten Jr., "The New Landscape of Adult Life," *Research in Human Development* 4, nos. 3–4: 239–52.

Immigration and Adult Transitions

Rubén G. Rumbaut and Golnaz Komaie

Summary

Almost 30 percent of the more than 68 million young adults aged eighteen to thirty-four in the United States today are either foreign born or of foreign parentage. As these newcomers make their transitions to adulthood, say Rubén Rumbaut and Golnaz Komaie, they differ significantly not only from one another but also from their native-parentage counterparts, including blacks and whites. The authors document the demographic changes in the United States over the past forty years and describe the ways in which generation and national origin shape the experiences of these newcomers as they become adults.

Rumbaut and Komaie point out that immigrant groups experience gaps in social, economic, and legal status that are even greater than the gaps between native whites and blacks. By far the most-educated (Indians) *and* the least-educated (Mexicans) groups in the United States today are first-generation immigrants, as are the groups with the lowest poverty rate (Filipinos) *and* the highest poverty rate (Dominicans). These social and economic divides reflect three very different ways immigrants enter the country: through regular immigration channels, without legal authorization, or as state-sponsored refugees. For many ethnic groups, significant progress takes place from the first to the second generation. But, say the authors, for millions of young immigrants, a lack of legal permanent residency status blocks their prospects for social mobility. Having an undocumented status has become all the more consequential with the failure of Congress to pass comprehensive federal immigration reforms.

In the coming two decades, as the U.S. native-parentage labor force continues to shrink, immigrants and their children are expected to account for most of the growth of the nation's labor force, with the fastest-growing occupations requiring college degrees. Rumbaut and Komaie stress that one key to the nation's future will be how it incorporates young adults of immigrant origin in its economy, polity, and society, especially how it enables these young adults to have access to, and to attain, postsecondary education and its manifold payoffs.

www.futureofchildren.org

Rubén G. Rumbaut is a professor of sociology at the University of California–Irvine. Golnaz Komaie received her Ph.D. from the University of California–Irvine in 2009.

I mmigration, a transformative force, has produced striking demographic changes in the American population over the past few decades, especially among its young adults. As recently as 1970, only 4 percent of the approximately 48 million young adults (aged eighteen to thirty-four) in the United States were foreign born. That proportion was the lowest since the U.S. Census Bureau began keeping records on nativity in 1850. But by 2008, when the number of young adults had grown to more than 68 million, almost 30 percent of them were either foreign born or of foreign parentage. These new first and second generations of immigrant origin are steadily growing and changing the ethnic composition and stratification of the nation's young adult population. What is more, their transitions to adult roles—leaving the parental home, finishing school, entering into full-time work, getting married, having children—not only differ significantly by generation and ethnicity, but often stand in marked contrast to patterns observed among their native counterparts who are conventionally assumed to set societal standards.

In this article we sketch a comparative portrait of young adults in the United States in the first years of the twenty-first century, focusing on new patterns of ethnic diversification and of widening socioeconomic and legal inequalities in early adulthood. We analyze data from the latest Current Population Survey and review recent research on young adults of immigrant origin. We focus particularly on generational differences between the foreign-born first and "one and a half" generations and the U.S.-born second generation (of foreign parentage), who are mainly of Latin American and Asian origins, compared with native-parentage young adults, who are overwhelmingly non-Hispanic blacks and whites. We consider structural barriers faced by sizable segments of immigrant youth, especially the undocumented and the less-educated poor, in their transitions to adulthood and discuss possible policy options.

Young Adults in an Age of Migration

No assessment of adult transitions in the United States can fail to pay heed to the ways in which contemporary young adulthood has been increasingly shaped by international migration. After four decades of accelerating migration flows, by 2008 about 41 million foreign-born men and women were living in the United States, most of them having arrived after 1990, primarily from Latin America and Asia. That population has been growing by about 1 million annually, in both legal and unauthorized statuses. *These immigrant flows consist primarily of young adults and their children.* Of the 41 million foreign born, 44 percent arrived in the United States as young adults between the ages of eighteen and thirty-four, and another 40 percent arrived as children under the age of eighteen, in due course to "come of age" and make their own transitions to adulthood in their adoptive society.[1]

Moreover, given the youthful age structure and higher fertility rates of the immigrant population, a new second generation—the U.S.-born children of the immigrants—has been growing rapidly. By 2008, the U.S.-born second generation (with one or two foreign-born parents) totaled more than 32 million; 20 percent of them were young adults aged eighteen to thirty-four, and nearly half (46 percent) were under eighteen—that is, they were still mainly children and teenagers. As this new second generation reaches adulthood in large numbers within the next decade or two, its impact will be increasingly and widely felt throughout the society—in higher education, the labor market, sports and popular culture, criminal justice and religious institutions, the mall, and the ballot box—all the more so in the urban centers where they are concentrated.[2]

As this new second generation reaches adulthood in large numbers within the next decade or two, its impact will be increasingly and widely felt throughout the society.

These new Americans are not a homogeneous population. They differ greatly in their national origins and cultural backgrounds, in their areas of geographic concentration, and in their patterns of socioeconomic mobility and legal status. Before turning to an examination of their transitions to adult roles, we consider briefly their ethnic diversity, ethnic geography, and ethnic inequality.

The Ethnic Diversity of Early Adulthood
Contemporary immigration has led to the formation of new U.S. ethnic groups. Their extraordinary ethnic diversity is belied by the fact that newcomers from more than 150 countries with profoundly different cultures and histories have been officially classified, through the use of one-size-fits-all pan-ethnic categories, as "Hispanics" and "Asians," similar to the older broad racial classifications of "blacks" and "whites." Still, the advent of these newcomers is clearly reflected in the changing ethnic and generational makeup of young adulthood. Among all young adults,

non-Hispanic blacks and whites are overwhelmingly native-stock populations, while Hispanics and Asians are overwhelmingly foreign-stock groups: about 90 percent of whites and blacks are native-born of native-born parents (third or higher generations), but about 80 percent of Hispanics and 94 percent of Asian ethnics are either foreign born or of foreign parentage (first or second generation). This sharp divide reflects the recency of the migration of the latter groups, and underscores the central importance of nativity and generation in the experience of ethno-racial groups in contemporary America. The magnitude of the ethnic shift will become more pronounced as a result of continuing international migration (especially from Latin America, the Caribbean, and Asia), the higher fertility of immigrant women in the United States, and the aging and lower fertility of the white native population. For instance, Hispanics, who according to the U.S. Census Bureau surpassed African Americans as the largest minority group in the United States in 2003, now account for one of every five young adults nationally—and much larger proportions in states and counties of Hispanic concentration, including California, Texas, New York, and Florida.[3]

Lumping millions of newcomers into "Hispanic" and "Asian" pan-ethnic categories, however, conceals fundamental differences between the scores of nationalities that are bound and glossed by those labels. Of the 19 million first- and second-generation young adults between the ages of eighteen and thirty-four, more than half come from the Spanish-speaking countries of Latin America, but fully 35 percent from a single country: Mexico. Salvadorans and Guatemalans together add 5 percent more, Puerto Ricans 4 percent, and Dominicans and Cubans 2 percent each. Together, this handful of Latin

American groups makes up nearly 50 percent of all first- and second-generation young adults in the United States. Similarly, despite far greater diversity among a score of Asian-origin groups, five of them make up another 16 percent of first- and second-generation young adults: Filipinos, Chinese, and Indians account for 4 percent each, and Vietnamese and Koreans for 2 percent each. Those ten ethnic groups thus constitute nearly two-thirds of all eighteen- to thirty-four-year-olds of foreign birth or parentage.

Their countries of origin are the largest sources of immigration to the United States, and they represent the principal types of migration flows (undocumented laborers, professionals, refugees). More than half of all Mexican, Salvadoran, and Guatemalan immigrants in the United States today are undocumented; those groups make up 70 percent of the estimated 11.6 million unauthorized immigrants (Mexicans alone account for three-fifths of the total).[4] Indians, Chinese (including Taiwanese), Koreans, and Filipinos have predominated among the "brain drain" flows of professional immigrants. And Cubans and Vietnamese are by far the two largest groups admitted as state-sponsored political refugees. Accordingly, although they by no means exhaust the extraordinary diversity of contemporary immigration, those ten groups (five "Hispanics," five "Asians") will be considered separately in the analyses that follow.

The Ethnic Geography of Early Adulthood

The nearly 30 percent of all young adults in the United States who come from immigrant origins (whether first or second generations) are not distributed evenly across the country; rather, they are highly concentrated in particular states and localities, especially in California, where 55 percent of *all* its young

adults are first or second generation, and in a handful of metropolitan regions. For example, nearly three-fifths of *all* persons eighteen to thirty-four in Southern California (59 percent), the San Francisco Bay Area (58 percent), and the New York metropolitan area (56 percent) are of foreign birth or parentage, as are fully two-thirds of the young adults of greater Miami and of Texas cities along the Mexican border from El Paso to Laredo, McAllen, and Brownsville. By contrast, outside of that handful of regions, the proportion of young adults in the rest of the United States who are of immigrant origin is less than one-fifth. Thus, studies of young adults in New York, Los Angeles, San Diego, and Miami encounter very different populations than are found in areas less touched by contemporary immigration.[5]

Those areas of immigrant concentration, in turn, differ greatly by the ethnic composition of the young adults who settle there. Consider the top ten groups noted earlier. Of the 6.5 million first- and second-generation Mexican young adults in the United States, more than a fourth are concentrated in Southern California alone (primarily along the corridor from Los Angeles to San Diego)—as are more than a fourth of all Salvadorans and Guatemalans between eighteen and thirty-four and a fifth of all Filipinos, Vietnamese, and Koreans. More than two-thirds of all Dominican young adults in the United States reside in metropolitan New York, as do nearly a third of Puerto Ricans and a fifth of the Chinese. Greater Miami alone accounts for well over half of all Cuban young adults. The Indians are more dispersed, but still 15 percent are found in greater New York.

Ethnic Inequalities

Until recently, social inequalities among Americans (and among young adults in particular) have been seen through a prism of black-white differences. Although major socioeconomic differences persist between native whites and blacks, the social and economic divides between immigrant-origin groups, who are overwhelmingly Hispanics and Asians, are even larger. The ethnic diversity of contemporary immigrants pales in comparison with the diversity of their social class origins. By far the most-educated (Indians) *and* the least-educated (Mexicans) groups in the United States today are first-generation immigrants, as are the groups with the lowest poverty rate (Filipinos) *and* the highest poverty rate (Dominicans)—a reflection of the fundamentally different ways they enter the country: through regular immigration channels, without legal authorization, or as state-sponsored refugees. And their differing legal status interacts with their human capital to shape distinct modes of incorporation.

"Brain drain" professionals mainly enter under the occupational preferences of U.S. law, which favor the highly skilled and educated. Also found among the first waves of refugee flows, these professionals are more likely to become naturalized citizens and, usually within the first generation, home-owners in the suburbs. The undocumented consist disproportionately of manual laborers with less than a high school education, whose legal vulnerability makes them economically exploitable and likely to be concentrated in central cities. Their children in turn tend to grow up in neighborhoods and attend schools where they are exposed disproportionately to peer groups involved with youth gangs and intergroup violence. Indeed, an unauthorized status can affect virtually every facet of an immigrant's life—especially during the transition to adulthood.[6] The size and concentration of this vulnerable young adult population

is significant. By 2008, more than a quarter of the foreign-born population—an estimated 11.6 million people—were undocumented immigrants, by far the largest number and share in U.S. history. Half (49 percent) of the undocumented were young adults eighteen to thirty-four, and another 13 percent were children under eighteen.[7] We turn now to examine generational and ethnic differences in the transition to adulthood and how adult transitions are affected by patterns of socio-economic and legal inequality among immigrant-origin groups.

Generational Differences in Adult Transitions

The exit from adolescence and entry into adult roles and responsibilities typically entails status transitions from school to work and from one's family of origin to the formation of new intimate relationships, notably via marriage and parenthood. Nationally, relative to patterns observed several decades ago, normative timetables for accomplishing such adult transitions have been prolonged.[8] Postsecondary schooling has lengthened for young people, and the exit from the parental household, the entry into full-time work, and decisions about marriage and children have been delayed. For example, data from the National Longitudinal Study of Youth show that, between 1985 and 2003, the proportion of young adults aged twenty to twenty-two still living with their parents increased from 45 percent to 57 percent.[9] And census data show that from 1950 to 2008 the median age at first marriage rose from twenty-three to twenty-eight for men and from twenty to twenty-six for women—the oldest on record for both.

Figure 1 graphs the percentage of young adults in the United States who are not living with their parents, are enrolled in school full

Figure 1. Transitions to Adulthood in the United States: Young Adults 18 to 34

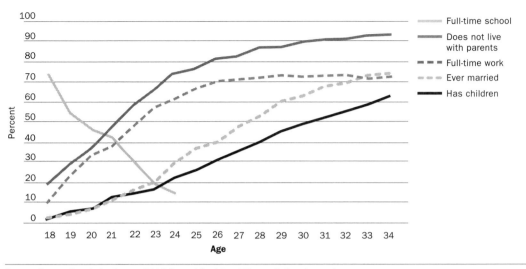

Source: Current Population Survey, 2008 (Annual Social and Economic Supplement).

time, are working full time, are married, and have children, for every year from age eighteen to thirty-four. The data again come from the 2008 Current Population Survey. Nationally, these data show that the most rapid shifts in the school-to-work transition, and in leaving the parental fold, occur between the ages of eighteen and twenty-four; the major changes in marriage and parenthood take place from age twenty-five to age thirty-four. For example, among all eighteen-year-olds in the United States, 80 percent were living with their parents, 75 percent were attending school full time, and only 10 percent were working full time. By age twenty-four, those figures had reversed: only 25 percent were still living with their parents and only 15 percent were attending school full time, while 62 percent were working full time. But among all twenty-four-year-olds, less than a quarter had had children (23 percent), and less than a third had ever married (29 percent); by age thirty-four, two-thirds had children and three-fourths had married.

Do these patterns hold for both immigrants and natives, or do they differ by generation? Figure 2 looks at each of these five measures for all young adults aged eighteen to thirty-four, broken down by generational cohorts. Within the foreign-born first generation, there are significant differences between immigrants who arrived in the United States as children and those who arrived as teens or young adults.[10] Thus, we distinguish the "1.0" (those who immigrated at age thirteen or older) and the "1.5" cohorts (those who immigrated as children under thirteen) from the second generation (native born with one or both parents foreign born) and the third and later ("3+") generations (native born with native-born parents).

As figure 2 shows, the first generation clearly stands out in their greater propensity to have completed the five major transitions to adulthood. Not surprisingly, the 1.0 generational cohort is the least likely to be living with their parents (only 8 percent)—who are most often left in the country of origin—and the least likely to be attending school (22 percent), the

Figure 2. Transitions to Adulthood by Generational Cohorts: Young Adults 18 to 34

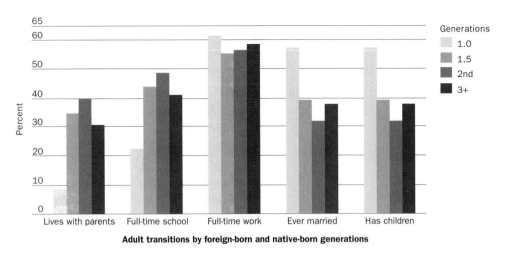

Adult transitions by foreign-born and native-born generations

Source: Current Population Survey, 2008 (Annual Social and Economic Supplement).

most likely to be working full time (61 percent), and by far the most likely to be married (57 percent) and to have children (42 percent).

In contrast, the U.S.-born second generation is the least likely to have achieved those conventional markers of adult status—leaving home, finishing school, entering the workforce, getting married, and having children. It is the second generation that stands out in every instance, rather than the first (1.0 or 1.5) or the third and later (3+), that is, U.S.-born children of U.S.-born parents. Indeed, second-generation young adults are by far the most likely to live with their (immigrant) parents (40 percent), as will be elaborated below; they are also the most likely to be attending school (49 percent) and by far the least likely to be married (32 percent) and to have children (25 percent).

The 1.5 generation, classic in-betweeners, falls in between the 1.0 and the second generations in virtually every indicator, but more closely resemble the latter (their U.S.-born counterparts, with whom they share the

circumstance of being raised in immigrant families while being educated and reaching adulthood in the United States). The native 3+ generations—who by definition set and reflect societal norms—in turn fall in between the first and second generations in these measures.

As noted, second-generation young adults are the least likely to have left the parental home. This trend is most pronounced during the *earliest* years (eighteen to twenty-four) of the transition: more than three out of five (61 percent) second-generation eighteen- to twenty-four-year-olds continue to live at home with their immigrant parents. As we will show, for young adults in immigrant families, staying at home helps to pool resources and minimize expenses, especially given the high cost of housing in major immigrant destinations like New York City, Miami, and Southern California.[11]

Despite general observations often made to the contrary about immigrants, it is worth underscoring that the 1.0 generation of young

Table 1. Adult Transitions among Young Men and Women, by Ethnicity and Generation, by Percent

Percent		Men and women, 18–24 only			Women only, 18–24 and 25–34			
Ethnicity	Generation*	Living with parents	Full-time school	Full-time work	Marriage		Children	
		18–24	18–24	18–24	18–24	25–34	18–24	25–34
Native parentage								
Black	3+	49.2	35.2	33.5	8.9	40.0	30.2	65.5
White	3+	53.0	42.4	40.2	18.7	71.4	16.3	56.8
Foreign parentage								
Mexican	1.0	12.4	4.7	57.4	59.2	81.7	47.0	77.1
	1.5	43.8	23.1	46.9	35.9	73.9	35.7	75.2
	2nd	57.1	32.5	40.8	25.4	67.9	28.7	65.8
Salvadoran/ Guatemalan	1.0	9.6	5.5	59.6	44.4	72.5	34.7	67.5
	1.5	46.5	23.8	52.2	42.4	62.4	39.0	60.5
	2nd	64.1	43.4	33.5	13.8	48.3	15.2	51.8
Puerto Rican**	1.0	24.2	22.9	39.9	38.3	69.6	43.1	68.9
	1.5	45.6	29.2	42.6	20.3	49.1	29.7	68.0
	2nd	59.9	30.5	35.8	13.8	53.7	30.4	70.7
Dominican	1.0	31.6	23.3	43.4	31.2	71.2	30.0	74.7
	1.5	57.4	43.3	33.9	8.1	54.5	18.9	64.2
	2nd	66.9	48.4	25.7	7.6	54.8	13.9	52.7
Cuban	1.0	40.7	12.9	52.3	33.2	72.1	20.3	58.2
	1.5	56.1	32.1	44.9	23.8	75.6	20.2	64.7
	2nd	59.7	46.7	39.1	10.0	70.2	11.1	57.6
Vietnamese	1.0	37.6	46.6	28.5	24.8	78.3	8.5	56.0
	1.5	52.1	59.9	22.8	13.0	56.7	15.0	41.4
	2nd	53.9	60.5	30.4	6.2	38.8	6.1	31.9
Filipino	1.0	47.5	28.1	37.0	31.9	76.1	22.9	53.4
	1.5	55.5	55.7	36.6	8.9	56.6	9.9	45.6
	2nd	65.6	55.0	29.5	9.6	55.7	15.3	44.8
Korean	1.0	33.5	60.9	15.2	14.3	75.5	<1%	47.0
	1.5	58.9	57.9	29.1	6.7	56.6	4.4	36.5
	2nd	58.0	61.4	21.0	10.2	39.3	4.3	26.0
Chinese	1.0	27.2	68.4	20.4	10.9	71.5	2.9	37.9
	1.5	59.6	67.4	21.9	1.7	45.4	5.4	26.8
	2nd	66.7	65.7	21.5	3.5	46.0	1.3	25.5
Indian	1.0	19.1	41.4	30.8	53.6	92.0	8.8	63.0
	1.5	71.7	73.5	16.9	15.3	65.4	8.6	52.1
	2nd	75.0	71.0	18.1	2.7	51.0	1.4	25.8

Source: Current Population Surveys, 2003–2008 (Annual Social and Economic Supplement).
*   The first generation (foreign-born) is divided into two cohorts: 1.0 (13 or older at arrival) and 1.5 (12 or younger at arrival); the second generation is U.S.-born with one or both parents foreign-born; the third or higher (3+) generations are U.S.-born of U.S.-born parents.
** For Puerto Ricans, 1.0 and 1.5 are born on the island; 2nd is born on the mainland of island-born parents.

adults (but not the 1.5) is by far the least likely to reside with their parents; generally, the parents of most of those who immigrated as young adults (or even in their late teens) still reside in their countries of origin. For those who were the protagonists of the decision to migrate—to leave home, radically —immigration itself is a definitive adult transition. But for the children of immigrants raised in American communities, for whom the migration of their parents is an inherited circumstance, the process of "coming of age" has different meanings and obligations and evolves in fundamentally different contexts.

Ethnic Differences in Adult Transitions

Generational status, as determined by age at migration and by the nativity of self and parents, clearly makes a major difference in the modes of adult transitions. What about ethnicity? In previous analyses of young adults in the United States we found that Hispanics collectively (two-thirds of whom are of Mexican origin) were the most likely to have moved out of the home of their parents, to be married, have children, and be working full-time, while Asian-origin young adults as a whole were the most likely to be attending school and least likely to have children.[12] But as noted, such pan-ethnic categories often conceal more than they reveal.

Table 1 takes a closer look at ethnic differences and provides data on adult transitions for the ten largest ethnic groups of foreign parentage in the United States, broken down by generational status (1.0, 1.5, and second), compared with native-parentage white and black young adults. Because the greatest changes in the school-to-work transition and in the exit from the parental household occur from age eighteen to twenty-four, the left panel of table 1 focuses on that earlier phase for those transitions; then, with respect to the entry into marriage and parenthood, the right panel of the table compares women only in two age groups, eighteen to twenty-four and twenty-five to thirty-four.

Between age eighteen and age twenty-four, native-parentage whites and blacks exhibit relatively minor differences in the first three of these status transitions: whites were only slightly more likely than blacks to be living with their parents (53 to 49 percent), 7 points more likely to be attending school full time (42 to 35 percent), and 6 points more likely to be working full time (40 to 34 percent). With respect to marriage and children, however, differences are very sharp: between age eighteen and twenty-four, white women were two times more likely to have married (19 to 9 percent), while black women were two times more likely to have had children (30 to 16 percent). By age twenty-five to thirty-four, white women remained far more likely to have ever married (71 to 40 percent), while the childbearing gap had narrowed significantly (57 to 66 percent).

Intergroup and intergenerational differences in adult transitions among the ten foreign-parentage Hispanic and Asian ethnic groups are much more pronounced. For example, among 1.0-generation immigrants eighteen to twenty-four years old, only 5 percent of Mexicans, Guatemalans, and Salvadorans were attending school full time (while almost 60 percent were working full-time—characteristic of low-wage labor migrants). By comparison, for the same 1.0 cohort of eighteen to twenty-four-year-olds, full-time school attendance ranged from less than 25 percent for Cubans, Dominicans, and Puerto Ricans, to less than 50 percent for Filipinos, Indians, and Vietnamese, to more than 60 percent for Koreans and Chinese.

By the 1.5 and especially the second generation, within the span of one generation, full-time school attendance increases tremendously for most of these groups, indicative of rapid educational mobility. Among eighteen- to twenty-four-year-olds, for example, the share of Mexicans going to school full time increased to 23 percent in the 1.5 generation and 33 percent in the second generation; the respective rates for Salvadorans and Guatemalans were 24 percent and 43 percent; for Cubans, 32 percent and 47 percent; for Dominicans, 43 percent and 48 percent; and for all of the Asian groups, well above 50 percent in both the 1.5 and second generations, including two-thirds of the Chinese and nearly three-fourths of the Indians. In turn, the proportion of these groups who lived with their parents roughly corresponded to the proportions that attended school full time, and was inversely related to the proportion that worked full time.

Pursuing higher education leads many young adults to postpone marriage and children. Thus, it is not surprising to see that the groups most likely still to be in school full time (for example, second-generation Filipinos, Indians, Chinese, Koreans, and Vietnamese) are also the least likely to be married and to have children. But as was the case between native-parentage whites and blacks, the interethnic and intergenerational group differences are striking in these respects. As table 1 shows, the Mexicans and Puerto Ricans were by far the most likely to have had children in early adulthood (eighteen to twenty-four years old), but Mexican women were much more likely to be married than the Puerto Ricans (for whom the likelihood of nonmarital childbearing increases notably from the 1.0 to the 1.5 and second generations). The likelihood of both marriage and early parenthood among Mexican young women decreases notably from the 1.0 to the 1.5 and second generations. Salvadoran and Guatemalan young women also exhibit high rates of marriage and early childbearing in the first generation, but sharp decreases in the second generation. In contrast, Dominican, Cuban, and Filipino

women exhibit moderate and declining levels of childbearing from the first to the second generations, with the Cubans more likely to be married.

The Vietnamese, Korean, Indian, and Chinese women, in turn, exhibit very low levels of early childbearing (all in single digits), and very sharp declines from the first to the second generation in the proportion who get married. By ages twenty-five to thirty-four, only a fourth of second-generation Korean, Indian, and Chinese women and less than a third of the Vietnamese have had children, compared with more than half of the Cubans, Dominicans, Salvadorans, and Guatemalans, and two-thirds of the Mexicans and Puerto Ricans. These differences in adult transitions, in turn, are rooted in and reflect wide differences in socioeconomic inequality and mobility among these groups. We now turn to those considerations.

Socioeconomic Inequality and Mobility in Early Adulthood

Table 2 examines key indicators of educational and economic inequality. The data are again presented for the ten largest ethnic groups of foreign parentage in the United States, broken down by generational status (1.0, 1.5, and second), compared with native-parentage white and black young adults. The left panel of the table presents data on those at the two poles of educational attainment— college graduates and high school dropouts— and the ratio of the two. The right panel of the table presents the percentage of young adults who are low-wage laborers, below the poverty line, and lacking private health insurance (itself a reflection of job instability in early adulthood).[13]

As the data make clear, these diverse groups of newcomers, who account for a substantial

Table 2. Socioeconomic Inequality among Young Adults 18 to 34, by Ethnicity and Generation

Percent		Educational attainment			Economic status		
Ethnicity	Generation*	College graduate**	High school dropout	Ratio of college graduates to high school dropouts	Low-wage labor***	Below the poverty line	Lacking private health insurance
Native parentage							
Black	3+	17.9	17.8	1.01	40.1	25.6	48.9
White	3+	35.2	10.8	3.26	32.0	10.7	27.2
Foreign parentage							
Mexican	1.0	4.2	61.4	0.07	79.2	27.5	76.4
	1.5	7.4	41.8	0.18	54.6	19.8	63.0
	2nd	14.8	23.6	0.63	37.0	15.4	49.8
Salvadoran/ Guatemalan	1.0	5.0	64.1	0.08	75.6	19.9	74.9
	1.5	11.2	37.8	0.30	47.0	13.8	55.7
	2nd	32.0	19.8	1.62	29.1	9.9	48.6
Puerto Rican	1.0	14.9	23.9	0.63	45.4	30.9	51.2
	1.5	11.2	28.0	0.40	33.2	23.0	51.6
	2nd	13.1	23.6	0.56	32.2	21.6	51.8
Dominican	1.0	11.9	27.5	0.43	53.6	21.7	56.1
	1.5	17.8	28.1	0.63	34.0	22.8	60.0
	2nd	27.4	22.6	1.21	29.1	19.6	59.0
Cuban	1.0	16.5	17.2	0.96	44.7	16.9	53.1
	1.5	22.3	14.3	1.56	18.5	11.4	42.0
	2nd	47.6	10.6	4.48	17.8	10.9	33.5
Vietnamese	1.0	27.1	18.4	1.47	58.6	11.6	46.3
	1.5	47.8	8.8	5.45	29.0	10.3	41.7
	2nd	51.7	8.6	6.04	24.4	15.0	37.2
Filipino	1.0	54.5	3.5	15.45	26.4	4.6	28.0
	1.5	37.4	7.8	4.79	26.7	6.7	28.9
	2nd	46.5	7.6	6.14	21.8	7.2	24.9
Korean	1.0	66.6	4.1	16.10	15.1	23.7	39.7
	1.5	58.0	5.2	11.09	17.2	8.6	30.0
	2nd	59.0	7.5	7.83	18.8	14.5	39.1
Chinese	1.0	65.6	8.4	7.85	22.2	20.8	35.2
	1.5	64.2	9.5	6.74	21.7	11.8	34.5
	2nd	79.1	7.6	10.37	14.1	7.3	23.0
Indian	1.0	88.4	2.0	44.03	7.2	8.2	15.9
	1.5	70.3	7.1	9.94	18.9	7.8	28.7
	2nd	86.2	7.0	12.33	4.2	8.9	18.7

Source: Current Population Surveys, 2003–2008 (Annual Social and Economic Supplement).
* The first generation (foreign-born) is divided into two cohorts: 1.0 (13 or older at arrival) and 1.5 (12 or younger at arrival); the second generation is U.S.-born with one or both parents foreign-born; third or higher (3+) generations are U.S.-born of U.S.-born parents.
** College graduation rates are reported only for 25- to 34-year-olds.
*** Employed in jobs with Duncan socioeconomic index (SEI) scores below 25.

share of all young adults in the United States, are situated at the polar ends of the opportunity structure. Educational, occupational, and economic inequalities between native-parentage whites and blacks—the quintessential "color line" in American life—seem narrow compared with the gulf that now separates most Asian and Hispanic young adults. For example, native whites are twice as likely to have college degrees as blacks (35 to 18 percent), while dropout rates among blacks are 7 points higher (18 to 11 percent). The ratio of college graduates to high school dropouts among whites is more than 3 (there are three times more college graduates than dropouts), while the ratio among blacks is 1 (there are as many college graduates as there are high school dropouts). A third of whites (32 percent) are employed in low-wage jobs at the bottom of the occupational structure, compared with 40 percent of blacks. A quarter (26 percent) of black young adults are below the poverty line, compared with 11 percent of whites. And nearly half (49 percent) of blacks eighteen to thirty-four lack private health insurance, compared with 27 percent of whites.

In sharp contrast is the profile that emerges of foreign-parentage Latin American and Asian young adults. Many Asian young men and women enter at the top of the educational hierarchy from the get-go: in the 1.0 generation, an extraordinary 88 percent of the Indians had bachelor's or advanced degrees (more than 50 points above the proportion of native whites), while only 2 percent failed to complete high school (their ratio of college graduates to dropouts is an astronomical 44). Also in the 1.0 generation, two-thirds of the Chinese and Koreans are college graduates, as are more than half of the Filipinos, and 27 percent of the Vietnamese (who entered mainly as refugees), while their proportions with less than a high school diploma are in the single digits (the sole exception are the 1.0 Vietnamese, at 18 percent). By the second generation, those high levels of educational attainment remain very high (all well above the level of native whites), or, as in the case of the Chinese and Vietnamese, increase significantly (to 79

percent and 51 percent, respectively), while their high school dropout rates remain in single digits, well below that of native whites.

Latino young adults enter at the bottom of the educational hierarchy, although wide differences exist between ethnic groups. In the 1.0 generation, only 5 percent or fewer of the Mexicans, Salvadorans, and Guatemalans had college degrees, while over 60 percent had not finished high school. However, significant progress takes place from the first to the second generation, with college graduation rates increasing to 15 percent for Mexican Americans and 32 percent for Salvadorans and Guatemalans, and high school dropout rates decreasing to between 20 and 25 percent (still higher than that of African Americans). The Puerto Rican profile largely stays flat: from the 1.0 to the 1.5 to the second generation the rate stays about the same, with the dropout rate (around one in four) nearly double the proportion that earns college degrees (around one in eight). For the Dominicans the share of college graduates increases from the 1.0 (12 percent) to the second generation (27 percent), but their dropout rates remain very high (around one in four). The Cubans show significant progress in college graduation levels (tripling from 16 percent in the 1.0 cohort to 48 percent in the second generation) and moderate declines in high school dropouts (from 17 to 11 percent, matching the rate for whites).

In the 1.0 generation, the Mexicans, Salvadorans, and Guatemalans (the groups with the largest proportion of undocumented immigrants—an issue to which we will return) also enter at the bottom of the occupational hierarchy, with more than three out of four mired in the lowest rungs of the U.S. labor market, and a nearly identical proportion lacking health insurance. About half of 1.0-generation Dominicans, Puerto Ricans, Cubans, and Vietnamese also work in low-wage jobs. Their poverty rates are correspondingly high, and more than half of all of them lack private health insurance. However, most noticeably for the Mexicans, Salvadorans, and Guatemalans (who, in the second generation, are U.S. citizens by birthright), again intergenerational progress is rapid, as table 2 indicates.

Although the process of intergenerational change is only hinted at with these data, the formation of new patterns of urban ethnic inequality in early adulthood seems evident.

At the other end of the economic spectrum, reflecting the patterns of educational attainment already noted, the economic situation of the various Asian young adult ethnic groups is significantly better, as measured by the indicators listed in table 2. Groups that start out economically advantaged in the 1.0 generation (for example, the single-digit poverty rates seen among the Filipinos and Indians) maintain that advantage; others show intergenerational progress into the second generation (for example, decreasing poverty rates among the Chinese and decreasing low-wage employment among the Vietnamese). Poverty rates and lack of health care coverage for the Vietnamese and Koreans remain above those of native whites, but below the levels of African American young adults. Although the process of intergenerational change is only hinted at

with these data, the formation of new patterns of urban ethnic inequality in early adulthood seems evident. And as we will elaborate, that inequality is widened further still by the fact that millions of young immigrants lack legal permanent residency status, blocking their prospects for social mobility.

Leaving Home and "Giving Back" among Young Adult Children of Immigrants

By most any measure, coming of age is taking longer these days. In the process, parents are also assisting their adult children longer. Robert Schoeni and Karen Ross recently calculated how much material support parents provide for their grown-up children, using data from the 1988 special Time and Money Transfers Supplement to the Panel Study of Income Dynamics (PSID), and decennial census data from 1970 to 1990.[14] The PSID is a longitudinal, nationally representative sample—but it was drawn in 1968, before the new era of large-scale immigration to the United States, and thus the sample is representative of a predominantly native-parentage population. Specifically, the authors examined how much time and money the sample of 6,661 young adults between the ages of eighteen and thirty-four received from their families over the study period. It found that parents provided roughly $38,000 in material assistance for food, housing, education, or direct cash assistance throughout the transition to adulthood, or about $2,200 a year from age eighteen to age thirty-four. Of course, the amount of material assistance depended greatly on parental income. For example, parents (especially middle-income parents) used their financial resources to help their children pay for college, help them with the down payments for their first homes, or to defray some of the costs associated with having children. In addition, the authors estimated that the number of young adults still living at home with their parents had led to a 19 percent increase in parental contributions. In short, the overall trend has been for parents to assist their children well into their thirties.

Are these trends and patterns equally applicable to the first and second generations of foreign-born or foreign-parentage young adults today? Earlier we noted that the 1.0 generation was by far the least likely to live with their parents—indeed, young adult immigrant workers in the United States frequently send remittances to support their parents and families "back home," all the more as their economic prospects improve.[15] In sharp contrast, the 1.5 and most notably the second generations of particular ethnic groups are living in the parental home longer than young adults of native parentage, especially white natives. Yet a series of studies of young adults of immigrant origin in Southern and Northern California, Miami, New York City, and elsewhere suggest that the pattern of support in immigrant families more often flows reciprocally or even in the opposite direction than that indicated by data on preponderantly native-parentage families. Such results have been reported since the 1980s by studies based on both structured surveys and qualitative interviews.

For example, a longitudinal study in the San Francisco Bay area led by Andrew Fuligni followed a sample of about 1,000 adolescents of both immigrant and non-immigrant families from middle school through high school and into young adulthood; the majority had immigrant parents from Mexico, Central America, the Philippines, China, Taiwan, and other countries. It found a greater sense of obligation and indebtedness to the family (measured by three multiple-item scales)

among Latin American and Asian youth, which was significantly associated with high levels of academic motivation; moreover, high school graduates from immigrant Latin American families were significantly more likely than their peers from non-immigrant families to provide financial assistance to their parents and siblings.[16]

The Immigrant Second Generation in Metropolitan New York (ISGMNY) study, led by Philip Kasinitz, John Mollenkopf, and Mary Waters, compared five foreign-parentage groups (Chinese, Dominicans, South Americans, West Indians, and Russians) with native-parentage white, black, and Puerto Rican young adults between the ages of eighteen and thirty-two.[17] They conducted a telephone survey of a sample of 3,415 during 1998–2000, as well as follow-up open-ended interviews with 333 of those respondents. The high cost of housing in New York City presented a major hurdle to achieving some of the traditional benchmarks of adulthood, including leaving the parental home; but the 1.5- and second-generation groups were more likely to live with their parents than natives. Of all the groups in the sample, the Chinese stayed at home the longest, followed by Russians, South Americans, and West Indians. Native-parentage whites were the most likely of all the groups in their sample to move out of the parental home, either living alone or with roommates throughout most of their twenties. The authors note that living at home has important implications for socioeconomic mobility. Those living at home were more likely to be enrolled in school, and those attending college while living with their parents were able to avoid incurring heavy debt. By living with their immigrant parents, the 1.5 and second generations were less likely to be working yet able to save money to buy a home, benefiting them in the long run.

In a related analysis based on qualitative data from the ISGMNY project, Jennifer Holdaway illustrates how the high cost of housing in New York City has affected the transition to adulthood. Given the high cost of real estate and rents in Manhattan and the surrounding boroughs, many young New Yorkers cannot afford to leave the parental home. One-fourth of New York renters carry a "severe rent burden" of more than 50 percent of household income.[18] The high housing costs lead many young New Yorkers to postpone moving out of their parents' homes. Although nationally about half of eighteen- to twenty-four-year-olds were living independently of their parents, only 17 percent were doing so in the New York metropolitan area. Among thirty- to thirty-four-year-olds, only 55 percent were independent, compared with more than 90 percent nationally. Even at the higher age range, many more New Yorkers continue to live with their parents than elsewhere in the nation; again, this finding is especially true for the children of immigrants.

Holdaway shows how the disposition of many second-generation young adults to stay at home makes it much easier for them to attend and finish college and get a foothold in the New York housing market. In contrast, "native-born minorities, who share with whites the idea that becoming an adult means moving out of their family home but rarely have the resources to do so, find themselves at a disadvantage compared with most of the second generation in this respect."[19] In fact, a small but significant number of 1.5- and second-generation respondents were engaged in "multi-generational living." Some families chose to live on different floors in the same building or purchase large homes that can accommodate multi-generation families. By living together, it was possible to combine

parenthood with continuing education or full-time work; while young parents went to work, grandparents assisted with child care. This practice was most common among Chinese, West Indian, South American, and Russian families. Very few native-parentage whites, blacks, and Puerto Ricans engaged in such living arrangements even though many would have benefited from them.[20]

In addition to being able to save money and pool resources by living together, second-generation youth provide significant financial and social support *to* their immigrant parents. For instance, in a study of young adults (mostly Mexican, Filipino, Vietnamese, Laotian, Cambodian, and Chinese) participating in the Children of Immigrants Longitudinal Study (CILS) in San Diego, Linda Borgen and Rubén Rumbaut found that many of them seek to "take care of" their immigrant parents and even contribute financially to their parents' future retirement.[21] In-depth follow-up interviews with 134 CILS respondents (a one in ten systematic sample ranging in age from twenty-three to twenty-seven) found that 39 percent were supporting their parents financially (giving them money directly or paying their mortgage, rent, food, and other bills), another 6 percent were planning concretely to contribute financially to their parents, and 5 percent were contributing their labor in their parents' business. Of the remaining half who were not making payments to or otherwise supporting their parents, 10 percent were living on their own without any assistance from their parents (including 4 percent who were putting themselves through college while working and living independently), and 9 percent had strained or severed relations with the parents (involving a history of family conflict or dysfunction, alleged abuse, drug addiction, prison). Only in a third of the cases

(31 percent) were the immigrant parents supporting their young adult children financially, either partially (27 percent) or fully (4 percent).

For some of these young adults, financial independence coincides with a sense of family financial security, not just their own individual security. A prominent theme in the CILS study, seen across ethnic groups, concerned the family's concerted efforts to minimize expenses, pool resources, and accumulate capital. Just over half of the families in CILS were homeowners by the mid-1990s, a rate of homeownership that had been aided by opportunities to get cheaper mortgages on real estate during the economic slump of the early 1990s, especially for the more advantaged immigrant professionals, or military personnel (mostly Filipino).[22] But in other cases, the young adults themselves strove to become the family's first-time homeowners, with plans to shelter their parents.

The arrangements of San Diego's immigrant parents and their young adult children differed in several ways from conventional American adulthood norms of departing the parental household and setting up a separate home. First, there was no insistence that grown children leave their parents' home after age eighteen or twenty-one or even after marriage. Second, shared bedrooms and familial living space were common. Third, the children often embraced a range of responsibilities to assist their immigrant parents. And fourth, as in New York, given the costly affordability quotient in the region for single living, shared familial habitation made economic sense even for those who felt the "Americanized" urge to live independently. In San Diego, immigrant parents often shared their homes with their adult children, but as often as not, the children purchased or

contributed substantial sums securing shelter for their parents or for their parents and themselves together.

For some of these young adults, financial independence coincides with a sense of family financial security, not just their own individual security.

In some cases young adult children look at their earnings as part of the family's income, as documented by the Southeast Asian Refugee Youth Study in the late 1980s in San Diego.[23] The research combined qualitative and survey data to produce detailed case histories of Vietnamese, Cambodian, and Hmong young adults. One was Van Le, then a twenty-six-year-old medical student at the University of California and one of ten children of a Vietnamese refugee family whose father had died soon after arriving in the United States in 1976. In their family, as the children grew up and entered the work world, each was required to give a "tax" back to the mother. Van gave the money he earned as an undergraduate in work-study employment to his mother, and he expected to pay a "tax" when he became a practicing physician. The down payment for the house she lived in was given by the two employed oldest sisters, who also made the monthly house payments. His mother's low-paying job in electronics assembly was just enough to cover food and daily living expenses, but it would have been impossible for her to live in that house without the family tax system. Those who remained in his mother's house were expected to pay half of their salary to her. The tax was seen as "generosity," given without resentment, and treated as a filial obligation of child to parent. In fact, whenever a child married, one condition was that the new spouse accept the tax system, as did the American-born husband of Van's eldest sister. This system of taxing was flexible enough that if grandchildren were born, the tax would be reduced.

A recent study based on forty in-depth interviews with 1.5- and second-generation middle-class Mexican young adults in the Los Angeles area illustrates three patterns of "giving back" to their immigrant families: providing total financial support of their parents or younger siblings, or both; becoming the "safety net" for their parents, siblings, and relatives during times of hardship; and providing regular financial support to supplement their parents' incomes.[24] The authors found that about one-fifth of the respondents fully supported their immigrant parents—as did Adrián, a second-generation Mexican-American teacher with a master's degree: "Ever since I started working when I was 14 I have given them everything I could. Now it's at about $1,000 a month…just to help them out." He also paid all of the household bills. María, a second-generation entrepreneur with two young children, similarly supported her mother: "I pay her rent, I give her money, I take her to the doctors, I buy her prescriptions. I take care of my Mom."

The most common form of giving back by the children of Mexican immigrants was providing monthly supplemental income to their parents. Half of the respondents in this study gave their parents between $200 and $1,000 every month for household expenses and also helped them in non-financial ways: translating documents, drafting letters,

making phone calls, accompanying them to work-related and medical appointments. The more successful often came to the rescue of their immigrant parents in times of economic crisis—like Lupe, a second-generation thirty-four-year-old vice president of a national financial services institution, who gave her parents $5,000 to make their mortgage payment and cover their household bills. Even when she was in college Lupe had financially rescued her father, whose landscaping business was in jeopardy, by giving him $10,000 from her school loans, which she was still paying back. She also agreed to co-sign for the loan used to purchase her father's new truck, which he could not obtain on his own because of his credit record. The authors note that those who grew up poor (but were not poor now) were more likely to "give back" to their parents, relatives, and the co-ethnic community, and to display a "collectivist orientation," while those who grew up middle-class exhibited an individualistic orientation resembling conventional American norms.

Immigration, Legal Status, and the Transition to Adulthood

In 2008, of the more than 68 million young adults aged eighteen to thirty-four in the United States, nearly one in five (18 percent) was foreign-born; astonishingly, almost half of those immigrant young adults, or nearly 6 million, were estimated to be unauthorized (most "entered without inspection," while as many as 40 percent entered legally but then overstayed their visas).[25] The undocumented immigrant population has more than tripled since the early 1990s; one-fourth is in California, although increasingly it has been dispersing to new destinations. For foreign-born young adults, an undocumented status blocks access to the opportunity structure and paths to social mobility. It has become all the more consequential since the passage of draconian federal laws in 1996, the advent of the "war on terror" after September 11, 2001, and the failure by Congress to pass comprehensive federal immigration reforms. Undocumented young adults are coming of age amid a hostile political backlash and rising animus toward immigrants. Hundreds of thousands of immigrants have been deported ("removed") over the past decade, separating families and leaving behind, as of 2005, at least 1.6 million spouses and children, many of whom are U.S. citizens—a figure that has significantly increased since 2005, with the expansion of the enforcement budget for Immigrations and Customs Enforcement under the newly created Department of Homeland Security.[26] Federal raids of workplaces and private homes and other enforcement campaigns have been intensified. Hundreds of new laws and ordinances seek to achieve social control at the local level—restricting access to drivers' licenses, education, employment, housing, even library cards. States such as South Carolina have banned all undocumented young adults from the state's community colleges. Not surprisingly, the 2007 National Survey of Latinos found that 53 percent of all Hispanic adults in the United States (about a fourth of whom are undocumented immigrants) feared that they, a family member, or friend would be deported.[27] Federal, state, and local enforcement actions have continued since that survey was taken, throughout 2008 and into the Obama administration.

Adult transitions in these circumstances, most saliently the entry into higher education, are invariably shaped by young adults' legal residency status. Undocumented youth do not qualify for federal financial aid or, in forty states, for in-state tuition.[28] In Arizona, for example, the passage in 2006 of Proposition 300, which restricts in-state

tuition and financial aid to legal residents, quickly resulted in a drop in enrollment at local community colleges and public universities. Some 300 students were estimated to have dropped out of the University of Arizona in Tucson, and as many as 1,000 students from Pima Community College were affected by the passage of this new legislation.[29] In California, one of ten states where undocumented students are allowed to pay in-state tuition, only 1,620 undocumented students were estimated to have enrolled in the University of California and California State University systems in 2005—a minuscule fraction of the 630,000 students enrolled in the UC and CSU systems, let alone the 2.5 million in all of California's public higher education, including community colleges.[30] The severe economic recession since late 2007, exacerbated by bank failures, home foreclosures, and the state's deep budget deficit, had by 2009 seriously undermined California's "master plan" of universal access to public higher education—and those bearing the brunt have been the poor and the most vulnerable.

Consider the case of Karina de La Cruz, an eighteen-year-old undocumented student from San Pedro in Los Angeles County, who struggles to remain a full-time student at University of California–Los Angeles. Born in Mexico, Karina crossed the border illegally into the United States with her family when she was four years old. The family settled in San Pedro, where her mother worked in a fish cannery seven days a week to make ends meet. Karina graduated from San Pedro High School and was accepted to UCLA. She is the first in her family to attend college (as is typically the case with students in these circumstances) and hopes one day to get a job as a psychologist. Without legal status, however, she is ineligible for most forms of state and

Adult transitions in these circumstances are invariably shaped by young adults' legal residency status.

federal financial aid. UCLA costs about $17,500 a year for in-state fees, books, transportation, and living expenses. Karina won a scholarship from a College Bound program that also held a fundraiser on her behalf, but those funds could cover fees and tuition for only two quarters. Moreover, Karina lives in a cramped apartment with her two brothers, sister-in-law, aunt, and infant niece; she must make an eighty-mile round-trip commute by bus to attend her classes, has few friends at UCLA, and has no safety net. She is not optimistic about her future job opportunities: she realizes that even if she is able to earn her bachelor's degree, most companies will not hire someone who is undocumented.[31] Karina's story illustrates just how difficult it is for undocumented students to remain in school full-time, even when they can pay in-state tuition (as in California) and even when they are highly motivated and academically engaged (as is Karina). For undocumented students in states where in-state tuition is not available, the chances of graduating from college are slimmer still.

Roberto Gonzales' research in the greater Los Angeles area, based on more than a hundred in-depth interviews with undocumented young adults who were born in Mexico and came to the United States as children with their parents, shows how legal status shapes the adult transitions and life chances of 1.5-generation unauthorized immigrants,

including schooling, full-time employment, and marriage.[32] Ramón Betancourt, one of the respondents, exemplifies the difficulties that undocumented youth face in even the most routine day-to-day activities. Ramón migrated to the United States with his mother at the age of ten. Although he has spent most of his life in the United States, he cannot legally work, drive, or vote. Ramón has not finished high school, struggles to find work, and is constantly looking over his shoulder. Without a diploma and a legal means to work, Ramón has spent most of his adult life piecing together odd jobs to support his girlfriend and two children. He started working for himself doing landscaping and painting, but work is not always steady. Child care is expensive, so Ramón's girlfriend stays at home with the children. She too is undocumented and faces the same fears and blocked mobility as Ramón. After spending five years—and having two children—together, they want to get married, but have been advised not to, as their marriage may cut off any possibilities for either of them to regularize their status. Ramón's younger brother, José, who was born in Santa Ana, California, stands in sharp contrast. He is twenty-four, married, and the father of three children. The two brothers grew up in poverty, but José earned his high school diploma through a local continuing education program, passed the tests for his California driver's license after several unsuccessful attempts, and opened up a bank account with hopes of establishing credit and saving money. Although his path to adulthood has been problematic and he too struggles to make ends meet, José remains optimistic and hopes for a good life for his family; his optimism is bred by the circumstance that unlike his older brother, he was born in the United States and is a citizen by birthright.[33]

Of the nearly 12 million undocumented immigrants estimated to be in the United States today, about 13 percent are children under age eighteen who have been raised in and acculturated to American contexts. They cannot be denied access to public elementary or secondary education under the equal protection clause of the Fourteenth Amendment of the U.S. Constitution, as the Supreme Court ruled in *Plyler v. Doe* (1982). But when they complete their secondary education—from the moment they reach early adulthood—they confront formidable barriers. They are subject to detention and deportation regardless of how old they were when they arrived, how they have conducted their lives, or how remarkable their school or community ties and accomplishments. An estimated 65,000 (who have lived in the United States for more than five years) graduate from high school each year, yet perhaps only 5 percent of them ever go to college. As they commence their transitions to adulthood, they face huge economic as well as legal obstacles. A large proportion lives below the poverty line (39 percent versus 17 percent for native-born children).[34] Without a means to adjust their legal status— which is derived from their parents, and they generally have no right to legal permanent residency through any other route—they are ineligible for most forms of college financial aid, cannot apply for a driver's license, and are excluded from the legal workforce, creating a growing pool of acculturated young adults who are being forced further underground instead of forging educational credentials and occupational skills.[35]

The Development, Relief, and Education for Alien Minors (DREAM) Act, a bipartisan bill introduced in Congress in 2001 and reintroduced repeatedly since (most recently in 2009), would permit undocumented students to apply for legal permanent residency if they remain in school through high school graduation and go on to college or military service. As proposed in the bill, before the date of its enactment into law, an applicant must have: entered the United States at the age of fifteen or younger and be under age thirty; must have been continuously present in the United States for at least five years; must have earned a high school diploma or its equivalent; and must have demonstrated good moral character. Undocumented young adults who meet these conditions would then be able to apply for a six-year "conditional" legal permanent status that would allow them to work, go to college, or join the military. If during this period they complete at least two years toward a four-year college degree, graduate from a two-year college, or serve at least two years in the U.S. armed forces, they could change their conditional status to permanent and become eligible to apply for U.S. citizenship. Estimates made in 2006 suggested that the bill could make 360,000 undocumented high school graduates aged eighteen to twenty-four eligible for conditional legal status (enabling most of them to enroll in college or the military), and make another 715,000 undocumented youth between the ages of five and seventeen eligible for conditional and then permanent legal status.[36] The act would give students like Karina an opportunity to pursue a postsecondary education, with full access to financial aid, as well as the means to enter the legal workforce and ultimately gain a pathway to citizenship.

Conclusion

Immigration in the United States is quintessentially the province of the young. Six out of seven immigrants arrive in early adulthood or as children accompanying their young adult parents. Relative to natives, their youthful age structure and higher fertility have combined to produce a rapidly growing, U.S.-born second generation, with median ages still in the teens, who will enter adulthood by the millions in the coming decade. As this process plays out, the transition to adulthood will become more significantly a generational story—made more complex by the much greater ethnic diversity and social inequalities that exist among young adults. Social scientists who study this period of the life course must take these new dynamics into account.

Before the end of the first decade of the twenty-first century, the foreign-born population of the United States surpassed 40 million, an unprecedented total that reflected the evolution of a new era of migration since the 1960s. Fifty years ago young baby boomers, overwhelmingly of native stock, were beginning their transition to adulthood in a society undergoing rapid social change. Today as those baby boomers approach retirement, eighteen- to thirty-four-year-olds are increasingly a foreign-stock population of diverse Latin American and Asian origins. Nationally, nearly 30 percent of American young adults already are of foreign stock—and that proportion doubles to 60 percent in key areas of immigrant concentration, notably in California, Florida, New York, and Texas. The transitions to adulthood of all these newcomers do not play out in the same way or in the same contexts.

Generational status matters. For the newcomers, adult status transitions—leaving the parental home, exiting (or prolonging) formal education, entering into full-time work, marriage, and having children—differ sharply between the first and second generations, and both differ in turn from conventional U.S. norms. Those patterns also vary by ethnicity and by socioeconomic and legal status. The new immigration has brought highly skilled professionals, labor migrants with little education, and refugees escaping harrowing circumstances. Some 1.5- and second-generation groups have made extraordinary strides in early adulthood, outdistancing middle-class natives both educationally and occupationally. But a significant segment of these young adult newcomers is falling behind. Most vulnerable—accounting for almost half of all young adult immigrants—are those who lack legal permanent residency.

The DREAM Act, a legislative initiative aimed at the most successful portion of that population, offers at best a partial policy remedy to a much larger social problem. That a divided Congress has allowed it to languish for nearly a decade, along with other measures aimed at comprehensive immigration reform, is shortsighted. As the native-parentage labor force continues to shrink in the United States in the coming decades—a process that will accelerate as the baby boom generation reaches retirement age—immigrants and their children are expected to account for most of the growth of the U.S. labor force, with the fastest-growing occupations requiring college degrees. California already lacks enough college graduates to meet demand.[37] A key to the future of California—and to that of a nation being transformed by immigration—will be how the rapidly expanding generation of young adults of immigrant origin is incorporated in its economy, polity, and society. Virtually every aspect of that incorporation will be affected by their access to and attainment of postsecondary education and the manifold payoffs to that education. For a sizable proportion of the nation's immigrant population, that access is now blocked. The predictable result of political inaction—exacerbated since 2007 by a deep and prolonged economic recession—will be enduring ethnic inequalities among young adults.

Endnotes

1. These estimates and those that follow are based on the 2008 Current Population Survey (CPS), Annual Social and Economic Supplement. The CPS is a household survey of representative samples of the civilian non-institutionalized adult population of the United States. It excludes persons living in group quarters (such as those in prison, nursing homes, or military barracks). For our purposes in this article, persons born in Puerto Rico (who are U.S. citizens) are classified as first generation, and those born in the mainland of island-born parents are classified as second generation. In 2008, about 1.1 million Puerto Rican young adults eighteen to thirty-four resided in the mainland; of them, 29 percent were first generation and 35 percent second generation.

2. Rubén G. Rumbaut, "The Coming of the Second Generation: Immigration and Ethnic Mobility in Southern California," *Annals of the American Academy of Political and Social Science* 620, no. 1 (2008): 196–236. See also Dowell Myers, *Immigrants and Boomers: Forging a New Social Contract for the Future of America* (New York: Russell Sage Foundation, 2007); and Marta Tienda and others, *Multiple Origins, Uncertain Destinies: Hispanics and the American Future* (Washington: National Academies Press, 2006).

3. U.S. Census Bureau, "Census Bureau Projects Tripling of Hispanic Population in 50 Years," 2004, www.census.gov/Press-Release/www/releases/archives/population/001720.html; "Hispanic and Asian Americans Increasing Faster than Overall Population," 2004, www.census.gov/Press-Release/www/releases/archives/race/00eighteen39.html; Tienda and others, *Multiple Origins, Uncertain Destinies* (see note 2).

4. Michael Hoefer, Nancy Rytina, and Bryan C. Baker, Office of Immigration Statistics, U.S. Department of Homeland Security, "Estimates of the Unauthorized Immigrant Population Residing in the United States: January 2008," February 2009.

5. For a comparative qualitative study of early adulthood in New York City, San Diego, Minneapolis-St. Paul, and rural Iowa, see Mary C. Waters and others, eds., *Coming of Age in America* (forthcoming).

6. Cecilia Menjívar, "Family Reorganization in a Context of Legal Uncertainty: Guatemalan and Salvadoran Immigrants in the United States," *International Journal of Sociology of the Family* 32, no. 2 (2006): 223–45. See also Roberto G. Gonzales, *Born in the Shadows: The Uncertain Futures of the Children of Unauthorized Mexican Migrants* (Ph.D. dissertation, Department of Sociology, University of California–Irvine, 2008).

7. Hoefer, Rytina, and Baker, "Estimates of the Unauthorized Immigrant Population Residing in the United States" (see note 4).

8. Richard A. Settersten Jr., Frank F. Furstenberg Jr., and Rubén G. Rumbaut, eds., *On the Frontier of Adulthood: Theory, Research, and Public Policy* (University of Chicago Press, 2005).

9. Carolyn Hill and Harry Holzer, "Labor Market Experiences and Transitions to Adulthood," in *The Price of Independence: The Economics of Early Adulthood*, edited by Sheldon Danziger and Cecilia E. Rouse (New York: Russell Sage Foundation, 2007).

10. Rubén G. Rumbaut, "Ages, Life Stages, and Generational Cohorts: Decomposing the Immigrant First and Second Generations in the United States," *International Migration Review* 38, no. 3 (2004): 1160–1205.

11. Waters and others, eds., *Coming of Age in America* (see note 5); Rubén G. Rumbaut, Golnaz Komaie, and Charlie V. Morgan, "Young Adults in Five Sites of the United States: New York City, San Diego,

Minneapolis-St. Paul, Detroit, and Iowa," The Network on Transitions to Adulthood, May 2007, www.transad.pop.upenn.edu/publications/wp.html.

12. Rubén G. Rumbaut and Golnaz Komaie, "Young Adults in the United States: A Mid-Decade Profile," The Network on Transitions to Adulthood, October 2007, www.transad.pop.upenn.edu/publications/wp.html.

13. Helen Levy, "Health Insurance and the Transition to Adulthood," in *The Price of Independence: The Economics of Early Adulthood*, edited by Danziger and Rouse (see note 9).

14. Robert F. Schoeni and Karen E. Ross, "Material Assistance from Families during the Transition to Adulthood," in *On the Frontier of Adulthood: Theory, Research, and Public Policy*, edited by Settersten, Furstenberg, and Rumbaut (see note 8), pp. 396–416.

15. Such remittances sent by immigrants worldwide to family members back home, which surpassed $300 billion in 2007 according to World Bank estimates, link communities across national borders and are vital to the economies of many sending countries. See Dean Yang, "How Remittances Help Migrant Families," *Migration Information Source*, December 2004, www.migrationinformation.org/Feature/display.cfm?iD=270.

16. Andrew J. Fuligni and Sara Pedersen, "Family Obligation and the Transition to Young Adulthood," *Developmental Psychology* 38, no. 5 (2002): 856–68. See also *Family Obligation and Assistance during Adolescence: Contextual Variations and Developmental Implications*, edited by A. J. Fuligni (San Francisco: Jossey-Bass, 2001); Carola Suárez-Orozco and Marcelo M. Suárez-Orozco, *Transformations: Immigration, Family Life, and Achievement Motivation among Latino Adolescents* (Stanford University Press, 1995).

17. Philip Kasinitz and others, *Inheriting the City: The Children of Immigrants Come of Age* (Cambridge and New York: Harvard University Press and Russell Sage Foundation, 2008). See also John Mollenkopf and others, "The Ever-Winding Path: Ethnic and Racial Diversity in the Transition to Adulthood," in *On the Frontier of Adulthood: Theory, Research, and Public Policy*, edited by Settersten, Furstenberg, and Rumbaut (see note 8), pp. 454–97.

18. Jennifer Holdaway, "If You Can Make It There ... The Transition to Adulthood in New York City," in *Coming of Age in America*, edited by Waters and others (see note 5).

19. Ibid.

20. Similarly, an exodus of tens of thousands of Cubans who came to Miami in daily "freedom flights" during 1965–73 brought a disproportionate number of elderly (since young adults of military age were not allowed to leave) and led to the formation of more three-generation Cuban households in Miami with resident grandparents than among any other U.S. ethnic groups. The grandparents in turn served as built-in child care providers, allowing young Cuban women to enter the labor force in much larger proportions than other Latin American immigrant groups. That dynamic played a significant role in the Cuban family economic "success story." See Lisandro Pérez, "Immigrant Economic Adjustment and Family Organization: The Cuban Success Story Reexamined," *International Migration Review* 20, no. 1 (1986): 4–20.

21. Linda Borgen and Rubén G. Rumbaut, "Coming of Age in 'America's Finest City': Transitions to Adulthood among Children of Immigrants in San Diego," in *Coming of Age in America*, edited by Waters and others (see note 5). The larger CILS study, carried out in the San Diego and metropolitan Miami areas, followed for a decade a panel of more than 5,000 1.5- and second-generation youth, representing seventy-seven different nationalities, from mid-adolescence to early adulthood. See Alejandro Portes and Rubén G. Rumbaut, eds., *The Second Generation in Early Adulthood*, special issue of *Ethnic and Racial Studies* 28, no. 6 (2005).

22. The foreign-born represented less than 5 percent of the 1.4 million active-duty personnel in the U.S. armed forces in 2008, including 8 percent of all navy personnel. Filipinos accounted for 23 percent of all foreign-born personnel, most of them serving in the navy and stationed in San Diego; Mexicans were a distant second, with 9 percent of the total. See Jeanne Batalova, "Immigrants in the U.S. Armed Forces," *Migration Information Source*, May 2008, www.migrationinformation.org/USFocus/display.cfm?ID=683.

23. Rubén G. Rumbaut and Kenji Ima, *The Adaptation of Southeast Asian Refugee Youth: A Comparative Study* (Washington: U.S. Office of Refugee Resettlement, 1988).

24. Jody Agius Vallejo and Jennifer Lee, "Brown Picket Fences: The Immigrant Narrative and 'Giving Back' among the Mexican-Origin Middle Class," *Ethnicities* 9 (2009): 5–31. The quotations from Adrián, María, and Lupe are from pages 15–16.

25. Hoefer, Rytina, and Baker, "Estimates of the Unauthorized Immigrant Population Residing in the United States" (see note 4).

26. Human Rights Watch, *Forced Apart: Families Separated and Immigrants Harmed by United States Deportation Policy*, HRW 18, no. 3 (2007), http://hrw.org/reports/2007/us0707.

27. Pew Hispanic Center, *2007 National Survey of Latinos: As Illegal Immigration Issue Heats Up, Hispanics Feel a Chill* (Washington: December 2007).

28. Arianna Green, "Longtime Residents Not Allowed In-State Tuition," *New York Times*, March 9, 2009.

29. Jesse McKinley, "Arizona Law Takes a Toll on Nonresident Students," *New York Times*, January 27, 2008.

30. See Roberto G. Gonzales, "Wasted Talent and Broken Dreams: The Lost Potential of Undocumented Students," *Immigration Policy in Focus* 5, no. 13 (October 2007) (Washington: Immigration Policy Center, American Immigration Law Foundation); and Roberto G. Gonzales, "Young Lives on Hold: The College Dreams of Undocumented Students," The College Board, April 2009, www.collegeboard.com/press/releases/204864.html.

31. Jason Song, "For an Illegal Immigrant, Getting into UCLA Was the Easy Part," *Los Angeles Times*, February 2, 2009.

32. Gonzales, *Born in the Shadows: The Uncertain Futures of the Children of Unauthorized Mexican Migrants* (see note 6).

33. Ibid, pp. 206–09.

34. Jennifer L. Frum, "Postsecondary Educational Access for Undocumented Students: Opportunities and Constraints," *American Academic* 3, no. 1 (2007): 81–107.

35. Gonzales, "Wasted Talent and Broken Dreams" (see note 30).

36. Jeanne Batalova and Michael Fix, "New Estimates of Unauthorized Youth Eligible for Legal Status under the DREAM Act," *MPI Immigration Backgrounder*, no. 1, October 2006, www.migrationpolicy.org/pubs/Backgrounder1_Dream_Act.pdf.

37. Hans P. Johnson and Deborah Reed, "Can California Import Enough College Graduates to Meet Workforce Needs?" *California Counts* 8, no. 4 (2007). San Francisco: Public Policy Institute of California.

On a New Schedule: Transitions to Adulthood and Family Change

Frank F. Furstenberg Jr.

Summary

Frank Furstenberg examines how the newly extended timetable for entering adulthood is affecting, and being affected by, the institution of the Western, particularly the American, family. He reviews a growing body of research on the family life of young adults and their parents and draws out important policy implications of the new schedule for the passage to adulthood.

Today, says Furstenberg, home-leaving, marriage, and the onset of childbearing take place much later in the life span than they did during the period after World War II. After the disappearance of America's well-paying unskilled and semi-skilled manufacturing jobs during the 1960s, youth from all economic strata began remaining in school longer and marrying and starting their own families later. Increasing numbers of lower-income women did not marry at all but chose, instead, non-marital parenthood—often turning to their natal families for economic and social support, rather than to their partners. As the period of young adults' dependence on their families grew longer, the financial and emotional burden of parenthood grew heavier. Today, regardless of their income level, U.S. parents provide roughly the same proportion of their earnings to support their young adult children.

Unlike many nations in Europe, the United States, with its relatively underdeveloped welfare system, does not invest heavily in education, health care, and job benefits for young adults. It relies, instead, on families' investments in their own adult children. But as the transition to adulthood becomes more protracted, the increasing family burden may prove costly to society as a whole. Young adults themselves may begin to regard childbearing as more onerous and less rewarding. The need to provide greater support for children for longer periods may discourage couples from having additional children or having children at all. Such decisions could lead to lower total fertility, ultimately reduce the workforce, and further aggravate the problem of providing both for increasing numbers of the elderly and for the young. U.S. policy makers must realize the importance of reinforcing the family nest and helping reduce the large and competing demands that are being placed on today's parents.

www.futureofchildren.org

Frank F. Furstenberg Jr. is the Zellerbach Family Professor of Sociology at the University of Pennsylvania.

The striking changes in the timing and sequencing of adult transitions charted by other articles in this volume have been accompanied by equally dramatic transformations in the institution of the family. In this article I examine how the Western, and most particularly the American, family is affecting and, in turn, being affected by the newly extended social timetable for entering adulthood. I review a growing body of social science research on the family life of young adults and their parents that identifies a set of puzzles and issues that require further investigation, and take note of the enormous policy implications of this new schedule for the passage to adulthood, not just for the family but also for the larger society.

During the final third of the twentieth century, the institution of the family did undergo a radical shift in form and function for reasons that social scientists still only partially understand.

I begin by identifying some of the sweeping changes in Western family systems—in the institution of marriage, in gender-based divisions of labor, and in the meaning of parenthood—that have complicated and extended the life course of young adults. I then address young adults' lengthening co-residence with their parents, a topic that is attracting increasing research interest. Next I explore family formation patterns among young adults: the move from the natal family to what used to be called the "family of procreation," though that term is becoming obsolete because of the sizable fraction of couples who remain childless. After briefly examining intergenerational exchanges among young adults and their parents, I conclude with a brief discussion of policy issues that arise from the changes in early adulthood and the family. Clearly, this is a larger bundle of issues than can be fully addressed in a single article, but I want to highlight what researchers have learned so far and what remains to be discovered to inform policy choices that promote both successful young adult transitions and the long-term welfare of families.

The Changing Family and the Changing Course of Early Adulthood

Contrary to a popular misconception that Western family systems have only recently undergone widespread change, the form and function of the family in the West have been changing for as long as reliable records exist.[1] Marriage, fertility, patterns of parent-and-child co-residence, parenting practices, and indeed virtually anything that can be measured by family demographers and historians have fluctuated over time. As economic conditions, demographic patterns, cultural beliefs, and social institutions have varied, the family has responded and adapted. In this sense, the "traditional" family has no golden past.[2] But during the final third of the twentieth century, the institution of the family did undergo a radical shift in form and function for reasons that social scientists still only partially understand.

The advent of "the post-modern family," as it is sometimes called, has been marked by sharp increases in women's labor force participation, a gradual breakdown of the gender-based division of labor, a precipitous

Figure 1. Proportion of Youth in School, by Age Cohort, 1950–2007

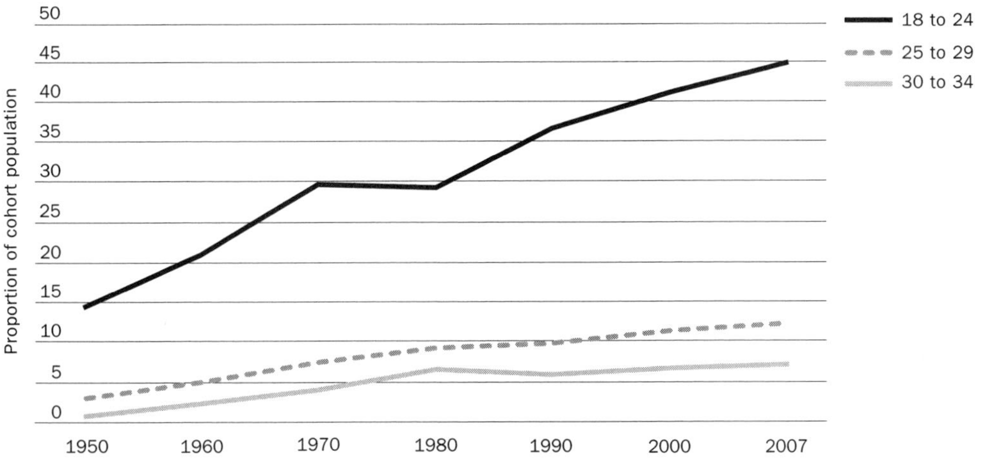

Sources: U.S. Census Bureau, Current Population Survey, October, 1961, 1970, 1980, 1990, 2000, 2007.

fertility decline (owing in part to postpone- ment of marriage and parenthood and in part to the growing number of childless couples), and rising rates of divorce, cohabitation, and nonmarital childbearing.[3] Many converging forces helped to alter family practices. Rising levels of education among women provided a growing demand for employment after marriage. Economic pressures to maintain or increase consumption propelled women into the labor force. Improved contraception allowed women to postpone childbearing. Ideological changes led to increased demands for equality in the marketplace and at home. The confluence of these forces reinforced a decline in the patriarchal family, which had persisted well into the twentieth century in the West and still prevails in many regions of the world.[4]

Many of these same social, economic, techno- logical, and cultural changes have also been prolonging early adulthood.[5] Although family scholars have not explicitly linked family change and the new schedule of adult transi- tions, there are many reasons to believe that

the two are closely related. All the conditions implicated in transforming the family during the final third of the twentieth century have helped to delay and complicate the passage to adulthood. For example, the advances in women's education that have been linked to their growing participation in the labor force also tend to delay marriage and parenthood.[6]

Young people today, men and women alike, aspire to jobs that require postsecondary education. It simply takes more time than it did even a half-century ago to gain a job that is secure enough to form and support a family.[7] Couples do not invariably wait to marry or to have children until they complete their school- ing or get a secure job, but they have more compelling reasons to do so than they did in the years after World War II, when it was still common to enter full-time, relatively well-paid (often union) work before completing high school, much less college. It follows, then, that marriage and the onset of childbearing generally take place far later in the life span than they did in the postwar period, because a growing proportion of young adults realize

Figure 2. Proportion of Youth Living at Home, by Age Cohort, 1960–2007

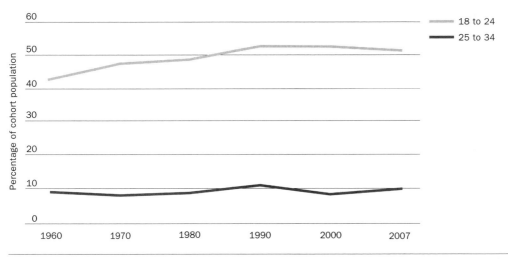

Sources: U. S. Census Bureau, 1960 Census of Population, PC(2)-4B, table 2; 1970 Census of Population, PC(2)-4B, table 2; 1980 Census of Population, PC80-2-4B, table 4; Current Population Survey, March and Annual Social and Economic Supplements, 1990, 2000, and 2007.

they cannot make sound family decisions until their economic fortunes are established.[8] Figure 1 shows the increase in the share of young adults remaining in school. Figures 2, 3, and 4 show the dramatic delays in the age of home-leaving, marriage, and childbearing in the United States. Similar trends can be observed in Canada and Europe.[9]

It is probably no coincidence that the expansion of higher education beginning in the late 1950s corresponds with the rising age of first marriage in the United States, as it did in Europe a decade later. Beginning in the 1960s, the decline of manufacturing jobs also began to undermine the prevailing pattern of early marriage in the United States. As well-paying unskilled and semi-skilled jobs disappeared, the single-earner family became less tenable for most Americans. Education through high school and beyond was no longer a luxury but a necessity for both men and women who aspired to middle-class employment and earnings.

Perhaps related to the delay of marriage, young people, and women in particular, began to engage in sexual relationships earlier and with no immediate intention to marry. The availability of reliable birth control for women and access to legal abortion no doubt made it possible for young people to escape the seemingly inevitable consequences of sex. As marriage age climbed, fewer young adults who became pregnant elected to marry, in part because they had begun to feel that settling down into family life so early was undesirable.[10] Family demographers and sociologists have also argued that the rising marital instability during the 1960s and early 1970s, tied to early marriage and shotgun weddings, made young people more sensitive to the risks associated with a hasty decision to marry. Women, in particular, became more concerned about having enough education and work experience to support themselves should they remain or become single.[11]

Figure 3. Proportion of Youth Married, by Age Cohort, 1950–2007

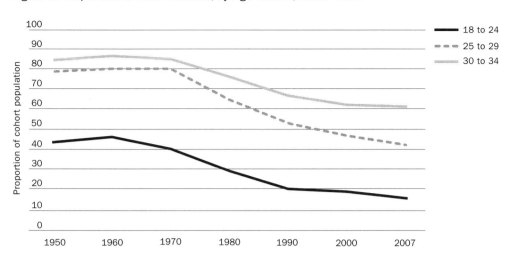

Sources: Historical Census of the United States, Millennial Edition Online, edited by S. B. Carter and others (Cambridge University Press, 2006), table Aa614-683: Population, by Marital Status, Sex, and Race: 1880–1990; U.S. Census Bureau, Current Population Survey, March 2000 and 2007.

The growth of the consumer economy, stimulated by advertising and mass marketing, may have also contributed to the desire of couples to increase their earning potential before marrying. Although solid evidence is lacking on couples' perceptions of what they need to set up an independent household, it is likely that the demand for more material goods and the perceived and actual cost of rearing children affected couples' choices about whether and when to marry and have children. Overall, childbearing became a more conscious decision as new forms of contraception allowed, or perhaps even required, couples to make deliberate choices. Moreover, as women became more independent, they began to take more control over family building, timing parenthood to fit their expanded roles in the household economy.[12]

Finally, childrearing itself changed as parents began to view their responsibilities differently. Men were under greater pressure to become actively involved as parents, perhaps feeding into the belief that it was better to wait to have children.[13] Some scholars have argued that parents began to perceive the importance of investing in "quality" children who could compete in a growing skills-based economy.[14] The growth of inequality in the United States beginning in the 1970s may have also contributed to the perception that, for children to succeed later in life, parents must invest more in them over a longer time span.[15] Early autonomy from the natal household, so valued at mid-century, gave way to a longer period of co-residence. Parents, it appears, increasingly believe that their children need their support longer than they did a half-century ago, and youth feel less compelled to leave the natal home in late adolescence and their early adult years.[16]

I have sketched some of the overlapping sources of change in family patterns and in the length of adult transitions without reference to variations in gender, ethnicity, or social class.

Figure 4. Proportion of Female, Ever-Married Youth with at Least One Child, by Age Cohort, 1950–2006

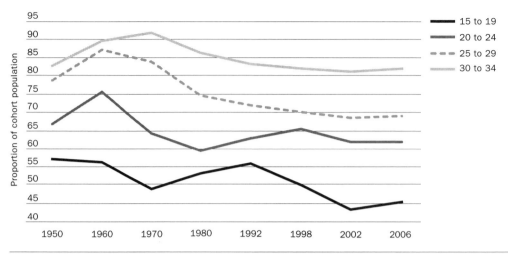

Sources: U.S. Census Bureau, Census of the Population: 1950 Special Report, Fertility, Part 5; Census of the Population: 1960 and 1970, vol. 1, Characteristics of the Population, Part 1, U.S. Summary; Current Population Survey, June, 1980, 1992, 1998, 2002, 2006.

Although I will address some of these differences later, some general comments about these variations are appropriate here.

Men and women have become more alike over the course of the past century in how they move into adult roles.[17] Class differences, however, have increased.[18] Youth from all economic strata are remaining in school longer and marrying later, but young adults from less-advantaged households are finding it increasingly difficult to adhere to an orderly and predictable sequence of education, full-time employment, home-leaving, cohabitation or marriage, and parenthood.[19] In more privileged families, youth more often adhere to the traditional sequence but take far longer to complete the demographic milestones of successful passage to adulthood and remain financially dependent on their parents while they complete their education.[20] In short, young adults without resources find it difficult to attain independence on the traditional (early) schedule, while those with ample

family support spend more time gaining necessary credentials to become economically self-sufficient. Dependency on parents for both the advantaged and disadvantaged sometimes extends late into the third decade of life, albeit for different reasons. In either case, the financial and emotional burden on families has grown in ways that were almost unimaginable just a half-century ago.

Changing Patterns of Co-Residence and Home-Leaving

The impression that American youth are remaining at home much longer now than they once did, while not inaccurate, is nonetheless often exaggerated in the mass media.[21] As shown in figure 2, the period of co-residence with parents has lengthened notably since the 1960s, when youth left home at a very young age. Today's home-leaving patterns are, in fact, much closer to those of the early 1900s. But though the two patterns are similar, the driving forces behind them are very different: more young adults remained with their parents longer at the beginning of the twentieth century not because they were dependent on them but because they were obliged to contribute to the family economy.[22]

All the increase in the age of home-leaving in the United States since the 1960s is attributable to delayed marriage.[23] Unmarried young adults are, of course, more likely to reside with their parents than those who wed. Consequently, with couples marrying later, youth in their late teens and early twenties moved out of the home more slowly than they had during the postwar years when couples married earlier. This trend is especially pronounced if young adults are continuing their education, as was the case during the decades of the 1970s and 1980s. The rate of co-residence declined slightly between 1990 and 2000, perhaps because a strong economy during much of the 1990s afforded young adults the opportunity to move out on their own, although co-residence with parents will likely increase during the first decade of the century owing to the recession of 2008.

The trend toward a later exit from home in the United States parallels that in almost all Western nations, although with considerable variation, particularly in Europe. In the Nordic countries, for example, youth leave home in their late teens, largely owing to the availability of state support. By contrast, lack of state support and long-standing cultural norms favor an extended period of co-residence among youth in Mediterranean nations, lasting for men into their mid-thirties.[24]

Here in the United States, nearly half of all young adults in their late teens and early twenties still live with their parents. That fraction drops below one in seven by the late twenties and below one in ten by the early

thirties.[25] By international standards, Americans still leave home relatively early. Women are typically younger than men when they leave home because they complete college earlier, form cohabiting unions earlier, and marry about two years earlier, on average, than men. Regionally, co-residence is substantially higher among families in the Northeast than elsewhere, likely because of the higher costs of housing, higher rates of college attendance, and later entry into full-time employment.[26] The rapid growth of immigrant families may have also contributed to the rise of co-residence in the early adult years, although as Rubén Rumbaut and Golnaz Komaei note in their article in this volume, this trend would probably emerge only among second-generation immigrants because foreign-born residents often migrate in their early adult years without their families.

Whereas cohabitation or marriage is generally associated with earlier home departure, single parenthood often works in the opposite direction: young mothers who do not enter a union before bearing a child typically remain in the parental home for several years and receive financial support and child care from their parents. Indeed, the federal Temporary Assistance to Needy Families (TANF) program and parallel state assistance programs for young parents have required co-residence for teen mothers, a policy that was aimed both at restricting public assistance and at assuring greater parenting supervision for children of young mothers. Whether young parents and their children do better if they remain in their natal home is an unsettled question. In a longitudinal study of teen parents in Baltimore, I found that mothers and their children did better if they lived with the young mother's parents for one or two years, but if they failed to move out thereafter, they fared somewhat worse, perhaps owing to differences between the families that moved out and those that remained at home.[27]

In general, youth are more likely to remain at home when their biological parents are still living together. In particular, divorce and remarriage among parents have been associated with earlier home-leaving among young adults and with earlier provision and receipt of assistance.[28] Youth who grow up living with their mothers only are distinctly less likely to receive help from or provide assistance to their fathers in later life, while children growing up apart from their mothers are not as likely to curtail contact and exchange with their mothers when they reach adulthood. In short, divorce and remarriage tend to create a matrilineal tilt to kinship ties in the United States.[29]

Research has documented not only the lengthening of home-leaving but also the quality of the relations between co-residing parents and young adult children. Studies report that bonds are close, particularly when the young adults are on a clear path toward moving out. For example, those who remain at home in their early and mid-twenties get along better with their parents when they are studying, working, or looking for work than when they are having serious difficulties moving toward independence.[30] Results of the third wave of the Add Health study, a nationally representative, longitudinal sample of young adults between the ages of twenty and twenty-four, reveal that relations with mothers are closer than those with fathers, particularly nonresident fathers (author's tabulations). This finding, replicated in numerous studies, indicates the partial withering of paternal relationships outside of marriage.[31] To some degree, paternal involvement remains something of a "package deal" that comes with marriage or at least cohabitation.[32]

Few studies, however, have examined the texture of family life when young adults reside in the natal household. For example, what kinds of rules, routines, and understandings emerge regarding household obligations, expenses, and the comings and goings of young adults and other family members? Qualitative reports from parents and youth and perhaps analysis of time diaries would go a long way in filling this gap. The media frequently speculate about the irresponsibility of youth in their dealings with their parents, but very little solid evidence substantiates the presumed tensions.

What happens inside families on a day-by-day basis when young adults co-reside with their parents remains a largely unexplored topic. Whether parents provide continued guidance, set expectations, and provide assistance in promoting development after the adolescent years is a topic for further research. Both anecdotal evidence and studies of parental spending give every reason to believe that parents continue to invest heavily, both financially and emotionally, in their young adult children. What is lacking is good qualitative evidence on how parents and young adults work things out.

Along this same line, researchers know more about the timing of home-leaving than about how either young adults or their parents manage the process.[33] For example, how much do young people consult or involve their parents in the decision to leave, and how much advice, support, and resources do parents provide as young adults depart? Analysts could learn a great deal about the impact of the process on both young adults and their parents by following both parties during and after the departure from the home. According to census data, of every six young adults who move out, one moves back in at some point before age thirty-five.[34] Reverse transitions appear to be occasioned by financial setbacks, career changes involving a return to school or bouts of unemployment, and the dissolution of cohabitation and marriages.[35] Sharon Sassler and her colleagues conducted one of the few qualitative studies on the strategies of managing a return to home. The study reveals the dilemmas of economic dependency in early adulthood for both parents and youth, as well as the ways that young adults cope with receiving support from their parents while still psychologically considering themselves "adults."[36] Renegotiating authority inside the family turns out to be a challenging task when youth continue to rely on their parents for economic support, though it appears that many learn ways of achieving greater equality inside the family. Whether and how this negotiation differs in the households of the foreign-born is a question that merits further attention.

Differing Pathways to Family Formation among Young Adults

In the recent past, the maturational steps of leaving home and marrying were tightly sequenced.[37] During the middle years of the twentieth century, young people left home to marry and have children as soon as they had the wherewithal to do so, and not infrequently before they had adequate resources and secure employment.[38] Today the process of family formation (entering unions and having children) has become less orderly and more protracted.[39] The onset of sexual relations and marriage today is typically separated by at least five years, and often more. Cohabitation, and sometimes parenthood, occurs in the intervening years. Marriage has become a culminating event, still indicating social maturity, but social maturity increasingly occurs well before marriage.[40]

The process of family formation today, more than in the recent past, is shaped by education and employment opportunities.[41] And now, more than ever, the sequence and timing of family formation in the United States differs sharply by socioeconomic status. Family formation has long differed in timing and sequence (for example, pregnancy or parenthood before marriage) between poor and less-educated youth and better-off youth who manage to complete college.[42] But now, despite consistent evidence that young adults, regardless of social class, continue to endorse the importance of marriage and parenthood, there is a growing perception among less-advantaged youth that marriage is less attainable.[43]

Nonetheless, youth and parents from less-advantaged families continue to favor an earlier departure from the home than do those of more advantaged means.[44] Advantaged youth are far more likely to attend a residential college and possibly graduate school (which the Census Bureau classifies as still living with parents), enjoying a period of semi-autonomy that may or may not include part-time work and cohabitation. By contrast, youth from lower-income families, if they attend college at all, are likely to do so while still residing with their parents.[45]

Complicating the home-leaving process for lower-income youth, particularly women, is the growing likelihood of non-marital parenthood. Forty percent of all first births now take place outside marriage, and almost all are to young women who have not completed college. Although rates of teenage pregnancy and childbearing have declined during the past fifteen years (until 2006, that is), nearly half of all young adults with a high school education or less become parents in their late teens and early twenties.[46] These pregnancies are generally unplanned, and relatively few of the parents are fully prepared to take on the economic responsibilities of supporting a family. Data from the Fragile Families Study, a long-term examination of family formation among largely young, largely poor urban couples who are having a child, reveal the fluidity of the relations between the partners over time.[47] Although a substantial minority of nonmarital births to young adults is to couples who are cohabiting at the time of the pregnancy, these unions often are ephemeral, only rarely resulting in marriage, even though most young parents in the Fragile Families Study profess a desire to wed eventually.[48]

In the past, most of these young parents would have wed before or shortly after the birth of the child. Today, however, they perceive, correctly given the evidence, that the benefits of a hasty marriage are few. Many of the fathers lack job experience, are beset by mental health problems, or have been involved in the criminal justice system.[49] For economic and social support, young mothers often turn to their families rather than to their partners, who cannot provide steady assistance. In a long-term study of teenage mothers in Baltimore, I found a deep pessimism, especially among the parents of the pregnant teens, about the wisdom of relying on the men who fathered their children. As one mother told her daughter, "It don't do your child no good if his father can't take care of him."[50]

In recent decades, a growing number of low-income and less-educated white and Hispanic couples have joined African Americans in forming families before they are economically independent.[51] Thus, the traditional ordering of school, employment, home-leaving, and family formation has broken down for an ever larger share of youth

growing up in less than advantaged circumstances. Compared with the relatively weak bonds established between sexual partners and even prospective parents, bonds with natal families among these young adults are strong, particularly their reliance on families for economic assistance and practical help in childrearing. In the Baltimore study, it was common for young parents to remain at home and coordinate child care with their parents. And many of the young children in turn regard their grandmothers as a, if not the, primary parent figure in their lives. Fathers often continue to see their children, but over time, many become shadowy figures in their lives, creating further difficulties in the early adult years.[52]

Youth from disadvantaged circumstances with limited prospects for a well-paid job or a partner with solid earnings increasingly opt for cohabitation, which has become a weak form of matrimony.

Among disadvantaged African Americans, marriage often takes place, if it does at all, long after the onset of childbearing and following a series of cohabitations. This pattern is becoming common as well in other disadvantaged racial and ethnic minorities, though considerable variation exists by ethnic and national origin. A study I conducted with Rachel Margolis found that this pattern of delayed marriage after childbearing is emerging among less-educated whites as well, suggesting that socioeconomic status is linked to the decision to postpone marriage even when childbearing occurs.[53]

Youth from disadvantaged circumstances with limited prospects for a well-paid job or a partner with solid earnings increasingly opt for cohabitation, which has become a weak form of matrimony. More than ever, cohabitation provides a temporary basis for childbearing and childrearing, but its major appeal is that it does not require a high level of commitment or even contentment. Nonetheless, as noted earlier, for most, marriage remains the ultimate or preferred status, a symbol of economic success often deferred long after parenthood.[54]

The contrast in how college-educated young adults (most of whom are also from more affluent families) form families is striking. In-depth interviews with nearly 500 young adults in four sites conducted by the Mac-Arthur Network on Transitions to Adulthood show that most college-educated young adults complete their education and gain some work experience before marrying and certainly before having children.[55] Like their less-educated counterparts, these well-educated couples also cohabit for lengthy periods before marrying, but such relationships typically do not result in parenthood, presumably because of more reliable contraceptive practice, sometimes backed up by abortion.[56] It is still quite rare for affluent couples to have a child outside of marriage, although a few elect to have children in common-law or consensual unions.[57]

The search and commitment process among highly educated young adults provides time to test the durability of relationships.[58] Acquiring the "marriage mentality," as some better-educated young people explained in

in-depth interviews, requires time and experience that is often acquired by living together.[59] In short, the pattern of forming marriages and deciding whether and when to have children has become more deliberate among well-educated young adults. This slower pace may be paying off: evidence is accumulating that marital dissolution among the highly educated has declined over time.[60]

Researchers know far less about the family formation patterns of young adults who grow up in families with modest resources, many of whom obtain some college or complete an associate's degree. There is likely more variety among the middle stratum in the timing and sequence of marriage and parenthood. It would be useful to investigate how these young adults manage both to move away from home and to establish their own families. They face some of the hazards of family formation experienced by low-income and less-educated youth, such as unplanned parenthood, but they possess greater resources to manage more stable unions.

Family formation in the United States today differs not only by social class but also by geographical region. Throughout large parts of the South and Midwest, young adults still follow the early marriage patterns of previous generations, dictated in part by traditional and religious values.[61] To a considerable degree, these values collide with the economic and emotional realities of contemporary life that make marriage a more difficult undertaking than it was a half-century ago. At that time couples were perhaps more willing to put up with less-than-perfect unions because they were unprepared or unwilling to divorce. At least one study finds that young adults sort themselves according to who remains in the community and who leaves to get higher education or seek work. The less-educated "stayers" often subscribe to an early schedule of family formation while those who move to urban areas or out of state adopt a pattern of later marriage and parenthood.[62]

Families with higher incomes contribute more in material assistance, although, measured as a share of income, lower-income families still provide considerable support.

The family formation patterns, not to mention co-residence patterns, of gay young adults largely remain unexplored by researchers. Over time, there is reason to expect that enough data will accumulate to permit a direct examination of this hitherto invisible segment of the young adult population. It is an open question whether they adopt the same timing for forming lasting relationships and, now, increasingly entering parenthood, as their heterosexual counterparts.

Relations between Young Adults and Their Parents across Households

The prolongation of adult transitions raises a series of questions about how relationships change as young adults move out of the household, and how patterns of material and emotional assistance between young adults and their parents are altered by living apart.[63] Long-term data, as noted, are best suited to investigating how exchange patterns are altered as young adults make the passage to adulthood. Several long-term studies such as Add Health and the Panel Study of Income

Dynamics (PSID) have recently included modules on intergenerational transfers, providing much-needed information on exchanges between young adults (living both inside and outside the home) and their parents. These data are just becoming available, so most of what researchers know comes from information that may incompletely reflect the relatively recent extension of early adulthood.

Analyzing data collected in the PSID in 1988, Robert Schoeni and Karen Ross find that parental support for a young adult was substantial even two decades ago.[64] For their adult children between the ages of eighteen and thirty-four, parents provide, on average, $2,200 a year in today's dollars. Put differently, parents' economic contributions to their children amount to an additional one-third of what they spend during the first eighteen years of their children's lives. Financial assistance declines from a high of nearly $3,500 a year between age eighteen and age twenty, to about $2,300 annually from age twenty-five to twenty-six, to a little more than $1,500 a year by the early to mid-thirties. Time contributions by parents are similarly high during the early adult years, trailing off in the late twenties and early thirties.[65]

Family contributions increase in large part because of education and longer periods of time in the household. As might be predicted, families with higher incomes contribute more in material assistance, although, measured as a share of income, lower-income families still provide considerable support. There is little or no difference by social class in time contributions.[66] From the growing research on the determinants of intergenerational transfer, analysts know that parents are more willing to provide support for children with special needs, for educational advancement, in times of immediate crisis such as unemployment or union dissolution, and for children who have children themselves.[67]

The Long-Term Consequences of Later Adulthood: Some Unaddressed Policy Issues

Parents who are called on to provide economic and emotional assistance during a more protracted period of their children's semi-dependency may wonder whether these investments will erode or enhance their own economic security later in life. Arguably, greater transfers to their children reduce parents' savings for retirement, but they might also prompt children to return greater assistance to their parents later in life. Whether rising parental concerns about the adequacy of Social Security and pensions will reduce their investment in young adults remains an open issue. Martin Kohli and several colleagues are finding from their analysis of European data that the flow of assistance from parents to children persists into the latter decades of life.[68] That trend holds true both in northern Europe, where autonomy comes relatively early, and in southern Europe, where it comes far later.[69] Researchers can learn much from such cross-national comparisons about the societal determinants of interfamilial exchanges.[70] Social security systems in both Europe and North America have permitted parents to provide financial aid to their offspring for a longer period. Does the generosity of the welfare system in providing aid to elders, support for education, and living expenses to young adults have consequences for patterns of investment by parents in their young adult offspring? And how in turn does the generosity of the welfare system affect patterns of exchange later in life?

The United States devotes relatively little public spending to supporting young adults. Spending for higher education, health care, and job benefits is meager to modest, although such investments appear to be increasing in the Obama administration. The relative paucity of public support has placed a heavier burden on families during young adults' increasingly protracted and uncertain transition to independence. The burden is particularly heavy for the families of vulnerable young adults, those with special needs and limited resources, whose families may be unable to provide necessary assistance after they reach the age of majority.[71] In this country, much of the media attention about the prolongation of early adulthood has been directed to what is happening in affluent families. Far less is known about what happens to less well-off youth as they navigate the passage to adulthood, and particularly about the critical role that parents play (or fail to play) as their children struggle to complete their education, enter the labor market, form relationships, and have children.

The analysis by Schoeni and Ross revealed that a large fraction of parents extend assistance to their children in the early adult years and that, regardless of income, parents provide roughly the same proportion of their family income. That assistance, however, may be insufficient to meet the needs of grown children because many low-income parents simply lack the resources to give much in the way of direct financial assistance. When families cannot help out, youth are often left to flounder on their own. There is a pressing need for publicly provided health care, education and training, and social services for youth whose families cannot support them as they navigate the passage to economic self-sufficiency.

At a societal level, the United States and the rest of the developed world face a growing policy dilemma: the need to invest in children and youth while continuing to support the economic, health, and social needs of a growing population aged sixty-five and older. The dilemma has been largely managed so far by family exchange from the elderly to the young. The current public system of support for seniors is underfinanced, however, and many observers are talking about the need to reduce Social Security benefits to preserve the system. Cutting back on those benefits, though, may have unforeseen consequences for the ability of parents to invest in their young adult children. With less support from their parents, the middle generation may be required to cut back on their support for their own children to help out their parents. Low-income families, especially, may face competing demands from elderly parents and their young adult offspring.

Is it possible that the new job description for parents—the requirement that they provide greater support for children over longer periods—might discourage couples from having additional children or even having children at all?[72] It does not seem farfetched to suggest that couples may begin to factor the long-term responsibilities of rearing children into their planning for their own retirement. If the economic burdens of rearing children become intolerable, potential parents may elect not to assume those costs. Such family decisions would lead to lower total fertility and ultimately reduce the workforce, thus further aggravating the problem of providing both for the elderly and for the young.

Conclusion
That the passage to adulthood has become more protracted and the sequence of transitions less orderly and predictable is well

documented. Although I have touched on some of the reasons why the timetable has changed, I have emphasized the consequences of the change for young adults, their families, and the larger society.

Social scientists, having relied for too long on anecdotal reports from the mass media about the direct effects of the later transition to adulthood, are now conducting their own independent research. So far, though, researchers still know far more about the demography and economics of the change than about its implications for family life and practices. Recent evidence from the General Social Survey shows that families generally accept that it now takes their children longer to pass the milestones that mark economic independence and social maturity. How parents and their young adult offspring are managing this longer period of co-residence and economic dependency remains less well understood. More fine-grained information on daily routines, rules and understandings, and exchanges of time, money, and support among co-resident parents and children should make it possible to chart how this new timetable for growing up affects the family. It also remains to be seen whether and how this period of semi-autonomy (or semi-dependency, if the glass is seen as half empty) changes the path of psychosocial development. Using new and more discriminating measures of development during the early adult years, analysts will be able to examine more directly whether and how the experience of adult transitions fosters psychological development, a topic that has remained largely unexplored.

The new schedule of adulthood has complicated family formation itself, particularly for the less-advantaged members of American society. Moving out of the natal household has become precarious for those with limited means. Unlike the not-so-distant past, when marriage provided an easy (though not always a successful) route out, fewer young adults today are willing to commit to a permanent union, in part because they lack the resources and the mind-set to settle down and in part because they lack confidence that marriage provides the security that it once did. These conditions help to explain why parenthood now often precedes marriage for many young adults growing up in disadvantaged households. By contrast, for youth from advantaged families who are able to complete college, the extended period of growing up brings few costs and many benefits. The longer educational process provides greater opportunities for self-exploration, including the search for stable life partners. Delaying marriage and parenthood, it appears, results in wiser marriage choices and consequently more stable family situations and more positive environments for childbearing and childrearing. This class divide in the early adult transition risks reinforcing social advantage and disadvantage in family formation in the next generation.[73]

The body of research on the connections between young adults and their parents across households is growing. Clearly, parents continue to channel support and economic assistance to their adult children after they leave home. But exactly how, when, and why do parents extend help, and how is it reciprocated in both the short term and the long term? Much also remains to be learned about how such family assistance affects both the givers and the receivers of help. How intergenerational exchange is affected by the distribution of resources in the larger society also requires more investigation. I have argued that the United States, with its relatively underdeveloped welfare system, relies more on the family to invest in young adults than do many nations in Europe. The heavy burden placed on families may come at a price if young adults begin to regard childbearing as too onerous and perhaps not sufficiently rewarding. Although there may be no immediate policy prescription for addressing this problem, it is essential to recognize the importance of strengthening the family nest and reducing the immense and competing demands that are being placed on today's parents.

Endnotes

1. William J. Goode, *The Family* (Englewood, N.J.: Prentice-Hall, 1962); L. Stone, "The Historical Origins of the Modern Man" (fifth annual O. Meredith Wilson Lecture in History, Department of History, University of Utah, 1981), pp. 1–25; Goran Therborn, *Between Sex and Power: Family in the World, 1900–2000* (Oxford: Routledge Press, 2004).

2. Steven Ozment, *Ancestors: The Loving Family in Old Europe* (Harvard University Press, 2001); Michael Gordon, ed., *The American Family in Social-Historical Perspective* (New York: St. Martin's Press, 1978).

3. Elisabeth Beck-Gernsheim, *Reinventing the Family: In Search of New Lifestyles* (Oxford: Polity Press, 2002); Anthony Giddens, "The Global Revolution in Family and Personal Life," in *Family in Transition,* edited by Arlene S. Skolnick and Jerome H. Skolnick (Boston: Pearson Education, Inc.), pp. 26–31; Ronald Lesthaeghe, "The Second Demographic Transition in Western Countries: An Interpretation," in *Gender and Family Change in Industrialized Countries,* edited by Karen Oppenheim Mason and Ann-Magritt Jensen (Oxford: Clarendon Press, 1995), pp. 17–62.

4. Therborn, *Between Sex and Power* (see note 1); Cynthia B. Lloyd, *Growing Up Global: The Changing Transitions to Adulthood in Developing Countries* (Washington: National Academies Press, 2005).

5. Frank F. Furstenberg Jr., Rubén G. Rumbaut, and Richard A. Settersten Jr., "On the Frontier of Adulthood: Emerging Themes and New Directions," in *On the Frontier of Adulthood: Theory, Research, and Public Policy,* edited by Richard A. Settersten, Frank F. Furstenberg, and Rubén G. Rumbaut (University of Chicago Press, 2005), pp. 3–25; Michael Shanahan, "Pathways to Adulthood in Changing Societies: Variability and Mechanisms in Life Course Perspective," *Annual Review of Sociology* 26 (2000): 667–92; Arnold Thornton, Linda Young-DeMarco, and Frances Goldscheider, "Leaving the Parental Nest: The Experience of a Young White Cohort in the 1980s," *Journal of Marriage and the Family* 56 (1993): 216–29.

6. Andrew J. Cherlin, *Marriage, Divorce, Remarriage* (Harvard University Press, 1992); Frances K. Goldscheider and Linda J. Waite, *New Families, No Families? The Transformation of the American Home* (Berkeley, Calif.: University of California Press, 1991); Karen Oppenheim Mason and Ann-Magritt Jensen, *Gender and Family Change in Industrialized Countries* (Oxford: Clarendon Press, 1995); Michael J. Rosenfeld, *The Age of Independence: Interracial Unions, Same-Sex Unions, and the Changing American Family* (Harvard University Press, 2007); Barbara Schneider and Linda J. Waite, *Being Together, Working Apart* (Cambridge University Press, 2005).

7. Sheldon Danziger and Cecilia Elena Rouse, eds., *The Price of Independence: The Economics of Early Adulthood* (New York: Russell Sage Foundation, 2007); Timothy M. Smeeding and Kathleen Ross Phillips, "Cross-National Differences in Employment and Economic Sufficiency," *Annals of the American Academy of Political and Social Science* 580 (2002): 103–33.

8. Elizabeth Fussell and Frank F. Furstenberg, "The Transition to Adulthood during the Twentieth Century: Race, Nativity, and Gender," in Settersten and others, *On the Frontier of Adulthood* (see note 5), pp. 29–75; Frank F. Furstenberg and others, "Growing Up Is Harder to Do," *Contexts* 3 (2004): 42–47.

9. Francesco C. Billari, Stefano Mazzuc, and Fausta Ongaro, "Leaving Home: A Comparative Analysis of ECHP Data," *Journal of European Social Policy* 12 (2002): 259; Elizabeth Fussell, "The Transition to Adulthood in Aging Societies," *Annals of the American Academy of Political and Social Science* 580 (2002): 16–39;

Anne H. Gauthier and Maria Iacovou, "Regional Differences in the Transition to Adulthood," *Annals of the American Academy of Political and Social Science* 580 (2002): 40–69; Karl Ulrich Mayer, "Life Course and Life Chances in a Comparative Perspective," in *Analyzing Inequality: Life Chances and Social Mobility in Comparative Perspective,* edited by Stefan Svallfors (Palo Alto, Calif.: Stanford University Press, 2005), pp. 17–55.

10. Frank F. Furstenberg, *Destinies of the Disadvantaged: The Politics of Teen Childbearing* (New York: Russell Sage Foundation, 2007).

11. Kathryn Edin and Maria Kefalas, *Promises I Can Keep: Why Poor Women Put Motherhood Before Marriage* (Berkeley, Calif.: University of California Press, 2005); Lawrence L. Wu and Barbara Wolfe, eds., *Out of Wedlock: Causes and Consequences of Nonmarital Fertility* (New York: Russell Sage Foundation, 2001).

12. Mason and Jensen, *Gender and Family Change* (see note 6).

13. Michael E. Lamb, *The Role of the Father in Child Development* (New York: Wiley, 2003).

14. Hilary Levey, "Outside Class: A Historical Analysis of American Children's Competitive Activities," in *Childhood in American Society,* edited by Karen Sternheimer (New York: Allyn and Bacon, Inc., 2009), pp. 342–54.

15. Annette Lareau, *Unequal Childhoods: Class, Race, and Family Life* (London: University of California Press, 2003).

16. Furstenberg and others, "Growing Up" (see note 8).

17. Fussell and Furstenberg, "The Transition to Adulthood" (see note 8).

18. Frank F. Furstenberg, "The Intersections of Social Class and the Transition to Adulthood," *New Directions for Child and Adolescent Development* 119 (2008): 1–10; Sara S. McLanahan, "Fragile Families and the Reproduction of Poverty," *Annals of the American Academy of Political and Social Science* 621 (2009): 111–31.

19. Ronald Rindfuss, "The Young Adult Years: Diversity, Structural Change, and Fertility," *Demography* 28 (1991): 493–512.

20. Robert F. Schoeni and Karen E. Ross, "Material Assistance from Families during the Transition to Adulthood," in Settersten and others, *On the Frontier of Adulthood* (see note 5), pp. 396–416.

21. Rick Settersten and Barbara Ray, *Slouching toward Adulthood: Why Young People Are Taking So Long to Grow Up and What It All Means* (New York: Ballantine, forthcoming).

22. John Modell, *Into One's Own: From Youth to Adulthood in the United States, 1920–1975* (Berkeley, Calif.: University of California Press, 1989).

23. Rosenfeld, *The Age of Independence* (see note 6).

24. Francesco C. Billari, Dimiter Philipov, and Pau Baizan, "Leaving Home in Europe: The Experience of Cohorts Born Around 1960," Working Paper WP2001-014 (Rostock, Germany: Max Planck Institute for Demographic Research, 2001); Martine Corijn and Erik Klijzing, eds., "Transitions to Adulthood in Europe," special issue, *European Journal of Population* 18 (2002).

25. Rubén G. Rumbaut, "Young Adults in the United States," Working Paper 4, Network on Transitions to Adulthood, 2006.

26. Rubén G. Rumbaut, Golnaz Komaie, and Charlie V. Morgan, "Demographic Profile of Young Adults in the Five Cities" (Philadelphia: Network on Transitions to Adulthood, May 2007); Mary Elizabeth Hughes, "Home Economics: Metropolitan Labor and Housing Markets and Domestic Arrangements in Young Adulthood," *Social Forces* 81 (2003): 1399–1429.

27. Frank F. Furstenberg, Jeanne Brooks-Gunn, and S. Philip Morgan, *Adolescent Mothers in Later Life* (Cambridge University Press, 1987).

28. Frances K. Goldscheider and Calvin Goldscheider, "The Effects of Childhood Family Structure on Leaving and Returning Home," *Journal of Marriage and the Family* 60 (1998): 745–56.

29. Nicholas H. Wolfinger, "Parental Divorce and Offspring Marriage: Early or Late?" *Social Forces* 82 (2003): 337–53.

30. William S. Aquilino, "Two Views of One Relationship: Comparing Parents' and Young Adult Children's Reports of the Quality of Intergenerational Relations," *Journal of Marriage and the Family* 61 (1999): 858–70; William S. Aquilino and Khalil R. Supple, "Parent-Child Relations and Parents' Satisfaction with Living Arrangements When Adult Children Live at Home," *Journal of Marriage and the Family* 53 (1991): 13–27; Debra Umberson, "Relationships between Adult Children and Their Parents: Psychological Consequences for Both Generations," *Journal of Marriage and the Family* 54 (1992): 664–74.

31. Frank F. Furstenberg Jr. and Andrew Cherlin, *Divided Families: What Happens to Children When Parents Part* (Harvard University Press, 1991).

32. Paul Amato, Sandra J. Rezac, and Alan Booth, "Helping between Parents and Young Adult Offspring: The Role of Parental Marital Quality, Divorce and Remarriage," *Journal of Marriage and the Family* 57 (1995): 363–74; Teresa M. Cooney and Peter Uhlenberg, "Divorced Men and Their Adult Children after Mid-Life," *Journal of Marriage and the Family* 52 (1990): 677–88.

33. For exceptions, see Sharon Sassler and Frances Goldscheider, "Revisiting Jane Austen's Theory of Marriage Timing: Changes in Union Formation among American Men in the Late 20th Century," *Journal of Family Issues* 25 (2004): 139–66; Lara Descartes, "Put Your Money Where Your Love Is: Parental Aid to Adult Children," *Journal of Adult Development* 13 (2006): 137--47.

34. Rumbaut, "Young Adults in the United States" (see note 25).

35. See, for example, Goldscheider and Goldscheider, "The Effects of Childhood Family Structure" (see note 28).

36. Sharon Sassler, Desiree Ciambrone, and Gaelan Benway, "Are They Really Mama's Boys/Daddy's Girls? The Negotiation of Adulthood upon Returning to the Parental Home," *Sociological Forum* 23 (2008): 670–98.

37. John Modell, Frank F. Furstenberg, and Theodore Hershberg, "Social Change and Transitions to Adulthood in Historical Perspective," *Journal of Family History* 1 (1976): 7–32.

38. Hugh Carter and Paul C. Glick, *Marriage and Divorce: A Social and Economic Study* (Harvard University Press, 1976); John R. Weeks, *Teenage Marriages: A Demographic Analysis* (Westport, Conn.: Greenwood Press, 1976).

39. Rindfuss, "The Young Adult Years" (see note 19).

40. Jeffrey Jensen Arnett, *Emerging Adulthood: The Winding Road from Late Teens through the Twenties* (Oxford University Press, 2004); Furstenberg and others, "Growing Up" (see note 8); Settersten and others, eds., *On the Frontier of Adulthood* (see note 5); Shanahan, "Pathways to Adulthood" (see note 5).

41. Stephen F. Hamilton and Mary Agnes Hamilton, "The Transition to Adulthood: Challenges of Poverty and Structural Lag," in *Handbook of Adolescent Psychology,* edited by Richard Lerner and Laurence Steinberg (New York: Wiley, 2009), pp. 492–526; Furstenberg and others, "On the Frontier of Adulthood" (see note 5).

42. William Axinn and Arland Thornton, "The Influence of Parental Resources on the Timing of the Transition to Marriage," *Social Science Research* 21 (1992): 261–85; Kim M. Lloyd and Scott J. South, "Spousal Alternatives and Marital Dissolution," *Social Forces* 74 (1995): 1097–1119; Modell, *Into One's Own* (see note 22).

43. Edin and Kefalas, *Promises I Can Keep* (see note 11); Maureen Waller, *My Baby's Father* (Cornell University Press, 2002); Marcia Carlson, Sara S. McLanahan, and Paula England, "Union Formation in Fragile Families," *Demography* 41 (2004): 237–61; Christina Gibson-Davis, Kathryn Edin, and Sara S. McLanahan, "High Hopes but Even Higher Expectations: The Retreat from Marriage among Low-Income Couples," *Journal of Marriage and Family* 67 (2005): 1301–12.

44. Furstenberg and others, "Growing Up" (see note 8); Tom Smith, "Coming of Age in Twenty-First Century America: Public Attitudes Towards the Importance of Timing of Transitions to Adulthood," *Ageing International* 29 (2004): 136–48.

45. John Bynner, "Origins of Social Exclusion: Risk Factors Affecting Young Children," presentation at Her Majesty's Treasury (HMT) seminar (1988); Jeylan Mortimer, *Working and Growing up in America* (Harvard University Press, 2003); Smeeding and Phillips, "Cross-National Differences in Employment and Economic Sufficiency" (see note 7).

46. Rachel Margolis and Frank F. Furstenberg, "Social Class Differences in the Timing of First Sex, First Birth and First Marriage," presentation at the American Sociological Association annual meeting, San Francisco, Calif., August 2009.

47. Cynthia Osborne, Wendy Manning, and Pamela Smock, "Married and Cohabiting Parents' Relationship Stability: A Focus on Race and Ethnicity," *Journal of Marriage and Family* 69 (2007): 1345–66; Cynthia Osborne and Sara S. McLanahan, "Partnership Instability and Child Wellbeing," *Journal of Marriage and Family* 69 (2007): 1065–83.

48. "Fathers' Risk Factors and Their Implications for Healthy Relationships and Father Involvement," *Fragile Families Research Brief* 37 (2007): 1–3; "Predictors of Homelessness and Doubling-Up among At-Risk Families," *Fragile Families Research Brief* 43 (2008): 1–3.

49. Leonard Lopoo and Marcia Carlson, "Marriageability among the Partners of Young Mothers," *Social Service Review* 82 (2008): 253–71; Raymond Swisher and Maureen Waller, "Confining Fatherhood: Incarceration and Paternal Involvement among Nonresident White, African American, and Latino Fathers," *Journal of Family Issues* 29 (2008): 1067–88.

50. Furstenberg, *Destinies of the Disadvantaged* (see note 10), p. 108.

51. Margolis and Furstenberg, "Social Class Differences" (see note 46).

52. Waller, *My Baby's Father* (see note 43).

53. Margolis and Furstenberg, "Social Class Differences" (see note 46).

54. Cherlin, *Marriage, Divorce, Remarriage* (see note 6); Edin and Kefalas, *Promises I Can Keep* (see note 11); Gibson-Davis, Edin, and McLanahan, "High Hopes but Even Higher Expectations" (see note 43).

55. Patrick Carr and Maria Kefalas, *Hollowing out the Middle: The Rural Brain Drain and What It Means for America* (New York: Beacon Press, 2009); Mary Waters and others, *Coming of Age in America* (Berkeley, Calif.: University of California Press, forthcoming).

56. Rachel K. Jones, Jacqueline E. Dorrach, and Stanley K. Henshaw, "Contraceptive Use among U.S. Women Having Abortions in 2000–2001," *Perspectives on Sexual and Reproductive Health* 34 (2002): 294–304.

57. Margolis and Furstenberg, "Social Class Differences" (see note 46).

58. Valerie Kincade Oppenheimer, "A Theory of Marriage Timing," *American Journal of Sociology* 94 (1988): 563–91.

59. Maria Kefalas and others, "Marriage Planners and Marriage Naturalists: How the Transition to Adulthood Structures Marriage," Working Paper, Department of Sociology, St. Joseph's University.

60. David Ellwood and Christopher Jencks, "The Spread of Single-Parent Families in the United States since 1960," in *The Future of the Family,* edited by Daniel Patrick Moynihan, Timothy Smeeding, and Lee Rainwater (New York: Russell Sage Foundation, 2004), pp. 25–65; Joshua Goldstein and Catherine Kenney, "Marriage Delayed or Marriage Forgone? New Cohort Forecasts of First Marriage for U.S. Women," *American Sociological Review* 66 (2001): 506–19.

61. Carr and Kefalas, *Hollowing out the Middle* (see note 55).

62. Ibid.

63. An abundant research literature on patterns of intergenerational exchange spans several decades, although most of the studies focus on the latter stages of the life course. See, for example, Alice Rossi and Peter Rossi, *Of Human Bonding: Parent-Child Relations Across the Life Course* (New York: Aldine, 1990).

64. Schoeni and Ross, "Material Assistance from Families" (see note 20).

65. See also Teresa M. Cooney and Peter Uhlenberg, "Support from Parents over the Life Course: The Adult Child's Perspective," *Social Forces* 71, no. 1 (1992): 63–84; Teresa Swartz, Mayumi Uno, and Kirsten Caroline O'Brien, "Providing Scaffolds and Safety Nets or Enabling Slackers? Parental Support of Contemporary Young Adults," presentation at the Amercian Sociological Association annual meeting, San Francisco, Calif., August 2009.

66. Schoeni and Ross, "Material Assistance from Families" (see note 20).

67. Alan Booth and others, eds., *Intergenerational Caregiving* (Washington: Urban Institute Press, 2008); Cooney and Uhlenberg, "Support from Parents" (see note 65).

68. Martin Kohli and others, eds., *Time for Retirement: Comparative Studies of Early Exit from the Labor Force* (Cambridge University Press, 1991).

69. Claudine Attias-Donfut, James Ogg, and Francois Charles Wolff, "European Patterns of Intergenerational Financial and Time Transfers," *Journal of Ageing* 2 (2005): 161–73.

70. Francesco Billari and Aart Liefbroer, "Intergenerational Ties: What Can Be Gained from an International Perspective?" in *Intergenerational Caregiving*, edited by Alan Booth and others (Washington: Urban Institute Press, 2008), pp. 53–66.

71. D. Wayne Osgood and others, eds., *On Your Own without a Net: The Transition to Adulthood for Vulnerable Populations* (University of Chicago Press, 2005).

72. Fussell, "The Transition to Adulthood" (see note 9).

73. Sara S. McLanahan, "Diverging Destinies: How Children Are Faring under the Second Demographic Transition," *Demography* 41 (2004): 607–27.

Programs and Policies to Assist High School Dropouts in the Transition to Adulthood

Dan Bloom

Summary

Dan Bloom of MDRC examines policies and programs designed to help high school dropouts improve their educational attainment and labor market outcomes. So called "second-chance" programs, he says, have long provided some combination of education, training, employment, counseling, and social services. But the research record on their effectiveness is fairly thin, he says, and the results are mixed.

Bloom describes eleven employment- or education-focused programs serving high school dropouts that have been rigorously evaluated over the past thirty years. Some relied heavily on paid work experience, while others focused more on job training or education. Some programs, especially those that offered paid work opportunities, generated significant increases in employment or earnings in the short term, but none of the studies that followed participants for more than a couple of years found lasting improvements in economic outcomes. Nevertheless, the findings provide an important foundation on which to build.

Because of the high individual and social costs of ignoring high school dropouts, the argument for investing more public funds in services, systems, and research for these young people is strong. The paucity of conclusive evidence, however, makes it hard to know how to direct resources and magnifies the importance of ensuring that all new initiatives provide for rigorous evaluation of their impacts.

Bloom concludes with recommendations for policy and research aimed at building on current efforts to expand and improve effective programs for dropouts while simultaneously developing and testing new approaches that might be more effective and strengthening local systems to support vulnerable young people. He stresses the importance of identifying and disseminating strategies to engage young people who are more seriously disconnected and unlikely to join programs. A recurring theme is that providing young people with opportunities for paid work may be useful both as an engagement tool and as a strategy for improving long-term labor market outcomes.

www.futureofchildren.org

Dan Bloom is co-director of the Health and Barriers to Employment Policy Area at MDRC.

The transition to adulthood is likely to be perilous and rocky for young people who drop out of high school. In fact, even those who earn a high school diploma or a General Educational Development (GED) certificate face increasingly long odds of success if they do not go on to get at least some postsecondary education or training. Young people from low-income families are substantially less likely than their higher-income peers to move smoothly through school, making it much more difficult for them to earn family-sustaining wages and, potentially, to reach other adult milestones such as marrying.

Through a variety of school reforms beginning in preschool and running through high school, U.S. educators are working to prevent young people from getting off track. For the foreseeable future, however, the nation will also need "second-chance" systems and programs to re-engage and re-direct young people who leave the public school system. The research record on the effectiveness of such programs is fairly thin and the results are mixed, but there are some positive findings on which to build. Moreover, the individual and social costs of neglecting this problem are potentially enormous.

I begin by describing the magnitude and consequences of the dropout problem, with a particular focus on the heterogeneity of the dropout population. Next, I describe what researchers know about the effectiveness of programs designed to assist young people who leave school before graduation, focusing mainly on how the programs affect participants' educational attainment and labor market outcomes. I conclude with some recommendations for policy and research that would build on the current evidence base to expand and improve effective programs for dropouts while simultaneously developing and testing new approaches that might be more effective and strengthening local systems to support vulnerable young people.

The Magnitude and Consequences of the Dropout Problem

National studies estimate that 3.5 million to 6 million people between the age of sixteen and twenty-four are high school dropouts— meaning that they have not earned a high school diploma and are not now enrolled in high school.[1]

Dropouts come disproportionately from low-income and minority families. According to the National Center for Education Statistics (NCES), the share of sixteen- to twenty-four-year-olds who are out of school and lack a diploma or GED is 4 percent in the highest income quartile and 17 percent in the lowest quartile. Similarly, the dropout rate is 6 percent for whites, 12 percent for blacks, and 20 percent for Hispanics.[2] Moreover, the dropout problem is heavily concentrated in a subset of high schools that are themselves concentrated in large northern and western cities and in the South.[3]

Experts disagree about how to calculate high school graduation rates. Surprisingly, they even disagree about whether the national dropout rate has been rising or falling in the past thirty years and whether racial disparities in graduation rates have been declining or growing.[4] It seems clear, however, that over this period several developments have amplified the negative consequences of dropping out of school. First, well-documented changes in the labor market have dramatically reduced the availability of well-paying jobs for young people, particularly young men, without postsecondary education. Adjusted for inflation, the earnings of young men with no high school diploma dropped 23 percent between 1973 and 2006 (the earnings of young men with only a high school degree dropped about the same percentage).[5]

Even before the current recession began, growing numbers of young dropouts were entirely disconnected from both school and work. More than half of all sixteen- to nineteen-year-old high school dropouts had no paid employment in 2007. Declining employment among dropouts is one symptom of a broader collapse in the youth labor market. In just eight years—from 1999 to 2007—the share of all sixteen- to nineteen-year-olds with no paid employment during the entire year rose from 44 percent to 59 percent.[6]

Second, changes in sentencing and other criminal justice policies have sharply increased the number of young adults who are incarcerated. The rate of incarceration in the United States stayed relatively flat for most of the twentieth century and then exploded beginning in the late 1970s. More than 2 million Americans (most of them young men) are now in prison or jail—many for offenses that would not have led to prison terms thirty years ago.[7] Spending time in prison not only strains family ties but also depresses future earnings.And high school dropouts are much more likely than their more educated peers to become involved with the justice system. More than two-thirds of state prison inmates have no high school diploma—though a substantial share has earned a GED while incarcerated.[8]

Trends in labor market conditions and incarceration may have made it harder for high school dropouts to reach other adult milestones. As discussed by Sheldon Danziger and David Ratner in their article in this

volume, it is difficult to prove a causal relationship between earnings trends and marriage trends. The correlations, however, are striking. In 1970, 68 percent of male dropouts between age twenty-two and thirty-two were married; in 2007, after earnings for dropouts had dropped precipitously, the marriage rate for this group had fallen to 26 percent. One study found earnings a key predictor of marriage rates for young men. Similarly, although trends in out-of-wedlock births are affected by many factors, having children outside of marriage is strongly correlated with education. In 2006, a startling 67 percent of births to female high school dropouts under age thirty were out-of-wedlock (by contrast, the out-of-wedlock birth rate was 10 percent for women under thirty with a master's degree).[9]

Diverse Population

High school dropouts are a heterogeneous group. In the first place, they leave high school for many different reasons. In a 2005 survey of more than 400 dropouts, about 47 percent reported that a major reason for their decision to drop out was that "classes were not interesting." Overall, 62 percent said they were receiving grades of "C's and above." At the other end of the spectrum, 35 percent of respondents identified "failing in school" as a major reason why they dropped out. For many dropouts, the major reasons for leaving school—needing to get a job (32 percent) or to care for a family member (22 percent) or becoming a parent (26 percent)—were not directly related to school itself.[10]

Second, dropouts follow different trajectories after leaving school. Most try to continue their education. The National Education Longitudinal Study tracked a sample of young people who entered high school in 1988 and were scheduled to graduate in 1992. About 20 percent of the sample dropped out of high

Figure 1. Status in 2000 of 100 People Who Were Eighth Graders in 1988

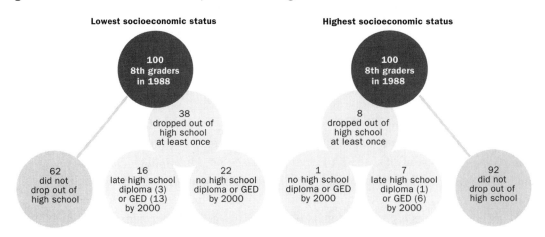

Source: Authors' calculations based on Cheryl Almeida, Cassius Johnson, and Adria Steinberg, *Making Good on a Promise: What Policymakers Can Do to Support the Educational Persistence of Dropouts* (Boston: Jobs for the Future, 2006).

school at least once. By 2000, eight years after their scheduled graduation date, nearly two thirds (63 percent) had earned a high school diploma or, much more commonly, a GED certificate, and 43 percent had attended a postsecondary institution. Presumably, more than 63 percent of the dropouts *attempted* to continue their education.[11]

As figure 1 shows, however, the above data mask huge differences by socioeconomic status. As noted, higher-income students are much less likely to drop out in the first place. And almost all of the higher-income dropouts earned a GED or diploma by 2000. By comparison, less than half of the low-income dropouts had a credential by 2000. Similarly, among those in the highest socioeconomic group, 67 percent of those who had a diploma or GED had enrolled in college, compared with 29 percent of those in the lowest group (numbers not shown in the figure).[12] Young people from higher-income families who drop out of school are often able to get back on track, while their lower-income peers are more likely to flounder.

Third, young people who leave school and then become disconnected face a variety of personal and situational obstacles. For example, a recent study focusing on New York City identified five overlapping groups of young people who are at particularly high risk of leaving school, not returning, and then ending up unemployed or out of the labor force: immigrant youth, young people with disabilities (learning disabilities or emotional and behavioral issues), young people involved in the justice system, youth aging out of foster care, and young mothers.[13]

Programming for Dropouts

Second-chance programs have long offered opportunities for young people who leave the K–12 education system without earning a diploma. Ranging from large national programs or networks like the Job Corps (more than 100 sites nationwide) and YouthBuild (more than 200 programs) to small independent programs run by churches or community-based organizations, these programs typically provide some combination of education, training, employment, counseling, and social services. Some, like the Job Corps, have dedicated streams of federal funding, while others piece together funding from the federal Workforce Investment Act of 1998 (WIA) and other state and local sources. Many target specific subsets of youth, such as those with disabilities or those in the foster care or juvenile justice systems, reflecting the availability of targeted funding for those groups. High school dropouts are typically overrepresented among these vulnerable populations, which are discussed by D. Wayne Osgood, E. Michael Foster, and Mark E. Courtney in their article in this volume. (Other programs for dropouts have broader eligibility criteria, but end up serving many young people from these same vulnerable groups.)

Not so long ago, second-chance programs that helped dropouts earn the GED credential were fairly clearly differentiated from traditional high schools. Today the landscape is far more varied. On the one hand, many school districts are developing "multiple pathways" initiatives that offer a wider range of high school options in an effort to prevent young people from leaving the K–12 system. For example, New York City's Office of Multiple Pathways has created Transfer Schools (small schools specifically designed for students who have fallen behind for their age or who have dropped out) and Young Adult Borough Centers (evening programs for older students operated by partnerships between schools and community organizations), along with new GED programs, all of which are supplemented by Learning to Work, a program that provides job readiness instruction and paid internships. On the other hand, some community-based programs with experience serving dropouts now operate charter schools or alternative high schools. For example, YouthBuild, a large national

network of programs known for serving dropouts and targeting the GED, now includes twenty-nine diploma-granting schools.

Moreover, although second-chance programs once viewed the GED credential as the ultimate goal, their aim now is increasingly to help former dropouts obtain postsecondary education, which has become a virtual prerequisite for admission to the middle class. The Gateway to College program, developed at Portland (Oregon) Community College and now operating in twenty-three other community colleges across the country, gives high school dropouts a chance to attend high school and college simultaneously. Gateway students begin as a group during the Foundation Term, during which they strengthen basic academic skills and adjust to college. Those who succeed in these courses gradually move into the regular college curriculum. Gateway relies on "average daily attendance" funding from the K–12 system even though students are enrolled at a community college.

In addition, the Bill and Melinda Gates Foundation has given grants to YouthBuild and other community-based youth employment programs to help them build pathways to postsecondary education for their participants. These college-focused efforts appear to be growing, though they are likely to serve a subset of dropouts with stronger academic skills.

Beyond specific programs, some cities are working to develop coherent youth "systems" to improve coordination among the many programs that serve specific subsets of disadvantaged youth or provide a narrow range of services using separate, targeted funding streams. Without a single agency or entity to take responsibility for ensuring that young people with few family supports make a successful transition to adulthood, many youth will fall through the cracks. The National League of Cities has profiled efforts by several cities to build collaboration across many public systems, including law enforcement, education, workforce development, and child welfare, to better serve disconnected youth.[14]

Program Effectiveness

Most programs that target high school dropouts have never been formally evaluated for effectiveness. Moreover, because the programs are often run by small community-based organizations, the most rigorous evaluation methods are probably not feasible or appropriate in many cases. The result is a gap between the strongly held views of practitioners who believe they know what constitutes "best practice" in youth programming, on the one hand, and the knowledge base researchers have built from rigorous evaluations, on the other.

Table 1 describes eleven rigorous evaluations of employment- or education-focused programs serving high school dropouts that have been conducted over the past thirty years (a few of the programs served both dropouts and in-school youth).[15] The table focuses on major studies that used random-assignment designs, in which eligible youth were placed, through a lottery-like process, either in a program group that had access to the program being studied or in a control group that did not.[16] The table does not include some specialized programs that were rigorously evaluated and may serve some dropouts, such as Multi-Systemic Therapy (a treatment approach for youth with serious behavior problems), or Structured Training and Employment Transitional Services (an employment model for young adults with developmental disabilities).[17]

Although the programs and studies can be categorized in many ways, table 1 groups them according to their primary service approach. The first three programs—the National Supported Work Demonstration, the Youth Incentive Entitlement Pilot program (YIEPP), and the Conservation and Youth Service Corps—relied heavily on paid work experience, while the next six—JOBSTART, the National Job Training Partnership Act, New Chance, the Center for Employment and Training (CET), Job Corps, and National Guard Youth ChalleNGe—focused more on job training or education. The last two—the Teenage Parent Demonstration and the Learning, Earning, and Parenting program (LEAP)—were mandatory, welfare-based programs that encouraged, supported, or required teenage mothers to work or go to school.

This classification scheme is useful in understanding the broad patterns of program effects, but it is far from perfect. For example, two of the work programs include a strong emphasis on education, and some of the training programs provide work experiences of some kind. More important, the simple categorization does not capture critical factors such as the program atmosphere or the types of ancillary services, supports, and activities provided to participants.

Overall, the evaluations tell a mixed story. In several, young people in the program group were substantially more likely than their control group counterparts to earn a GED or another credential. For example, in the Job Corps evaluation, 42 percent of the program group earned a GED within four years after entering the study, compared with 27 percent of the control group. Similarly, 38 percent of the program group earned a vocational or trade certificate, compared with only 15

Table 1. Selected Rigorous Evaluations of Programs for High School Dropouts

Evaluation (dates)	Target group	Program model	Sample size (number of sites)	Summary of results
Work programs				
National Supported Work Demonstration (1976–81)	17- to 20-year-old high school dropouts (one of four target groups)	Paid work experience, with graduated stress	861 youth (5 sites)	Large increases in employment initially, but no lasting impacts for youth target group
Youth Incentive Entitlement Pilot Projects (1977–81)	16- to 19-year-olds from low-income families who had not graduated from high school	Guaranteed part-time and summer jobs conditioned on school attendance	82,000 youth (17 sites)	Large, short-term increases in employment; no impacts on school outcomes
American Conservation and Youth Service Corps (1993–96)	Mostly 18- to 25-year-old out-of-school youth	Paid work experience in community service projects; education and training; support services	1,009 youth (4 sites)	Increases in employment and decreases in arrests, particularly for African American males; short follow-up
Education and training programs				
JOBSTART (1985–93)	17- to 21-year-old high school dropouts with low reading levels	Education, training, support services, job placement assistance	2,300 youth (13 sites)	Increases in GED receipt; few impacts on labor market outcomes (except in CET site)
National Job Training Partnership Act (out-of-school youth analysis) (1987–94)	Disadvantaged 16- to 21-year-old out-of-school youth	Education, job skills training, job placement, on-the-job training, and support services	5,690 youth (16 sites)	No earnings impacts for females or male non-arrestees, possibly negative impacts for male arrestees
New Chance (1989–92)	16- to 22-year-old teenage mothers who were high school dropouts	Wide range of education, employment, and family services	2,000 youth (16 sites)	Increases in GED receipt; no impacts on labor market outcomes
Center for Employment Training (CET) Replication (1995–99)	Disadvantaged, out-of-school youth, ages 16 to 21	Education and vocational training	1,500 youth (12 sites)	Few impacts on employment and earnings overall; some impacts for younger youth
Job Corps (1994–2003)	Disadvantaged youth, ages 16 to 24	Employment, education, and training in a (mostly) residential setting	15,386 youth (nationwide)	Earnings and employment impacts in years 3–4 of study period; impacts faded after year 4 according to administrative data. Results appear stronger for older youth (20 to 24 years old)
National Guard Youth ChalleNGe (2005–present)	High school dropouts, ages 16 to 18, who are drug free and not heavily involved with the justice system	Education, service to community, and other components in a quasi-military residential setting; 12-month post-residential mentoring program	3,000 youth (10 sites nationwide)	Early results show large increases in diploma or GED receipt and smaller gains in employment, college enrollment, and other outcomes
Mandatory welfare-based programs				
Teenage Parent Demonstration (1987–91)	Teenage parents receiving welfare	Mandatory education, training, and employment-related services; support services (case management, workshops, etc.)	6,000 youth (3 sites)	One of three programs increased high school graduation; increases in employment and earnings
Ohio Learning, Earning, and Parenting Program (LEAP)(1989–97)	Teen mothers under age 20 who are on welfare and do not have a GED or high school diploma	Financial incentives and sanctions based on school enrollment and attendance	7,017 teens (12 Ohio counties)	Increases in GED receipt and some earnings gains for initially enrolled teens

Sources: Rebecca Maynard, *The Impact of Supported Work on Young School Dropouts* (New York: MDRC, 1980); Judith Gueron, *Lessons from a Job Guarantee: The Youth Incentive Entitlement Pilot Projects* (New York: MDRC, 1984); JoAnn Jastrzab and others, *Impacts of Service: Final Report on the Evaluation of the American Conservation and Youth Service Corps* (Cambridge, Mass.: Abt Associates, 1996); George Cave and others, *JOBSTART: Final Report on a Program for School Dropouts* (New York: MDRC, 1993); Larry Orr and others, *Does Training for the Disadvantaged Work? Evidence from the National JTPA Study* (Cambridge, Mass.: Abt Associates, 1997); Janet Quint, Johannes Bos, and Denise Polit, *New Chance: Final Report on a Comprehensive Program for Young Mothers in Poverty and Their Children* (New York: MDRC, 1997); Cynthia Miller and others, *The Challenge of Repeating Success in a Changing World: Final Report on the Center for Employment Training Replication Sites* (New York: MDRC, 2005); Peter Schochet, John Burghardt, and Sheena McConnell, "Does Job Corps Work? Impact Findings from the National Job Corps Study," *American Economic Review* 98, no. 5 (December 2008); Dan Bloom and Megan Millenky, *21-Month Results from the National Guard Youth ChalleNGe Program Evaluation* (New York: MDRC, forthcoming); Ellen Eliason Kisker and others, *Moving Teenage Parents to Self-Sufficiency* (Princeton: Mathematica Policy Research, 1998); Johannes Bos and Veronica Fellerath, *Final Report on Ohio's Welfare Initiative to Improve School Attendance Among Teenage Parents* (New York: MDRC, 1997).

Table 2. Interim Results from the National Guard Youth ChalleNGe Evaluation

Outcome	Program group (percentage with outcome)	Control group (percentage with outcome)	Difference
Educational attainment			
High school diploma or GED	60.5	36.4	24.1***
High school diploma	22.0	16.3	5.7***
GED credential	48.3	21.9	26.5***
Any college credit	24.8	9.6	15.1***
Current activities			
Attending high school or GED prep	16.1	26.0	−9.9***
Taking college courses	11.6	7.0	4.6***
Working for pay	55.0	50.1	4.9*
Serving in military	10.9	6.2	4.7***
High school diploma or GED and in college, training, work, or the military	45.5	23.1	22.4***

Source: MDRC analysis of the National Guard Youth Challenge Evaluation 21-month survey. Asterisks indicate differences that are statistically significant, meaning that they are very unlikely to arise by chance. Differences marked with three asterisks are significant at the 1 percent level, those marked with two asterisks are significant at the 5 percent level, and those marked with one asterisk are significant at the 10 percent level. The 1 percent level denotes the highest degree of confidence that the program actually had an impact.

percent of the control group. Interim results from the National Guard Youth ChalleNGe evaluation show that about 61 percent of the program group and 36 percent of the control group earned a GED or diploma within twenty-one months after study enrollment (see table 2). The JOBSTART and New Chance studies reported similar findings.

Some of the programs, especially those that offered paid work opportunities, also generated significant increases in employment or earnings in the short term. For example, in the National Supported Work Demonstration, which provided subsidized (paid) jobs for up to twelve to eighteen months to dropouts aged seventeen to twenty, the difference in employment rates between the program and control groups was as high as 68 percentage points early in the follow-up period. Similarly, the Youth Entitlement project, which guaranteed part-time and summer jobs to all disadvantaged young people in certain geographic areas who

agreed to attend school, employed 76,000 youth and virtually erased the large gap between the unemployment rates for white and black youth. The Conservation and Youth Service Corps also provided subsidized jobs and generated some statistically significant increases in employment outcomes, particularly for African American males, over a relatively short follow-up period.

The Job Corps program did not rely on subsidized jobs but still managed to increase employment and earnings in the third and fourth years of the study period—and even longer for older participants (aged twenty to twenty-four at enrollment). Similarly, as shown in table 2, the National Guard ChalleNGe evaluation found that program group members were modestly more likely than their control group counterparts to be employed twenty-one months after entering the study.

The gains in credentials and short-term earnings are notable, but none of the studies that followed participants for more than a couple of years found lasting improvements in economic outcomes. Some of the studies (YIEPP and Conservation and Youth Service Corps) did not report or collect long-term data or are still ongoing (ChalleNGe). In other cases, early effects faded over time. For example, the Job Corps evaluation found that increases in employment and earnings faded by year five and did not reappear (though, as noted, earnings gains persisted for study participants who were aged twenty to twenty-four when they enrolled).[18]

JOBSTART, which operated in thirteen sites, showed no significant earnings gains overall during a four-year follow-up period, but the study measured large impacts in one site, the Center for Employment and Training in San Jose, California. However, as shown in table 1, when CET was replicated in twelve sites during the 1990s, an evaluation found no increases in earnings over a fifty-four-month follow-up period (women at the program sites that most faithfully implemented the model made shorter-term earnings gains, but these gains faded after year three).

Several of the studies measured non-economic outcomes such as crime involvement, drug use, health, and psychosocial development—again, with mixed results. Partway through the evaluation's follow-up period, the National Guard ChalleNGe program has produced modest decreases in crime convictions and improvements in some measures of psychosocial development. The Job Corps significantly reduced arrests, convictions, and time spent incarcerated over the first four years of the study period (these outcomes were not measured after the four-year point). The Conservation and Youth Service Corps reduced arrests overall and had a range of positive effects on non-economic outcomes

for African American study participants. For example, African American females were less likely to become pregnant and African American males improved in measures of personal and social responsibility. Few of the other programs generated impacts on these non-economic measures.

Overall, these findings do not support the common perception that "nothing works" for high school dropouts. Many of the positive effects produced by the programs, however, were modest or relatively short-lived. Moreover, the studies suggest that even some of the relatively successful programs may have difficulty meeting a strict benefit-cost test. The authors of the Job Corps evaluation concluded that the benefits produced by the program probably exceeded its costs (about $16,500 per participant) for older participants, but not for the full study sample. Nevertheless, the findings provide an important foundation on which to build.

One important study is not included in table 1 because it targeted in-school youth, but the findings may be relevant to the topic discussed here. A random-assignment evaluation of Career Academies, a high school-based model, found that it produced statistically significant increases in earnings over an eight-year follow-up period. Men in the program group earned about $30,000 more than their control group counterparts over the eight years even though they were no more likely to graduate from high school or go to college. The researchers suggest that the program's use of "career awareness and development activities," including job shadowing and work-based learning activities, may have contributed to the earnings gains.

Perhaps most interesting, the Career Academies produced significant effects on several adult transition milestones. At the end of the follow-up period, program group members were more likely to be living independently with children and a spouse or partner, and young men in the program group were more likely to be married and to be custodial parents.[19] These findings suggest that improving young people's economic prospects may ease their transition into other adult roles.

What Conclusions Can Be Drawn?

It is difficult to draw cross-cutting lessons from the evaluations in table 1 because there are many programs and not many unambiguously positive results. For example, the data do not support clear conclusions about whether paid work, a residential structure, or other program design elements are associated with more positive results in random-assignment studies. It is possible, however, to make a few general points.

First, although sustained positive effects would obviously be preferable, short-term effects are not unimportant. When programs achieve short-term increases in earnings or other outcomes, those effects are not erased if the program and control groups have similar outcomes later. Although many programs assert that they can alter the long-term trajectories of their participants, it is worth considering whether it is reasonable to expect even the strongest youth programs to produce effects that can still be measured many years later. Results like those achieved in the Career Academies evaluation, where earnings gains persisted eight years after students had completed high school, are very rare—and the Academies that were tested did not serve a highly disadvantaged group of young people. Some experts have raised the question of whether it is more appropriate to think of time-limited programs for dropouts

as inoculations, whose effects may last forever, or as vitamins, whose effects wear off if they are not taken consistently.

Some experts have raised the question of whether it is more appropriate to think of time-limited programs for dropouts as inoculations, whose effects may last forever, or as vitamins, whose effects wear off if they are not taken consistently.

Second, it is important to note that almost all the programs (and the control groups as well) involved youth who had volunteered to participate—and who thus had at least some motivation to change their lives. In fact, some of the programs extensively screened applicants and accepted only those who demonstrated strong motivation and commitment. Thus the young people who ended up in the control groups likely sought out other programs in the community and received some of the same kinds of services that program group youth received. The study results could thus be interpreted to mean that the tested programs did not do much better than other programs in their communities, but that all of the programs were relatively effective for motivated participants. That said, most of the evaluations also found that outcomes were relatively poor for both research groups. For example, in the Job Corps study, the average employed sample member earned only about $10,000 a year during the later years of the follow-up period. Similarly, in the JOBSTART study, only about 65 percent of sample members worked at all in the final year of the study period, and those who worked earned less than $9,000, on average. In other words, regardless of their effects, the programs' outcomes leave much room for improvement.

Third, it is possible that the difficulty in achieving sustained increases in economic outcomes may be traced, in part, to the educational goal of most programs—to help participants pass the GED exam. Many studies have concluded that the labor market does not, in fact, view the GED as equivalent to a high school diploma. In other words, GED holders earn significantly less than people with regular high school diplomas. Some studies have even questioned whether GED holders earn more than uncredentialed dropouts, though some recent studies suggest that the GED does have an economic payoff, at least for dropouts with low skills—although the payoff may take several years to appear. Studies have also shown that postsecondary education pays off as much for GED holders as for high school graduates, but only a small minority of GED holders complete even one year of postsecondary education.[20] These data may help explain why programs that substantially increased GED receipt did not lead to longer-term gains in employment or earnings.

Fourth, some youth experts have pointed to broader limitations of some of the program models, particularly those tested during the 1980s and early 1990s. Some have argued that these programs failed to engage youth long enough to make a lasting difference, in part because restrictions on federal funding under the Job Training Partnership Act system did not allow the programs to offer stipends or opportunities for paid work experience.[21]

Others maintain that some of the earlier youth programs were "deficit focused"—that is, they defined participants by their problems and sought to "fix" them. These experts recommend that programs should not only provide participants with training or a job, but also expose them to a range of settings, activities, and relationships that are thought to promote healthy development across a wide range of domains. One study identified these domains as cognitive, physical, social and emotional, ethnic identity, civic engagement, and career.[22] Young people from higher-income families are more likely than their lower-income counterparts to have positive experiences in these developmental areas in their families, schools, and communities. Programs may help to fill these gaps by exposing youth to responsible, caring adult role models; by creating a safe, positive group identity among participants; and by giving young people opportunities to act as leaders and to contribute to the broader society.

Among current programs, for example, YouthBuild helps young people work toward their high school diploma or GED while simultaneously learning job skills as they build or rehabilitate housing for homeless and low-income people. It emphasizes service and leadership development by giving young participants a key role in running the program. Participants also receive stipends or wages. Similarly, Service and Conservation Corps, descendants of the Depression-era Civilian Conservation Corps and of the American Conservation and Youth Service Corps evaluated in 1990 (see table 1), combine intensive community service with job training and education. Crews of participants work on conservation, urban infrastructure, and human services projects and receive stipends. A third such program, ChalleNGe, includes a five-month residential phase built around eight "core components" designed to promote positive development: service to community, leadership and followership, responsible citizenship, health and hygiene, life-coping skills, physical fitness, job skills, and academic excellence. In a final such example, City Year, participants devote a full year to community service and civic engagement, wearing uniforms to build a team identity and make their work highly visible to the community. Because the program is open to young people from a wide range of backgrounds, participants may be exposed to people quite different from themselves.

It is widely believed that programs built on positive youth development principles are more effective than others. Although this may well be the case, the evidence from rigorous evaluations is too thin to prove or disprove the hypothesis; several of the programs noted have not been rigorously evaluated. Moreover, it may be difficult to achieve consensus about which particular programs reflect youth development principles and which do not.

Tight structure and accountability may also be critical for young people who have grown up in chaotic environments and may help to counteract the potentially negative effects of placing many at-risk young people together in a program setting—effects sometimes called "deviant peer influences" or "peer contagion."[23] For example, the ChalleNGe program adopts a "quasi-military" approach: participants are divided into platoons and squads, live in barracks, have their hair cut short, wear uniforms, and are subject to military-style discipline. Their day is highly structured, with almost no "down time." Most of the staff are military veterans, retirees, or National Guard members. Although the program uses military structure, discipline, facilities, and staff to accomplish its objectives, program participation is voluntary, with no requirements for military service during the program or afterwards. Some experts have suggested that elements of the ChalleNGe model could be applied in non-residential settings and, indeed, a few military-style public high schools already operate in the United States.[24]

Finally, strong youth programs are focusing more on the transition for program graduates. Program effects may decay over time in part because youth have trouble maintaining momentum after they leave the structured, supportive program environment and confront a world where opportunities are limited. In addition, youth programs may have difficulty building strong links with employers, colleges, or other "post-program" resources for their participants. As noted, a number of youth programs have begun to build links to postsecondary education for their participants. Others have an "open door" policy that allows youth to maintain contact with the program for as long as they want or need to.[25] The ChalleNGe program includes a formal one-year Post-Residential Phase that is built around a structured mentoring program. Youth nominate their own mentors, who are then screened, trained, and supported by program staff. Studies suggest that well-implemented mentoring programs can have positive impacts for some young people, though the studies did not examine mentoring for high school dropouts.[26]

Future Directions

The individual and social costs of ignoring high school dropouts—or of focusing attention and resources only on those who show up in the criminal justice and welfare systems—are potentially enormous. Thus, the argument for investing more public funds in services, systems, and research for these young people is strong, even during a period when public resources will be severely constrained. It is clearly necessary to improve and expand prevention-oriented programs in the schools, beginning as early as preschool, but the need for strong second-chance programs for out-of-school youth is also obvious. As noted, in some cases, second-chance programs can operate within the K–12 education system, drawing on its relatively stable funding.

The challenge, again, is that the knowledge base on the effectiveness of second-chance programs is still thin. Relatively few programs have been rigorously tested, and even fewer have produced unambiguously positive results. The paucity of conclusive evidence makes it hard to know how to direct resources and magnifies the importance of ensuring that all new initiatives provide for rigorous evaluation of their impacts. Although states and localities will deliver or manage most of the services for these youth, the federal government plays a key role in funding, promoting innovation, and identifying and disseminating evidence about what works.

Some experts have suggested strategies for moving forward despite the lack of definitive evidence. For example, one recent proposal identified a number of "proven" and "promising" models for youth and called for creating a new federal grant program for disadvantaged youth that would replace the Work Investment Act youth funding stream (and possibly other existing funding streams). The new program, eventually reaching $10 billion a year, would provide both formula grants to states (with much of the funding passed through to cities) and competitive grants that would encourage neighborhood-level experimentation. Rigorous evaluation would be a requirement for programs receiving competitive grants.[27]

One possible model for testing innovative approaches might be the federal Youth Employment and Demonstration Projects Act (YEDPA), which spent more than $600 million on youth-focused research demonstration projects between 1978 and 1981. Lessons on the design, implementation, and management of the YEDPA demonstrations—a comprehensive review concluded that the program yielded some valuable evidence but tried to do too much too quickly—should inform any new efforts in this area.[28]

Whatever the specific format, a new round of youth-focused research might be structured around three general topics. The first would be how to improve outcomes for dropouts who enroll in youth programs or otherwise seek to continue their education or find jobs. The second would be how to identify and disseminate strategies to engage young people who are more seriously disconnected and unlikely to join programs. The final topic, not a focus of this paper, would be descriptive and process studies of local-level "systems" to support disconnected youth. A recurring theme in the discussion below is that providing young people with opportunities for paid work may be useful both as an engagement tool and as a strategy for improving long-term labor market outcomes.

Strengthening Programs for Youth Who Reengage
As noted, most dropouts eventually seek to continue their education or find jobs. Assessing, improving, and, where appropriate, expanding the programs that serve these young people is critical. In this section I describe three possible areas for investigation.

Existing Youth Programs. Many dropouts find their way to large programs or networks such as the Job Corps, YouthBuild, ChalleNGe, and the Service and Conservation Corps. These programs or networks often have relatively well-developed systems to ensure quality and disseminate program improvement strategies. A rigorous evaluation of the Job Corps has recently been completed, similar evaluations of ChalleNGe and the Service and Conservation Corps are under way, and an evaluation of YouthBuild is being planned as of this writing. If evaluation results are positive or even mixed, these programs should be expanded to serve more young people, while any shortcomings are being addressed simultaneously. Periodic smaller-scale, targeted evaluations could assess the progress of program improvement efforts or test the incremental impact of program enhancements, such as stronger transition services or tighter links with employers.

Other dropouts enter a wide variety of community-based programs funded by the Workforce Investment Act (WIA) and a wide array of other sources. Although the Department of Labor is planning a national evaluation of the WIA system, it is neither feasible nor appropriate to try to evaluate every program using a rigorous design, and it will always be difficult to ensure the quality and effectiveness of thousands of independent youth programs across the country. Measuring program outcomes is necessary, but does not ensure quality because programs that achieve good *outcomes* do not necessarily generate strong *impacts* (for example, they may serve youth who are relatively likely to succeed on their own). Initiatives like the National Youth Employment Coalition's Promising and Effective Practices Network (PEPNet) are designed to assess and enhance the quality of youth programs. Individual programs that appear particularly promising or innovative could receive financial incentives to participate in rigorous, federally funded evaluations. Those with positive results would be expanded or replicated.

It would be useful if some tests of existing youth programs could be structured as "differential impact studies" that assess the impact of particular program components. For example, it would be useful to understand the incremental impact of paid subsidized employment—a relatively expensive component—for particular categories of young people.

Measuring program outcomes is necessary, but does not ensure quality because programs that achieve good outcomes do not necessarily generate strong impacts.

GED Programs. Many dropouts do not enter "youth programs," but rather seek to continue their education by enrolling in classes to prepare for the GED. These classes may be offered at community-based organizations, schools, libraries, or community colleges. Each year 400,000 to 500,000 people pass the GED nationwide and more than 60 percent of them are under twenty-five years old.[29] Although it is preferable for students to earn a high school diploma whenever possible, for the foreseeable future large numbers of young people will take and pass the GED each year. The data cited earlier suggest that one reason for the GED's limited impact on labor market success is that most people who pass the test do not go on to get post-secondary training—even though 60 percent of those who pass the GED report that they took the test for "educational reasons."[30]

The past few years have seen the emergence of a number of small programs that focus on increasing the rates of postsecondary enrollment and success for GED recipients and other adult education students. Although college transition programming has a long history in high schools, it is relatively new to the adult education field. A study by the National Center for the Study of Adult Learning and Literacy has identified several models of college transition programs in the adult education sphere. The models include offering student workshops or individual advising about postsecondary options; enhancing the GED curriculum to include academic or study skills needed for college entry; and integrating basic skills and occupational training in a specific employment sector or occupation.[31]

These programs need not limit their focus to academic postsecondary programs. Occupational certificate programs may have a significant payoff in the labor market. A recent study found that median earnings after college were 27 percent higher for students with a certificate than for those who left college without a degree. Given the difficulty many low-income students have completing degree programs, the study concludes that some students struggling in associate's degree programs might be better off in certificate programs.[32] Another recent study projects substantial demand in coming years for "middle-skill" jobs that pay decent wages. Accessing these jobs often requires some postsecondary training (for example, an occupational certificate or an associate's degree), but not necessarily a bachelor's degree.[33] None of these data are meant to suggest that an associate's or a bachelor's

degree is not important, but rather that postsecondary occupational programs may help students build skills, raise their earnings, and move on toward a degree (particularly if programs can be structured to earn college credit). Community colleges would seem to be a natural venue for efforts to link adult education GED programs with postsecondary occupational programs. For example, Washington State's highly touted Integrated Basic Education and Skills Training (I-BEST) program combines basic skills and college-level occupational training in a community college setting, rather than expecting students to complete a GED before starting college-level coursework. Nonexperimental evaluations have found promising results.[34]

Strategies for Youth with Weak Academic Skills. Ongoing efforts to help dropouts access postsecondary education are exciting, but it is important to recognize that not all young people have the interest or the academic ability to attend college. Young people with weak reading and math skills must also have effective options.

As noted, some young people who are not interested in or qualified for academically focused postsecondary programs may benefit from occupationally oriented options. Jobs for the Future is seeking to develop intensive twelve- to twenty-four-month "Career First" programs that expand the limited options available for young people who want to find good jobs but are not prepared for college. In addition, some experts have argued that various forms of apprenticeships and internships are the most promising strategy to improve labor market outcomes for many disadvantaged youth.[35] When they are operating at a steady state, these models should be evaluated and, where appropriate, replicated.

For dropouts with very low levels of basic reading and math skills, postsecondary education, or even a GED, may not be a realistic short-term goal. Such youth may be neglected by programs whose focus is on helping participants pass the GED or find jobs relatively quickly. For example, some ChalleNGe and YouthBuild programs accept only young people who can read at a certain grade level. Ironically, the push to build links between youth programs and postsecondary education may unintentionally exacerbate this problem by encouraging programs to target dropouts who have the best chance to enter college. Experts report that programs targeting dropouts with very low reading and math skill levels are quite rare. The Youth Development Institute's Community Education Pathways to Success program is one model that seeks to help community-based organizations better serve youth who are not ready for GED programs, but much more research and experimentation is needed in this area. Research should focus not only on how best to teach young people with very low skills, but also on how best to retain them in programs long enough to make a difference. Paid work opportunities and performance-based financial incentives are two strategies that may be worth testing.

Although it is crucial to identify better ways to engage and teach young people with serious basic skills deficits, it is also important to acknowledge that some of them will not be able to obtain academic credentials. Unfortunately, today's labor market has few good jobs for this population. This reality magnifies the importance of work supports like the Earned Income Credit, which can provide almost $5,000 to low-income working families with children. The EIC, however, provides only a very small credit to childless workers and to noncustodial parents.

Recently several experts have proposed increasing the EIC for low-wage workers who are not custodial parents.[36]

Identifying Strategies to Engage Disconnected Youth

Almost all of the evaluations discussed above focused on youth who voluntarily came forward to join programs. But the reality is that many young people, both high school dropouts and struggling high school graduates, do not seek out programs. Advocates note, correctly, that the existing infrastructure of youth programs serves only a small fraction of the young people who need help. But it is also true that many youth programs struggle to recruit enough young people to fill their slots. Thus, a second goal of research should be to identify and disseminate effective strategies to engage profoundly disconnected young people who are unlikely to volunteer for programs like YouthBuild, the Job Corps, or ChalleNGe.

One way to help address this problem is to make the programs for reengaged dropouts more effective to help them attract more youth. It may also be possible to test systematically various strategies to locate and engage the most disconnected youth. Such strategies might involve financial incentives for participation, opportunities for youth to provide visible services to their communities, or approaches that embrace and incorporate youth culture into the program environment, an idea championed by the Youth Development and Research Fund.[37]

At a broader scale, engagement-focused demonstration projects might operate at the neighborhood level, seeking to saturate communities with work opportunities or other supports for youth. The Youth Entitlement project, described earlier, used this approach but mostly served in-school youth. A variation might be designed to engage more out-of-school youth. Projects of this type would also help to address the collapse of the youth labor market already noted. The much-discussed Harlem Children's Zone is another community-level model for engaging youth.[38] Although complex, geographically targeted initiatives are challenging to implement and evaluate, there may be synergistic effects from combining a range of proven program models in a single location.

Finally, though beyond the scope of this paper, it is important for researchers to consider the impact of mandatory programs for youth operating within enforcement-oriented systems like juvenile and criminal justice or child support enforcement. Although these programs compel participation, they could achieve positive impacts by using some of the same approaches as the voluntary programs already discussed. Anti-violence initiatives in Boston, Philadelphia, and elsewhere combine strict supervision with a range of supports to try to reach some of the highest-risk young people in the justice system.[39]

Conclusion

Young people who drop out of high school are a diverse group. Some will continue their education and get back on track, but many others, including a large share of dropouts from low-income families, will find it extremely hard to make a successful transition to adulthood in a labor market that offers fewer and fewer opportunities for workers with no postsecondary training or education.

The nation's schools, from preschool to high school, place a strong and appropriate emphasis on prevention-oriented programs and policies to keep students on track, but many thousands of youth nevertheless drop out every year, and the human and fiscal costs of neglecting them would be enormous. Many young people who leave school attempt to reengage as they mature, and both rigorous research and practitioner wisdom suggest that many second-chance programs are worthy of investment and expansion.

At the same time, much remains to be learned. It is important to keep assessing and strengthening existing programs, for example, by building stronger links to employers. It is also necessary to develop multiple pathways for youth who drop out. Some young dropouts have the interest and aptitude to move into academic postsecondary programs; others would do better in occupationally oriented programs; and still others need special approaches tailored to youth with very low levels of basic skills. Many young people at all skill levels might benefit from opportunities for paid work experience. Finally, it is critical to identify and disseminate lessons on how best to reengage the most disconnected young people, many of whom will need to be reached through public systems like juvenile and criminal justice or child support enforcement.

Endnotes

1. The National Center for Education Statistics estimates the number of dropouts at about 3.5 million. Analysis by the Center for Labor Market Studies at Northeastern University, which considers GED holders as dropouts, counts dropouts who are institutionalized, and uses a different estimation methodology, places the number of dropouts at about 6 million. National Center for Education Statistics, *The Condition of Education* (Washington: National Center for Education Statistics, 2009), table A-20-1; Center for Labor Market Studies, *Left Behind in America: The Nation's Dropout Crisis* (Boston: Northeastern University Center for Labor Market Studies, 2009). In this article, I focus mainly on high school dropouts. However, studies have found a large share of high school graduates not to be adequately prepared for work or college. Overall, about 45 percent of twenty-one-year-olds have a high school diploma or GED and are not enrolled in college; about 20 percent of that group is not employed. Many of the programs and policies discussed in this paper are potentially relevant to high school graduates as well as high school dropouts.

2. Data on dropouts by income are from 2006. See National Center for Education Statistics, *Digest of Education Statistics: 2007* (Washington: National Center for Education Statistics, 2008), tables 105 and 106. Data on dropouts by race and ethnicity are from 2007. See National Center for Education Statistics, *The Condition of Education* (Washington: National Center for Education Statistics, 2009), table A-20-1.

3. Robert Balfanz and Nettie Legters, *Locating the Dropout Crisis* (Baltimore: Center for Research on the Education of Students Placed at Risk, 2004).

4. For example, James Heckman and Paul LaFontaine write that "the true high school graduation rate…has been declining over the past 40 years [and]…majority/minority graduation rate differentials are substantial and have not converged over the past 35 years." Lawrence Mishel and Joydeep Roy conclude that "high school completion has grown significantly over the last 40 years and the black-white gap has shrunk significantly." James Heckman and Paul LaFontaine, "The American High School Graduation Rate: Trends and Levels," NBER Working Paper 13670 (Washington: National Bureau of Economic Research, 2007). Lawrence Mishel and Joydeep Roy, *Rethinking High School Graduation Rates and Trends* (Washington: Economic Policy Institute, 2006).

5. Andrew Sum, "The Deterioration of the Teen and Young Adult Labor Market in the U.S. and Their Adverse Consequences for Marriage, Out of Wedlock Childbearing, Young Family Economic Well-Being and Children in These Families," Powerpoint presentation (Boston: Northeastern University Center for Labor Market Studies, 2009).

6. Ibid.

7. Steven Raphael and Michael Stoll, "Why Are So Many Americans in Prison?" in *Do Prisons Make Us Safer?* edited by Steven Raphael and Michael Stoll (New York: Russell Sage Foundation, 2009).

8. Caroline Wolf Harlow, *Education and Correctional Populations* (Washington: Bureau of Justice Statistics, 2003).

9. Andrew Sum, "The Deterioration of the Teen and Young Adult Labor Market" (see note 5).

10. John Bridgeland, John DiIulio, and Karen Burke Morison, *The Silent Epidemic: Perspectives of High School Dropouts* (Washington: Civic Enterprises, 2006).

11. David Hurst, Dana Kelly, and Daniel Princiotta, *Educational Attainment of High School Dropouts 8 Years Later* (Washington: National Center for Education Statistics, 2004).

12. Cheryl Almeida, Cassius Johnson, and Adria Steinberg, *Making Good on a Promise: What Policymakers Can Do to Support the Educational Persistence of Dropouts* (Boston: Jobs for the Future, 2006).

13. Laura Wycoff and others, *Disconnected Young People in New York City: Crisis and Opportunity* (Philadelphia: Public/Private Ventures, 2008).

14. National League of Cities, *Beyond City Limits: Cross-System Collaboration to Reengage Disconnected Youth* (Washington: National League of Cities, 2007).

15. Table 1 lists the sources for the evaluation results discussed in the text.

16. For a more detailed synthesis that includes many of the same studies, see Susan Jekielek, Stephanie Cochran, and Elizabeth Hair, *Employment Programs and Youth Development: A Synthesis* (Washington: Child Trends, 2002). The Youth Incentive Entitlement Pilot Projects used a "saturation" approach in which all youth in particular neighborhoods or small cities were guaranteed jobs under certain conditions. Thus, it was not feasible to randomly assign individuals to program or control groups. Instead, the study compared YIEPP sites to other neighborhoods or cities. YIEPP served both in-school and out-of-school youth.

17. For more information on these programs, see Stuart Kerachsky and others, *The Impacts of Transitional Employment for Mentally Retarded Young Adults* (New York: MDRC, 1985); MST Services, *Multisystemic Therapy at a Glance* (Mt. Pleasant, S.C.: MST Services, 2005); Julia Littell, "Lessons from a Systematic Review of Effects of Multisystemic Therapy," in *Children and Youth Services Review* 27 (2005).

18. The Job Corps evaluation collected data on employment and earnings from both surveys and administrative records during the first four years of the study period, and from administrative records only in years five through ten. The positive effects on earnings and employment in years three and four were measured with both data sources, though they were much larger in the survey than in the records.

19. James Kemple, *Career Academies: Long-Term Impacts on Labor Market Outcomes, Educational Attainment, and Transitions to Adulthood* (New York: MDRC, 2008).

20. John Tyler, "The General Educational Development Credential: History, Current Research, and Directions for Policy and Practice," in *Review of Adult Learning and Literacy,* volume 5 (Boston: National Center for the Study of Adult Learning and Literacy, 2005).

21. Robert Ivry and Fred Doolittle, *Improving the Economic and Life Outcomes of At-Risk Youth* (New York: MDRC, 2003).

22. Rhonda Tsoi-A-Fatt, *A Collective Responsibility, A Collective Work: Supporting the Path to Positive Life Outcomes for Youth in Economically Distressed Communities* (Washington: Center for Law and Social Policy, 2008).

23. Kenneth Dodge, Thomas Dishion, and Jennifer Lansford, editors, *Deviant Peer Influences in Programs for Youth: Problems and Solutions* (New York: Guilford Press, 2007).

24. Hugh Price, "About Face: A Case for Quasi-Military Public High Schools," in *Educational Leadership* 65, no. 8 (May 2008); Daniel Donohue, *Designing a ChalleNGe-like Program for High School Dropouts*

and Students Who Are Drifting Through School, Disengaged and Repeating Grades (Fairfax Station, Va.: Donohue Associates, 2008).

25. Public/Private Ventures, "Serving High-Risk Youth: Lessons from Research and Programming" (Philadelphia: Public/Private Ventures, 2002).

26. Michael Karcher, "The Study of Mentoring in the Learning Environment: A Randomized Study of the Effectiveness of School-Based Mentoring," *Prevention Science* 9, no. 2 (June 2008); Joseph Tierney and Jean Grossman, *Making a Difference: An Impact Study of Big Brothers/Big Sisters* (Philadelphia: Public/Private Ventures, 2000).

27. Peter Edelman, Mark Greenberg, and Harry Holzer, "Youth Policy Proposals" (Washington: Georgetown Center on Poverty, Inequality, and Public Policy, 2008).

28. Charles Betsey, Robinson Hollister, and Mary Papageorgiou, editors, *Youth Employment and Training Programs: The YEDPA Years* (Washington: National Academy Press, 1985).

29. American Council on Education, *2007 GED Testing Program Statistical Report* (Washington: American Council on Education, 2008).

30. Ibid.

31. Cynthia Zafft, Silja Kallenbach, and Jessica Spohn, *Transitioning Adults to College: Adult Basic Education Program Models* (Boston: National Center for the Study of Adult Learning and Literacy, 2006).

32. Louis Jacobson and Christine Mokher, *Pathways to Boosting the Earnings of Low Income Students by Increasing Their Educational Attainment* (Washington: Hudson Institute Center for Employment Policy, 2009).

33. Harry Holzer and Robert Lerman, *The Future of Middle Skill Jobs* (Washington: Brookings Institution, 2009).

34. David Jenkins, Matthew Zeidenberg, and Gregory Kienzl, *Educational Outcomes of I-BEST: Findings from a Multivariate Analysis* (New York: Community College Research Center, 2009).

35. Robert Lerman, "Are Skills the Problem? Reforming the Education and Training System in the United States" in *A Future of Good Jobs?* (Kalamazoo, Mich.: W.E. Upjohn Institute for Employment Research, 2008).

36. See, for example: Gordon Berlin, *Rewarding the Work of Individuals* (New York: MDRC, 2007); Harry Holzer, Peter Edelman, and Paul Offner, *Reconnecting Disadvantaged Young Men* (Washington: Urban Institute Press, 2006).

37. Edward DeJesus, *Countering the Urban Influence* (Montgomery Village, Md.: Youth Development and Research Fund, 2005); Youth Development and Research Fund, *Listening to the Voices and Aspirations of Disconnected Youth* (Montgomery Village, Md.: Youth Development and Research Fund, 2007).

38. The Harlem Children's Zone is an ambitious, comprehensive initiative targeting one hundred blocks in Central Harlem. It includes a wide range of programs for children, from preschool through college, along with efforts to strengthen families and "reweave" the neighborhood's social fabric. The initiative's goal is to create a "tipping point" so that children are surrounded by supportive adults and peers. See www.hcz.org.

39. See, for example, Wendy McClanahan, *Alive at 25: Reducing Youth Violence through Monitoring and Support* (Philadelphia: Public/Private Ventures, 2004).

Young Adults and Higher Education: Barriers and Breakthroughs to Success

Thomas Brock

Summary

Although *access* to higher education has increased substantially over the past forty years, student *success* in college—as measured by persistence and degree attainment—has not improved at all. Thomas Brock reviews systematic research findings on the effectiveness of various interventions designed to help at-risk students remain in college.

Brock shows how changes in federal policy and public attitudes since the mid-1960s have opened up higher education to women, minorities, and nontraditional students and also shifted the "center of gravity" in higher education away from traditional four-year colleges toward nonselective community colleges. Students at two-year colleges, however, are far less likely than those at four-year institutions to complete a degree. Brock argues that the nation's higher education system must do much more to promote student success. Three areas, he says, are particularly ripe for reform: remedial education, student support services, and financial aid.

In each of these three areas, Brock reviews programs and interventions that community colleges have undertaken in order to raise completion rates. Some colleges have, for example, experimented with remedial programs that build social cohesion between students and faculty and integrate content across courses. Other colleges have tested student support service programs that offer counseling and advising that are regular, intensive, and personalized. Still others have experimented with ways to simplify the financial aid application process and incentivize students to earn good grades and persist in school.

Research shows that such programs and interventions can improve student outcomes, but Brock argues that more must be done to bring proven practices to scale and to test new ideas that might lead to better results. Institutions that most need help are those that provide the greatest access to nontraditional and underprepared students in community colleges and less selective universities.

www.futureofchildren.org

Thomas Brock is the director of the Young Adults and Postsecondary Education Policy Area at MDRC.

Few decisions matter more to a young person's future than the decision to attend college and earn a degree. As described by Sheldon Danziger and David Ratner in their article in this volume, college graduates have substantially better prospects in the labor market than peers who stop their formal education after high school. In fact, over a lifetime, an adult with a bachelor's degree will earn about $2.1 million—roughly one-third more than an adult who starts but does not complete college and nearly twice as much as one who has only a high school diploma.[1] College attendance and completion provide other benefits as well. For example, adults who have attended some college or earned a bachelor's degree are more likely to report "excellent" or "very good" health than those who have only a high school diploma, even when they have comparable incomes.[2] College is often where people form their deepest friendships and meet future spouses or partners. Finally, as Constance Flanagan and Peter Levine discuss in their article in this volume, research shows that educational attainment has positive effects on voting and other measures of civic engagement.[3]

Clearly, many of the benefits that accrue from a college education are explained by the knowledge, skills, and contacts that students gain from their time on campus and in the classroom. From a developmental standpoint, colleges and universities also provide a safe environment for young adults to explore new ideas and interests, interact with people who are different from themselves, and form their identity. For all these reasons, colleges and universities play an indispensable role in the transition to adulthood. At their best, they foster both intellectual and personal growth and prepare young people for productive lives at work and in society. Few public or private institutions have the capacity to do so much good for so many.

Access to higher education has increased substantially, although some racial and ethnic groups remain underrepresented. But success in college—as measured by persistence and degree attainment—has not improved at all.

My purpose in this article is to examine data on college enrollment and completion in the United States and to explore what might be done to help more young people benefit from the experience and complete college degrees. I begin by reviewing historical trends to show how the numbers and characteristics of college students have changed in the past forty years. *Access* to higher education, it turns out, has increased substantially, although some racial and ethnic groups remain underrepresented. But *success* in college—as measured by persistence and degree attainment—has not improved at all. I then examine some leading explanations for why college students do not succeed and review some research findings on interventions designed to help at-risk students overcome barriers. I conclude with some lessons and suggestions to guide policy makers, practitioners, and researchers.

The Changing Landscape of Higher Education: 1965–2005

Before 1965, American colleges and universities were rarefied places populated mostly by white males from middle- or upper-income families. In part, the lack of diversity reflected the fact that for much of the nation's history, a college education was not needed to make a decent living. Indeed, after World War II, the difference between the average wages of high school and college graduates was small and shrinking. After 1950, however, the trend moved in the opposite direction and accelerated as the demand for highly skilled labor increased.[4] In 1975, year-round workers with a bachelor's degree earned 1.5 times the annual pay of workers with only a high school diploma; by 1999, that ratio had risen to 1.8.[5]

Prevailing social norms and a limited federal role in higher education also served to keep higher education an exclusive domain before the 1960s. In many parts of the country, discriminatory laws and attitudes kept many blacks and other racial or ethnic minorities from pursuing a college degree. Prevailing attitudes about the role of women limited their college-going as well. Finally, before 1965, financial aid was not generally available for college students. The federal G.I. Bill had covered college costs for tens of thousands of veterans after World War II, but it, too, had "masculinized" campus life and had aided whites far more than African Americans.[6]

The mid-to-late 1960s marked a major turning point. Changes in federal policy, coupled with big changes in public attitudes and expectations, opened up higher education as never before. From a policy perspective, the passage of the Higher Education Act of 1965 was arguably the most important change, as it extended need-based financial assistance to the general population for the first time.[7] The federal role expanded in other ways, too, fueling growth on college and university campuses. Starting in 1963, for example,

the federal government launched a major program for facilities construction, targeting "developing institutions" like community colleges and historically black colleges and universities.[8] Federal spending on higher education increased exponentially, from $655 million in 1956 to $3.5 billion in 1966.[9]

During the same period, the civil rights movement influenced higher education by challenging public laws and practices that excluded blacks and other minority groups from attending some colleges and universities, particularly in the South. Early battles focused on winning admittance for individual students. In 1964, Congress passed the Civil Rights Act, which outlawed discrimination based on race in schools, public places, and employment and mandated equal opportunity for women. By the late 1960s, civil rights activists broadened their perspective to encompass poverty and income inequality and helped launch dozens of Great Society programs that funded education and job training programs targeted to low-income Americans.[10]

Demographic trends, combined with the social activism of the 1960s, also created pressure for change. As the baby boom generation reached maturity, young adults poured onto college campuses in record numbers. Colleges and universities became centers of protest, most famously against the Vietnam War, but also against all manner of social convention and custom.[11] Rules governing higher education were not above the fray. Questions of who should have access— and what role colleges and universities should play in confronting and reducing inequities in the larger society—were hotly debated. The "open admissions" movement gained currency during this era, most famously with the 1970 decision by the City University of

Figure 1. Fall Enrollment in Two- and Four-Year Degree-Granting Institutions, 1963–2005, by Millions

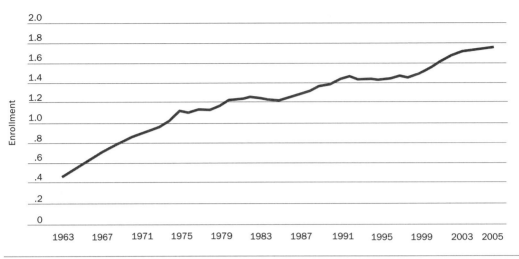

Source: T. D. Snyder, S. A. Dillow, and C. M. Hoffman, *Digest of Education Statistics 2007* (NCES 2008-022) (Washington: National Center for Education Statistics, Institute of Education Sciences, U.S. Department of Education, 2008), table 180.

New York to allow all high school graduates to pursue college degrees regardless of academic preparation. Other institutions across the country, notably community colleges, adopted similar policies.[12]

Trends in Student Enrollment and Demographics

The effects of changing laws and attitudes are evident in the dramatic rise in college enrollments depicted in figure 1. Total fall enrollment increased from just over 5.9 million students in 1965 to about 17.5 million students in 2005—a nearly 300 percent increase.[13] The rise was steepest through 1975 and was far greater than could be accounted for by population growth alone. To put the enrollment figures into perspective, in 1965 the number of young adults in the prime college-going years of eighteen to twenty-four was approximately 20.3 million; by 2005 that number had increased 44 percent, to about 29.2 million.[14]

Along with increased enrollments, the demographics of students attending colleges and universities changed. Figure 2 compares the characteristics of students by gender, race or ethnicity, and age starting in the 1970s, when the federal government first began reporting on student demographics. The top panel shows how the gender balance reversed between 1970 and 2005, from mostly male to mostly female. The second panel depicts the increase in the percentage of students from racial or ethnic minority groups, which more than doubled from 1976 to 2005. By far the largest percentage increases were among Hispanics and Asian and Pacific Islanders, though all minority groups experienced growth in college enrollment while the share of whites declined. Finally, the third panel shows an increase in the percentage of students aged twenty-five and older and a proportionate decline in those aged twenty-four and under. The U.S. Department of Education projects that the trend toward older students will continue in coming years.[15]

The shift in demographic characteristics hints at another significant development in the student population. The so-called traditional undergraduate—the high school graduate who enrolls full-time immediately after finishing high school, relies on parents for financial support, and either does not work during the school year or works only part-time—is now the exception rather than the rule. Only 27 percent of undergraduates met these criteria in 1999–2000. By comparison, in the same year, 28 percent of undergraduates met the Department of Education's definition of "highly nontraditional": they were likely in their twenties or older, working while going to school, and raising children (possibly as single parents), among other criteria. Some highly nontraditional students did not have a high school diploma.[16]

Patterns of Institutional Attendance

Government statistics show that a large majority of undergraduates enroll in four-year colleges and universities. At the same time, the "center of gravity" in higher education has gradually shifted, with community colleges playing a much more prominent role today than in the past. In 1969 (when the government adopted its current methodology for categorizing two- and four-year schools), 26 percent of all college students attended two-year institutions. By 2005, that figure had risen to 37 percent.[17]

The vast majority of students enroll in publicly funded colleges and universities. In 2005, private institutions accounted for about one-fourth of all undergraduates—a figure that has increased only slightly in the past decade. Nearly all of these students are enrolled in four-year institutions, though a small percentage of students is enrolled in private two-year colleges.[18] The advent of online courses may be changing higher

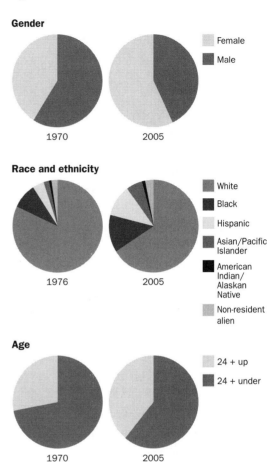

Figure 2. Characteristics of Students Attending College, by Gender, Race and Ethnicity, and Age, 1970 and 2005

Gender

1970 2005

Female
Male

Race and ethnicity

1976 2005

White
Black
Hispanic
Asian/Pacific Islander
American Indian/ Alaskan Native
Non-resident alien

Age

1970 2005

24 + up
24 + under

Source: Same as figure 1, tables 187, 217, and 181.

education again. Indeed, two of the five largest higher education institutions in 2005 rely principally on online instruction: the University of Phoenix, with an enrollment of more than 117,000 students, and Western International University, with an enrollment of nearly 51,000 students.[19]

Although the demographic composition of colleges and universities has become more diverse over the past forty years, the increased diversity is largely accounted for by nonselective institutions. Specifically, female, black, and Hispanic students are disproportionately enrolled in community colleges.[20] Nontraditional students are also much more likely to be enrolled in community colleges and to participate in distance education via the Internet.[21]

Trends in Persistence and Completion

Government statistics indicate that student outcomes differ markedly by type of institution attended. Specifically, undergraduates who begin at four-year colleges and universities are about twice as likely to complete a postsecondary degree as undergraduates who begin at two-year institutions. The five-year completion rate for students who began at a four-year college or university—taking into account certificates, associate's degrees, or bachelor's degrees—was 60 percent in the 1995–96 academic year. For students who began at a community college, the rate of completion was 32 percent.[22]

Many students take longer than five years to earn a degree: some are enrolled part-time, some change their majors, some need to drop out temporarily, and some have other reasons for the delay. Measures of *persistence* take into account those who have earned a certificate or degree as well as those who are still enrolled in college. Eighty percent of students who began at a four-year college or university in 1995–96 persisted after five years. Among students who began at a community college, the persistence rate was 52 percent. The data also show that students attending private institutions (both four-year and two-year) persist at higher rates than their counterparts at public institutions.[23]

Viewed historically, rates of completion at four-year institutions have been unchanged since the federal government began collecting data during the 1970s. A recent study suggests that there has been a slight uptick in the persistence rate at public four-year colleges.[24] Although that increase may seem contradictory, it likely reflects the longer time it now takes students in four-year colleges, particularly at less selective public institutions, to earn degrees.[25] Historical data on students attending community college go back only to 1990, but show no significant change in persistence or completion.[26]

Persistence and completion rates differ significantly by race and ethnicity and by gender. At public two- and four-year institutions, Asian and Pacific Islanders have the highest persistence and completion rates of any racial or ethnic group, followed by non-Hispanic whites, Hispanics, and non-Hispanic blacks. (The longitudinal studies commissioned by the government lack sufficient numbers of American Indians and Alaska Natives on which to report.) Asian and Pacific Islanders who entered public four-year institutions in 1995–96 were nearly twice as likely to earn a degree or still be in school after six years as non-Hispanic blacks who entered the same year. The story by gender is a bit more complicated. At public four-year institutions, women have slightly higher persistence and completion rates than men (a difference of about 5 percentage points); at public two-year institutions, the gender difference is reversed.[27] It is important to recall that because more women than men enroll in college, many more associate's and bachelor's degrees are awarded to women—a pattern that has held true at both two- and four-year institutions since at least the late 1980s.[28]

Despite these patterns, neither race and ethnicity nor gender is a good predictor of who will earn a college degree, owing to large variation within these demographic groups.

Research by Clifford Adelman for the Department of Education shows that the two best predictors are entering college immediately after finishing high school and taking a high school curriculum that stresses reading at grade level and math beyond basic algebra. Higher socioeconomic status is also a predictor, though only moderately so.[29] Consistent with these findings, being classified as a traditional student is another strong predictor of college completion. Conversely, all of the characteristics used to define nontraditional status—delayed entry into college from high school, working full-time, single parenthood, and so on—are considered "risk factors" because they are negatively correlated with persistence.[30] As noted, community colleges account for a disproportionate share of nontraditional students; they are also the institutions that raise the most concern about persistence and completion.

Summary of Trends and Key Issues

Access to higher education has been greatly expanded since the mid-1960s. More students are attending college—both in real terms and as a percentage of the population—and they are demographically more diverse. Actions taken by the federal government clearly played a major part in these trends, though larger economic, demographic, and social forces were also at play. Finally, the growth of nonselective institutions like community colleges and, more recently, online courses and programs has made it easier for people to attend college even if they lack good preparation or are working while going to school.

Despite these gains, college access remains problematic, and gaps in enrollment between certain racial and ethnic minority groups are substantial. In 2006, for example, 44 percent of whites between the ages of eighteen and twenty-four were enrolled in college,

compared with 32 percent of blacks and 25 percent of Hispanics.[31] Rates of college attendance for black and Hispanic males are particularly low. A recent national survey of college-qualified students who did not enroll in college underscores that college costs, availability of aid, and uncertainty about the steps needed to enroll in college remain significant deterrents.[32] Inadequate preparation for college is another factor, though with the rise of nonselective institutions, it is less a barrier to access than to success once students have enrolled in college.

From a public policy standpoint, it makes little sense to promote greater college access if students are failing once they get there. Figuring out how to boost college completion is the challenge. The United States has seen no progress on this measure since the advent of statistics on it and is losing ground to other nations in the share of the adult population with college degrees.[33] The costs of such failure—to students especially, but also to colleges, governments, and society at large—are extremely high. I next examine why some students don't succeed and what might be done in response.

Improving Academic Outcomes for Students in Higher Education

The search for solutions to the college persistence and completion problem begins with an understanding of its underlying causes. In his seminal book *Leaving College*, Vincent Tinto examines why students depart prematurely from both two-year and four-year institutions. He acknowledges that students come to college with different skills and abilities, varying personal motivation and objectives, and diverse external commitments that will influence their ability to succeed, but he argues that what happens to them *after* they arrive on campus is at least as important as what happened *before*. Specifically, he focuses on how well students are integrated into the classrooms and laboratories where instruction takes place and into the informal meeting places such as dormitories, cafeterias, and hallways. In all of these situations, he notes, the quality and frequency of interactions between students, faculty, and staff will shape students' experiences and determine how well they "fit" at a particular institution.[34] Other theorists have placed greater weight on how cultural norms and organizational structures and processes may affect student success, but generally support Tinto's dual emphasis on student attributes and institutional practices as the keys to understanding college persistence and completion.[35]

Some observers have argued that the problem of low persistence and completion would go away if primary and secondary schools did a better job of preparing students for college. There is certainly truth to this claim, and another article, if not a book, could be written on educational reforms and college preparatory programs that target younger students.[36] But these reforms and programs will always fail to reach some students, and blaming the nation's schools for poor college completion rates lets colleges and universities off the hook too easily. America's higher education system has many strengths, but it is far from perfect, and policy makers and institutions can do much more to promote greater student success. Three areas seem particularly ripe for reform: remedial education, student support services, and financial aid.

Rethinking Remedial Education

That many students arrive on college campuses unprepared to do college-level work is well known. Both two- and four-year institutions face this deficit, though the nation has made a conscious policy choice in recent

years to shift the primary teaching responsibility for remedial education to community colleges. The most recent data from the Department of Education indicate that 42 percent of freshmen at community colleges enroll in at least one remedial reading, writing, or mathematics course. At private and public four-year institutions, the figure ranges from 12 to 24 percent.[37]

Research and anecdotal evidence suggest that many students who are assigned to remedial education drop out of the classes (and often out of college) and that those who remain make slow progress. An analysis of data from the Department of Education's National Education Longitudinal Study shows that only 28 percent of remedial students in two-year colleges attain a degree or certificate within eight and one-half years of entry (compared with 43 percent of nonremedial students), and that 52 percent of remedial students in four-year colleges finish bachelor's degrees within this period (compared with 78 percent of students without remedial course work). The analysis also shows that remedial education delays time-to-degree for students in two-year colleges. Though seldom acknowledged, remedial education acts as a gatekeeper and quality control mechanism in most institutions.[38] It allows underprepared students access to campus facilities and resources, yet clearly divides them from students considered to be "college ready."

Is this the best that colleges and universities can do, or is it possible to remake remedial education so that greater numbers of students acquire basic skills and go on to earn college degrees? Many educators believe that change is possible, noting the propensity of remedial education classes to use outmoded teaching methods—including repetition and memorization of material that does not connect to students' interests—and to isolate and marginalize students from the rest of the college community.[39] Many reforms have been suggested or tried, but relatively few have been evaluated in a way that establishes a causal relationship between the reforms and educational attainment.[40]

Many reforms have been suggested or tried, but relatively few have been evaluated in a way that establishes a causal relationship between the reforms and educational attainment.

A notable exception is an evaluation of a Learning Communities program at Kingsborough Community College in Brooklyn, New York, one of four sites in a national demonstration project called Opening Doors.[41] The goal of Opening Doors was to test interventions designed to increase persistence and raise academic achievement among low-income community college students. At all of the Opening Doors sites, students were randomly assigned either to a program group that received an enhanced set of services or to a control group that experienced "business as usual" at the college. Random assignment ensures that the students in the program and control groups are similar at baseline; subsequent differences in educational attainment or other outcomes can therefore be attributed to the intervention, rather than to differences in student motivation or characteristics. The Opening Doors research was conducted by MDRC, in partnership with the MacArthur Network on Transitions to Adulthood. I discuss the other Opening Doors interventions later.

Kingsborough's Learning Communities program targeted incoming freshmen, the great majority of whom required remedial English. Students were placed into groups of fifteen to twenty-five to take three of their first-semester courses together: an English course (based on level of proficiency, but usually remedial); a regular college course like introductory psychology or health; and a student success course, taught by a college counselor, that covered time management, effective study habits, and other skills considered necessary to succeed in college. Faculty who taught in the Learning Communities were expected to coordinate assignments and meet periodically to review student progress. The idea was to build social cohesion between students and faculty and to make the subject matter more meaningful to students by integrating the content and helping students apply the concepts and lessons across the courses.[42]

More than 1,500 students participated in the Learning Communities evaluation and were, as noted, randomly assigned to either a program group that participated in Learning Communities or a control group that took regular, unlinked courses. The students were young (mostly seventeen to twenty years old), low-income, and highly diverse in terms of race and ethnicity. Researchers tracked program and control group members for two years and found that students in the Learning Communities were more likely to feel integrated at school and to be engaged in their courses and with fellow students and instructors. They also passed more courses and earned more credits during their first semester, moved more quickly through remedial English requirements, and were more likely to take and pass an English skills assessment test that was required for graduation. It is important to note that these effects, while statistically significant, were generally modest. For example, after four semesters, students in the program group earned an average of 33.2 college credits, compared with an average of 30.8 credits for the control group (a difference of 2.4 credits, or less than one standard college course). Moreover, contrary to expectations, the Learning Communities did not have an immediate effect on persistence. Kingsborough is only one test, however, and a new set of randomized trials is under way to determine whether similarly structured programs at six community colleges around the country will help students complete remedial English or math requirements and persist.[43]

As noted, one of the underlying concepts of Learning Communities is to make the course material more meaningful to students by linking the information covered in one class to the discussions and assignments in another class. Another way to make remedial education more meaningful is exemplified by Washington State's Integrated Basic Education and Skills Training (I-BEST) program. I-BEST offers "contextualized instruction," which integrates basic English and math skills into college-level career or technical training in fields such as nursing, early childhood education, automobile repair, and data entry. For example, nursing students in the I-BEST program attend English classes that emphasize medical terminology and writing used in health care settings. If students have trouble making sense of the words because of limited English proficiency, they receive additional help in learning basic language skills.

A recent evaluation comparing academic outcomes for 900 I-BEST participants with those of more than 31,000 students in regular remedial courses in Washington State community colleges found that I-BEST students had higher persistence rates, earned more credits toward a college credential, earned more occupational certificates, and showed greater increases on remedial education tests. The evaluation did not use a random-assignment design and therefore cannot eliminate the possibility that students who were selected into I-BEST were more motivated or had other characteristics that may have distinguished them from students in regular remedial courses, although the authors controlled for observed differences in student backgrounds and enrollment patterns. The results suggest that the model holds promise and should be subject to more rigorous experimental evaluation in the future.[44]

Another approach to reforming remedial education is to accelerate the pace at which students move through it. For example, students who test just below college level may be assigned to a short-term review class rather than a full-semester course. Alternatively, colleges may set up basic skills "immersion" courses that are shorter in duration but require more hours of attendance each week, to help students master the material more quickly. Such courses can be offered during the regular semester or during breaks between semesters.[45] Incoming students may also be targeted for intensive remediation before they start classes to help them do better on basic skills assessment tests and possibly avoid remediation altogether. A summer "bridge" program in Texas, for example, offers remedial English and math instruction along with general study skills to students who just finished high school and are about to enroll in a community college or public university. To date, researchers have not produced evidence on whether acceleration or immersion strategies improve student outcomes, though the Texas summer bridge program began undergoing a random-assignment evaluation in summer 2009.[46]

Many other promising remedial education reforms have been suggested or tried. The Carnegie Foundation for the Advancement of Teaching, for example, encourages adoption of pedagogical practices that emphasize "high structure" and "high challenge"—for example, giving students step-by-step guidelines for undertaking complicated academic tasks, while also engaging them in authentic debate and intellectual exchange. The foundation also encourages colleges and universities to adopt a strategy known as faculty inquiry, in which teachers formulate and explore questions about their students' learning and use the answers to improve their teaching.[47] Supplemental Instruction, another popular strategy, trains students who have passed remedial courses to lead study sessions for students currently enrolled in the courses; the leaders' job is to review difficult concepts and serve as role models outside the classroom.[48] Finally, many colleges and universities have developed remedial education laboratories or "success centers" where students can receive individualized tutoring, participate in study groups, and access computers loaded with instructional aids and review materials.

College completion rates in the United States are not likely to improve until substantially greater numbers of students break through the remedial barrier. For that reason—and because the nation already invests between $1 billion and $2 billion in remedial education programs—researchers must do much

more to identify effective practices.[49] The strategies I have outlined provide some promising venues for future evaluation; other ideas should be developed and tested as well. There is arguably no greater priority for research in higher education.

Enhancing Student Advising and Support Services

Some students may arrive at college knowing exactly what they need to do to accomplish their goals. Most, however, need guidance to figure out which courses to take and in what sequence, how to add or drop courses and apply for financial aid, and what resources are available to help them adjust to campus life. Even after they have been in college for awhile, many students need help knowing how to fulfill their major requirements, file for graduation or transfer, and resolve personal or academic problems that may interfere with their progress. One of the ironies in higher education is that institutions, such as Ivy League schools and highly selective liberal arts colleges, that enroll the best prepared and most traditional students tend to offer the most such guidance, while institutions that serve the least prepared and most nontraditional students tend to offer much less. In community colleges, counselor-to-student ratios of 1 to 1,000 are not uncommon.[50] A national survey of entering community college students found that 32 percent did not attend a freshmen orientation program and half did not meet with or recall seeing an academic adviser during their first four weeks of college.[51]

The primary reason why student services are so meager in some institutions is lack of funding. One study finds a general pattern in the United States of increased stratification in higher education and reductions in funding per student outside of top-tier institutions, affecting course availability, student-faculty ratios, and student services. The authors make a strong case that these reductions explain the increase in time-to-degree at less selective colleges and universities.[52] In California, for example, community colleges receive less than half the funding per full-time enrolled student that the state universities receive, and only about one-fifth as much as the University of California.[53] In addition, California community colleges are limited by state law in the percentage of their budget that can be devoted to non-instructional activities, which further constrains their ability to provide adequate support services.

Since the late 1960s, the federal government has funded TRIO programs (so-called because initially TRIO consisted of three programs) to serve and assist low-income, first-generation college students, and students with disabilities, to progress from middle school to post-baccalaureate programs. The largest and best-known TRIO program, Upward Bound, is geared toward helping disadvantaged high school students prepare for college. A smaller and lesser-known program, Student Support Services, provides funds for basic skills instruction, tutoring, academic advising, financial aid and career counseling, transfer and graduate school counseling, and mentoring to disadvantaged students on college and university campuses. In 2003–04, the Student Support Services program awarded more than 936 grants to colleges and universities and reached more than 200,000 students nationwide, about half of whom were in community colleges.

The Student Support Services program has not been subject to rigorous impact evaluation, though a Department of Education report indicates that it succeeded in reaching a needy target group. The report also states that more than two-thirds of full-time freshmen who received Student Support Services in community colleges persisted to their second year of college, and that 9 percent of these students earned an associate's degree at the end of two years.[54] Without a control group, however, it is impossible to know whether that record represents an improvement over what students would have accomplished on their own, had the extra services not been available.

The current financial aid system has significant flaws, but more money is available than students or the general public often realizes. The federal government now spends $18.6 billion a year on grant aid and an additional $70 billion on student loan programs.

As part of the Opening Doors demonstration discussed above, MDRC and the MacArthur Network on Transitions to Adulthood conducted random-assignment studies of two enhanced student services programs operating at community colleges. One of these programs, at Chaffey College in California, targeted a traditional group of community college students who were on probation because of poor grades or an excessive number of course withdrawals.[55] The program featured a College Success course, taught by a counselor, in which students addressed such topics as personal motivation, time management, college expectations, and note-taking and test-taking skills. The program also included additional counseling and required students to make use of the college's "Success Centers," where students could get help from instructors or tutors in reading, writing, or math.

Chaffey recruited nearly 900 students to participate in the evaluation during the first year, and close to 450 students during the second year. The students were generally young, and three out of five were female. Hispanics made up a slight majority; whites accounted for about a fourth of the sample. As in the other Opening Doors sites, students at Chaffey were randomly assigned to program and control groups. Control group members did not have access to the College Success class, but could take advantage of the Success Centers and any other campus resources on their own if they chose.

In its first year Chaffey's program was not implemented as planned. Word went out that the program was voluntary, and only about half the students who were assigned to the program group enrolled in the College Success class. Moreover, some of the counselors reported that they did not fully understand their roles or require students to visit the Success Centers. The evaluation of the first-year program showed no measurable effects. However, to the college's credit, administrators and staff came back together and addressed the major implementation problems before the second-year program began. Perhaps most important, after they informed students in the program group that enrollment in the College Success class was mandatory, participation rates rose to nearly 75 percent. The counselors were also better prepared and enforced the Success Center visits more consistently. The effects of the second-year program after two semesters

were large and significant. Students in the program group earned an average of 8.3 college credits, compared with an average of 5.6 credits for students in the control group. And almost twice as many students in the program group as in the control group got off probation and returned to good academic standing. The turnaround between the first- and second-year results underscores the importance not only of a good program model, but of strong implementation and high participation. Longer follow-up will be needed to determine whether the effects from the second-year program translate into increased persistence and degree completion at Chaffey.

The other enhanced student services program evaluated as part of the Opening Doors demonstration was operated by Lorain County Community College and Owens Community College, both in Ohio.[56] The Ohio program, it should be noted, targeted a different group of students than Chaffey: beginning freshmen and continuing students who had completed fewer than thirteen credits. Some of the students showed signs of academic trouble, but they were not on academic probation. The Ohio sample was also largely nontraditional, consisting mostly of working women in their mid-twenties. A little more than 2,100 students were randomly assigned to program and control groups.

For the program group, the Ohio colleges offered counseling and advising services that were much more regular, intensive, and personalized than they (or other community colleges) typically provide. The counselor-to-student ratio was less than 1 to 160, compared with 1 to 1,000 for students randomly assigned to the control group. In addition, the program paid students a modest stipend of $150 if they completed at least two counselor visits a semester. The enhanced counseling services lasted two semesters. Close to 90 percent of students in the program group saw a counselor at least once during this time, and results from a survey indicated that almost two-thirds of the program group reported having at least three academic advising sessions during their first year in the study, compared with only 40 percent of the control group. Even so, the intervention resulted in only a temporary improvement in persistence. Students in the program group were more likely to register for college after one semester in the program, but the effect went away as soon as the more intensive services ended. There was no effect on other key indicators of academic performance, such as credits earned.

The collective findings from the Chaffey and Ohio Opening Doors programs suggest that enhanced student services have the potential to improve student outcomes, but that researchers must do more to determine the precise ingredients of an effective program. The choice of target group seems to be one such ingredient, judging by the fact that the relatively young, traditional group of students at Chaffey seemed to benefit more from an intervention than a relatively older, nontraditional group of students in Ohio. Of course, the Chaffey students were also all on academic probation, which could mean they had more to gain from an intervention. The quality and intensity of the program also seemed to matter. The Chaffey model, with its combination of the College Success course, Success Center visits, and individualized counseling, was more intensive overall than the Ohio model, but it worked only when it was implemented well and when participation rates crossed a certain threshold. The Ohio program produced a positive impact on persistence while students were still receiving the enhanced counseling and advising, which suggests it may have had a more enduring effect if it had lasted longer than two semesters. As noted, more selective colleges and universities tend to provide intensive counseling and advising on an ongoing basis.

Making Financial Aid More Effective

In their article in this volume, Sheldon Danziger and David Ratner examine how uncertainty over how to pay for college and impediments to borrowing keep many young adults from attending college. As I discuss below, the current financial aid system has significant flaws, but more money is available than students or the general public often realizes. The federal government now spends $18.6 billion a year on grant aid and an additional $70 billion on student loan programs.[57] It also spends about $2 billion on the federal work-study program, which pays for up to 75 percent of the wages low-income students can earn at jobs on campus or with other participating employers.[58] Many states operate financial aid programs as well, supplementing the funds provided by the federal government.

Students are awarded some combination of these funds after completing a Free Application for Federal Student Aid (FAFSA). College financial aid offices make individual awards to students using a formula that takes into account the cost of attendance at the institution and the student's expected family contribution based on income and assets. Grant aid does not need to be paid back and is arguably the most important tool to promote college-going among low-income students, particularly because research shows that many low-income students are reluctant to take out loans, even when they have high levels of need.[59] Pell Grants provide the most funding and serve the most students, followed by the Supplemental Education Opportunity Grant. In 2006, Congress also established Academic Competitiveness Grants and SMART Grants to provide financial support to students from lower-income families who meet criteria related to academic achievement and course of study.[60]

Unlike federal grants, student loans are available to families in all income brackets, although only lower-income students may qualify for subsidized loans (meaning that the federal government pays the interest while students are enrolled in school). The federal government also funds an array of tax credits that enable students and their families to reduce their federal income tax obligation in relation to the tuition costs they pay each year. These tax credits primarily support middle- and upper-income families.[61]

Despite the large federal investment in financial aid, researchers know little about how effective the various federal programs are in promoting higher education attendance or completion. To determine how student aid affects college attendance, Susan Dynarski examined the Social Security Student Benefit program, which between 1965 and 1982 paid the college costs for eighteen- to twenty-two-year-old children whose parents had qualified for Social Security benefits but were deceased. The sudden elimination of the program made it possible to compare how students in similar circumstances responded before and after the change. Dynarski found that an offer of $1,000 in grant aid increased the probability of attending college by about 3.6 percentage points and also increased college completion. These estimates are consistent with other analyses of the effects of variation in tuition costs at public institutions within states and of a merit aid program in Georgia, known as the Helping Outstanding

Pupils Educationally (HOPE) scholarship (discussed further below).[62]

Although the effects of the federal government's financial aid programs may be uncertain, this much is clear: the present system has few supporters. Chief among the criticisms is that government aid has not kept up with the rising costs of college attendance; the various grant, loan, and tax credit programs are duplicative, inefficient, and not always successful in directing federal aid to the neediest students and families; and the process of applying for federal aid is needlessly complex.[63] The Obama administration has made the overhaul of financial aid a priority and has increased the value of the Pell Grant (from $4,731 to $5,350) and raised the tuition tax credit (from $1,800 to $2,500) as part of the American Recovery and Reinvestment Act.[64] The administration plans to make these changes permanent in its 2010 budget and to tie future increases in Pell Grants to the Consumer Price Index. It has also proposed to consolidate the tax credits into one program and make them refundable for low-income families and to restructure student loan programs so that they are provided directly through the federal government rather than through private lenders.[65] Finally, the administration recently announced plans to simplify the financial aid application process.[66]

A forthcoming evaluation of a program in Ohio and North Carolina that helped low-income families complete the federal financial aid application process indicates that FAFSA simplification may have a substantial payoff. The program targeted families with annual incomes below $45,000 and at least one household member between the ages of fifteen and thirty who did not have a college degree. The goal was not only to make families aware of how much aid they might qualify for if a family member attended a college or university but also to provide such information early enough to influence decisions about whether to apply to college and enroll. Through random assignment, one group of families received assistance from trained H&R Block employees to fill out the FAFSA, using information captured off their federal income tax forms; the other group received no such assistance, but could complete the FAFSA on their own. Early results indicate that the intervention produced substantial positive effects on financial aid receipt and college enrollment.[67]

Critics of the current financial aid system also charge that it does not do enough to encourage high academic achievement, persistence, and completion.[68] One strategy, popular among many states, is to create merit-based scholarship programs that reward students who have demonstrated their ability to earn good grades in high school and college. One of the best-known examples is the previously mentioned HOPE scholarship in Georgia, which now provides annual grants of up to $3,500 to students who graduated from a public high school with a 3.0, or "B," grade point average and who maintain that average in college.[69]

A comprehensive analysis of merit-based scholarship programs in seven states, including Georgia, found that the HOPE scholarship and other programs like it increased the probability of college attendance among college-age youth by 5 to 7 percentage points and that they encouraged students to attend four-year institutions rather than two-year schools. Some of the state programs also appeared to close racial and ethnic gaps in schooling.[70] Although this finding came as good news, there was also evidence that the

Georgia program increased course withdrawals, presumably because students worried about maintaining the required grade point average. It may also have contributed to overall grade inflation and price increases in the state's public university.[71] Finally, some observers have expressed concern that merit-based scholarships may crowd out need-based financial aid and go to students from more privileged backgrounds.[72]

A slight twist on the merit-based scholarship idea is the performance-based scholarship. MDRC and the MacArthur Network tested one version in Louisiana as part of the Opening Doors demonstration; another model was tested by researchers in Canada. Performance-based scholarships differ from merit-based scholarships in that they are predicated not on students' past performance, but rather on how students do *after* the scholarship is awarded. Students "earn" the scholarship as they get passing grades or meet other progress benchmarks. Performance-based scholarships may also include a student services component. The programs in Louisiana and Canada, for example, both hired counselors to monitor students' academic progress and help them satisfy scholarship conditions.

The Louisiana program, operated at two community colleges in the New Orleans area, offered $1,000 for each of two semesters ($2,000 total) if students stayed in college at least half-time and maintained a "C" average. The scholarships were paid in increments at the beginning, middle, and end of the semester, and program counselors monitored students' academic performance. Because state welfare funds were used to pay for the scholarship, eligibility was limited to students who were parents and whose household income was below 200 percent of the federal poverty level. A little more than 1,000 students enrolled in the study and were randomly assigned to program and control groups. Most were African American women in their twenties, and most had one or two children. The evaluation found that the scholarship program gave these students a substantial boost. They were more likely to register for college and attend full-time, even though only half-time enrollment was required to receive a scholarship. They were also more likely to persist in college. In the second semester of the program, 65 percent of the program group registered for courses, compared with 50 percent of the control group. Significant differences remained over four semesters. And, finally, students in the program group earned better grades and completed more course credits than those in the control group, earning on average 3.5 more credits (a little more than one standard college course) over four semesters. The study also found that students in the program had more social support and felt more confident that they would achieve their personal and academic goals.[73]

The Canadian study took place at a campus of a large, public, four-year university. Like the Louisiana program, the Canadian program —called the Student Achievement and Retention Project (STAR)—lasted two semesters. It differed in one major way: students received higher payments when they earned better grades. Students received a $1,000 payment if they earned grades between a "C+" and a "B" and up to $5,000 if they earned grades of "A-" or better. The Canadian program also targeted a more traditional group of students than the Louisiana program.

The Project STAR researchers randomly assigned more than 1,600 students, all first-year undergraduates, to three treatment

groups: one that received only the scholarship, one that received only enhanced counseling, and one that received the scholarship and the enhanced counseling combined. The combination of scholarships and counseling yielded the best results, including significant effects on grades and persistence. The scholarship alone also produced positive effects, but not as large; and the counseling alone produced no effects. Finally, the analysis showed that the positive effects were concentrated among women.[74]

If there is one overarching lesson from this review, it is that changes in higher education policies and practices can lead to improvements in college attendance, persistence, and completion.

Both the Louisiana and the Canadian studies point to the promise of performance-based scholarships in improving academic outcomes. The studies also suggest that researchers have more to learn about how best to design and implement such programs: which groups of students to target, what scholarship amount is optimal, and what role counselors should play, among other issues. A random-assignment study is now under way in New York, Ohio, New Mexico, and California to test variations of performance-based scholarships, including different models of service delivery and different target groups.[75] Another large random-assignment study in Wisconsin is testing the value added of a scholarship alone, without performance criteria, for low-income parents attending state colleges and universities.[76]

Conclusion

If there is one overarching lesson from this review, it is that changes in higher education policies and practices *can* lead to improvements in college attendance, persistence, and completion. That insight is evident from dramatic changes in the number and composition of students attending colleges and universities since the mid-1960s, when federal policy makers and college and university administrators acted aggressively to open higher education to excluded groups. It is also evident from the rigorous evaluations performed on various interventions designed to help college students succeed.

This is not to say that the problems of college access and completion are fully solved—far from it. Some groups, such as African American and Hispanic males, are sorely underrepresented on college campuses. Overall rates of degree attainment have not improved in decades. Time-to-degree is also increasing, particularly at two-year institutions. Remedial education programs often do a better job of weeding students out than helping them advance to college-level courses and degrees. Such trends run counter to the country's need for a sizable college-educated workforce in an era of global competition. Similarly, young people need a college degree to better their chance of landing a well-paying, stable job and supporting a family.

To boost college completion rates in the United States, policy makers and educators must act on two fronts. First they must encourage development and implementation of strategies that lead to greater student

success. I have identified several such strategies—learning communities and performance-based scholarships, for example—but much more needs to be done to bring proven strategies to scale and to incubate new ideas that might lead to better results. The Obama administration has put forth proposals to support such efforts, and several major philanthropies have indicated their intentions to invest in higher education reforms as well.[77] Given the severe financial pressures on most states and institutions, the challenge will be to make sure that new funds are used to make meaningful changes in existing programs and services, not to fill budget gaps or support business as usual.

Second, policy makers and practitioners must place much greater emphasis on evaluating reforms. Aside from the studies I have described, there is very little research that demonstrates the efficacy of most higher education interventions. Randomized control trials—the best means of establishing a causal connection between an intervention and student outcomes—are rare. Without clear evidence on what to do differently, colleges and universities are likely to continue the same kinds of programs and services that they have been running for years, and with similar results. Researchers must actively disseminate evaluation findings and technical assistance to help administrators, faculty, and staff adapt the most effective program strategies to their campuses.

A recurrent theme in this volume is the obstacles that face many young people making the transition to adulthood. William Bowen and Derek Bok make this point in their book on minority students in higher education, called *The Shape of the River*: "We often hear of the importance of keeping young people moving through the 'pipeline' from elementary school to high school to college, on through graduate and professional schools, and into jobs, family responsibilities, and civic life. But this image is misleading, with its connotation of a smooth, well-defined, and well-understood passage. It is more helpful to think of the nurturing of talent as a process akin to moving down a winding river, with rock-strewn rapids and slow channels, muddy at times and clear at others."[78]

The authors' words point to the need for a paradigm shift throughout higher education. To increase college persistence and completion, policy makers and educators must take a harder look at the needs and circumstances of the students they are serving and must ask what might be done to help them navigate more effectively the rocks and shoals of higher education. The answer is likely to require greater public investment in the institutions that provide the most access to nontraditional and underprepared students: community colleges and other less selective institutions.

Endnotes

1. U.S. Census Bureau, "The Big Payoff: Educational Attainment and Synthetic Estimates of Work-Life Earnings" (Washington: U.S. Census Bureau, July 2002).

2. Sandy Baum and Jennifer Ma, "Education Pays: The Benefits of Higher Education for Individuals and Society" (Washington: College Board, 2007), pp. 21–23.

3. Thomas S. Dee, "Are There Returns to Civic Engagement?" *Journal of Public Economics* 88 (2004): 1697–1720.

4. Donald R. Deere and Jelena Vesovic, "Educational Wage Premiums and the U.S. Income Distribution," in *Handbook of the Economics of Education*, vol. 1, edited by Eric Alan Hanushek and Finis Welch (Amsterdam: North-Holland, 2006), pp. 255–306.

5. U.S. Census Bureau, "The Big Payoff" (see note 1).

6. Wilson Smith and Thomas Bender, "Introduction," *American Higher Education Transformed: 1940–2005* (Baltimore: Johns Hopkins University Press), pp. 1–11.

7. Judith Eaton, "The Evolution of Access Policy: 1965–1990," in *Public Policy in Higher Education*, edited by. L. F. Goodchild and others (Needham Heights, Mass.: Pearson Custom Publishing, 1997), pp. 237–46.

8. Thomas Diener, *Growth of an American Invention: A Documentary History of the Junior and Community College Movement* (New York: Greenwood Press, 1986); Lawrence E. Gladieux and Thomas R. Wolanin, *Congress and the Colleges* (Lexington, Mass.: Lexington Books, 1976), pp. 1–14.

9. Gladieux and Wolanin, *Congress and the Colleges* (see note 8), pp. 12–13.

10. Taylor Branch, *Parting the Waters: America in the King Years, 1954–63* (New York: Simon and Schuster, 1988); Taylor Branch, *Pillar of Fire: America in the King Years, 1963–65* (New York: Simon and Schuster, 1998); Taylor Branch, *At Canaan's Edge: America in the King Years 1965–68* (New York: Simon and Schuster, 2006).

11. Todd Gitlin, *The Sixties: Years of Hope, Days of Rage* (New York: Bantam, 1993).

12. Eaton, "The Evolution of Access Policy: 1965–1990" (see note 7), pp. 237–46.

13. T. D. Snyder, S. A. Dillow, and C. M. Hoffman, *Digest of Education Statistics 2007* (NCES 2008-022) (Washington: National Center for Education Statistics, Institute of Education Sciences, U.S. Department of Education, 2008), table 180.

14. Population Division, U.S. Census Bureau, "Annual Estimates of the Population by Sex and Selected Age Groups for the United States: April 1, 2000, to July 1, 2007 (NC-EST2007-02)" (Washington: U.S. Census Bureau, May 1, 2008); Population Division, U.S. Census Bureau, "Resident Population plus Armed Forces Overseas—Estimates by Age, Sex, and Race: July 1, 1965" (Washington: U.S. Census Bureau, Internet Release Date: October 1, 2004.)

15. Snyder, Dillow, and Hoffman, *Digest of Education Statistics 2007* (see note 13), tables 181, 187, 217.

16. Susan Choy, *Findings from the Condition of Education 2002: Nontraditional Undergraduates* (NCES 2002-012) (Washington: National Center for Education Statistics, Institute of Education Sciences, U.S. Department of Education, 2002).

17. Snyder, Dillow, and Hoffman, *Digest of Education Statistics 2007* (see note 13), tables 180, 187.

18. Ibid., table 187.

19. Ibid., table 225.

20. Stephen Provasnik and Michael Planty, *Community Colleges: Special Supplement to The Condition of Education 2008* (NCES 2008-033) (Washington: National Center for Education Statistics, Institute of Education Sciences, U.S. Department of Education, 2008).

21. Susan Choy, *Findings from the Condition of Education 2002: Nontraditional Undergraduates* (see note 16).

22. Laura Horn and Rachel Berger, *College Persistence on the Rise? Changes in 5-year Degree Completion and Postsecondary Persistence Rates between 1995 and 2000* (NCES 2005-156) (Washington: National Center for Education Statistics, Institute of Education Sciences, U.S. Department of Education, 2004).

23. Ibid.

24. Ibid.

25. John Bound, Michael F. Lovenheim, and Sarah Turner, *Understanding the Decrease in College Completion Rates and Increased Time to the Baccalaureate Degree* (Ann Arbor, Mich.: Population Studies Center, University of Michigan Institute for Social Research, November 2007).

26. Horn and Berger, *College Persistence on the Rise?* (see note 22).

27. Lutz Berkner, Shirley He, and Emily Forrest Cataldi, *Descriptive Summary of 1995–96 Beginning Postsecondary Students: Six Years Later* (NCES 2003-151) (Washington: National Center for Education Statistics, Institute of Education Sciences, U.S. Department of Education, 2002), pp. 61 and 65.

28. Snyder, Dillow, and Hoffman, *Digest of Education Statistics 2007* (see note 13), table 178.

29. Clifford Adelman, *The Toolbox Revisited: Paths to Degree Completion from High School through College* (Washington: U.S. Department of Education, February 2006).

30. Choy, *Findings from the Condition of Education 2002: Nontraditional Undergraduates* (see note 16).

31. American Council on Education, *Minorities in Higher Education 2008: Twenty-Third Status Report* (Washington: American Council on Education, 2008).

32. Ryan H. Hahn and Derek Price, *Promise Lost: College-Qualified Students Who Don't Enroll in College* (Washington: Institute for Higher Education Policy, November 2008).

33. Organisation for Economic Co-operation and Development, *Education at a Glance: OECD Indicators 2007* (Paris: OECD Publishing, 2007).

34. Vincent Tinto, *Leaving College: Rethinking the Causes and Cures of Student Attrition* (University of Chicago Press, 1993).

35. See, for example, John M. Braxton, ed., *Reworking the Student Departure Puzzle* (Vanderbilt University Press, 2002).

36. See, for example, Monica Martinez and Shayna Klopott, *The Link between High School Reform and College Access and Success for Low-Income and Minority Youth* (Washington and Boston: American Youth Policy Forum and Pathways to College Network, 2005); and Michael Bangser, *Preparing High School Students for Successful Transitions to Postsecondary Education and Employment* (www.betterhigh-schools.org, August 2008).

37. Basmat Parsad and Laurie Lewis, *Remedial Education at Degree-Granting Postsecondary Institutions in Fall 2000* (NCES 2004-010) (Washington: National Center for Education Statistics, Institute of Education Sciences, U.S. Department of Education, November 2003).

38. Paul Attewell and others, "New Evidence on College Remediation," *Journal of Higher Education* 77 (2006): 886–924.

39. W. Norton Grubb, "Second Chances in Changing Times: The Roles of Community Colleges in Advancing Low-Skilled Workers," in *Low-Wage Workers in the New Economy: Strategies for Opportunity and Advancement,* edited by Richard Kazis and Marc S. Miller (Washington: Urban Institute Press, 2001), pp. 277–302; and Vincent Tinto, "Learning Communities and the Reconstruction of Remedial Education in Higher Education," paper prepared for the Conference on Replacing Remediation in Higher Education at Stanford University, January 26–27, 1998.

40. Henry M. Levin and Juan Carlos Calcagno, "Remediation in the Community College: An Evaluator's Perspective," *Community College Review* 35 (2008): 181–207; Thomas R. Bailey and Mariana Alfonso, *Paths to Persistence: An Analysis of Research on Program Effectiveness at Community Colleges* (Indianapolis, Ind.: Lumina Foundation for Education, January 2005).

41. Susan Scrivener and others, *A Good Start: Two-Year Effects of a Freshmen Learning Community Program at Kingsborough Community College* (New York: MDRC, 2008).

42. Ibid.

43. Mary G. Visher and others, *The Learning Communities Demonstration: Rationale, Sites, and Research Design* (New York: MDRC, 2008).

44. Davis Jenkins, Matthew Zeidenberg, and Gregor Kienzl, *Educational Outcomes of I-BEST, Washington State Community and Technical College System's Integrated Basic Education and Skills Training Program: Findings from a Multivariate Analysis,* Community College Research Center, Working Paper 16 (New York: Columbia University, Teachers College, Community College Research Center, May 2009).

45. The Carnegie Foundation for the Advancement of Teaching, *Basic Skills for Complex Lives: Designs for Learning in the Community College* (Stanford, Calif.: The Carnegie Foundation for the Advancement of Teaching, 2008).

46. See National Center for Postsecondary Research website: www.postsecondaryresearch.org/index.html?Id =Research&Info=Developmental+Summer+Bridges.

47. The Carnegie Foundation for the Advancement of Teaching, *Basic Skills for Complex Lives* (see note 45).

48. See International Center for Supplementary Instruction website: www.umkc.edu/cad/SI/overview.html.

49. The Institute for Higher Education Policy, *College Remediation: What It Is, What It Costs, What's at Stake* (Washington: The Institute for Higher Education Policy, December 1998).

50. Norton W. Grubb, "Getting into the World: Guidance and Counseling in Community Colleges," Community College Research Center, Working Paper 1 (New York: Columbia University, Teachers College, Community College Research Center, 2001).

51. Community College Survey of Student Engagement, *Committing to Student Engagement: Reflections on CCSSE's First Five Years* (Austin, Tex.: Community College Leadership Program, University of Texas–Austin, 2007).

52. Bound and others, *Understanding the Decrease in College Completion Rates and the Increased Time to the Baccalaureate Degree* (see note 25).

53. Colleen Moore and Nancy Shulock, *Beyond the Open Door: Increasing Student Success in the California Community Colleges* (Sacramento, Calif.: Institute for Higher Education Leadership and Policy, California State University, Sacramento, 2007).

54. U.S. Department of Education, Office of Postsecondary Education, Federal TRIO Programs, *An Interim Report on the Student Support Services Program: 2002–03 and 2003–04, with Select Data from 1998–2002* (Washington: U.S. Department of Education, 2007).

55. Susan Scrivener, Colleen Sommo, and Herbert Collado, *Getting Back on Track: Effects of a Program for Probationary Students at Chaffey College* (New York: MDRC, 2009).

56. Susan Scrivener and Michael Weiss, *Enhanced Student Services: The Effects of Two Programs in Ohio* (New York: MDRC, 2009).

57. New America Foundation, Federal Education Budget Project, "Education Policy Program: Federal Higher Education Programs—Overview" (www.newamerica.net/programs/education_policy/federal_education_budget_project/higher_ed [July 1, 2009]).

58. U.S. Government Accountability Office, *Student Aid and Postsecondary Tax Preferences: Limited Research Exists on Effectiveness of Tools to Assist Students and Families through Title IV Student Aid and Tax Preferences* (Washington: U.S. Government Accountability Office, July 2005).

59. Alisa F. Cunningham and Deborah A. Santiago, *Student Aversion to Borrowing: Who Borrows and Who Doesn't* (Washington: Institute for Higher Education Policy and Excellence in Education, 2008).

60. U.S. Government Accountability Office, *Student Aid and Postsecondary Tax Preferences* (see note 58).

61. Ibid.

62. Susan M. Dynarski, "Does Aid Matter? Measuring the Effect of Student Aid on College Attendance and Completion," *American Economic Review* 93, no. 1 (March 2003): 279–88.

63. See, for example, U.S. Department of Education, *A Test of Leadership: Charting the Future of U.S. Higher Education: A Report of the Commission Appointed by Secretary of Education Margaret Spellings* (Washington: U.S. Department of Education, 2006); and College Board, *Fulfilling the Commitment: Recommendations for Reforming Federal Student Aid* (www.collegeboard.com, September 2008).

64. U.S. Department of Education, "The American Recovery and Reinvestment Act of 2009: Education, Jobs, and Reform," program description from website (www.ed.gov/policy/gen/leg/recovery/factsheet/overview.html [February 18, 2009]).

65. U.S. Department of Education, "Education Secretary Duncan Highlights Budget Proposals to Increase College Access and Affordability," press release from website (www.ed.gov/news/pressreleases/2009/02 /02262009.html [February 26, 2009]).

66. U.S. Department of Education, "Obama Administration Announces Streamlined College Aid Application," press release from website (www.ed.gov/news/pressreleases/2009/06/06242009.html [June 24, 2009]).

67. Eric P. Bettinger and others, "The Role of Information and Simplification in College Decisions: Results from the H&R Block FAFSA Experiment" (Cambridge, Mass.: National Bureau of Economic Research, July 2009 draft).

68. U.S. Department of Education, *A Test of Leadership* (see note 63); and College Board, *Fulfilling the Commitment* (see note 63).

69. See Georgia college information website: www.gacollege411.org/FinAid/ScholarshipsAndGrants/ HOPEScholarship/overview.asp (July 1, 2009).

70. Susan Dynarski, "The New Merit Aid," in *College Choices: The Economics of Where to Go, When to Go, and How to Pay for It,* edited by Caroline M. Hoxby (University of Chicago Press, 2004), pp. 63–100.

71. Ibid.; Christopher Cornwell, David B. Mustard, and Deepa J. Sridhar, "The Enrollment Effects of Merit-Based Financial Aid: Evidence from Georgia's HOPE Scholarship," *Journal of Labor Economics* 24, no. 4 (2006): 761–86.

72. Lashawn Richburg-Hayes and others, *Rewarding Persistence: Effects of a Performance-Based Scholarship Program for Low-Income Parents* (New York: MDRC, 2009), pp. 9–10.

73. Ibid.

74. Joshua Angrist, Daniel Lang, and Philip Oreopoulos, "Incentives and Services for College Achievement: Evidence from a Randomized Trial," *American Economic Journal: Applied Economics* 1, no. 1 (January 2009): 136–63.

75. See project website for the Performance-Based Scholarship Demonstration: www.mdrc.org/project_31 _91.html.

76. See project website for the Wisconsin Scholars Longitudinal Study: www.wiscape.wisc.edu/research/ Details.aspx?id=17.

77. See note 65. Philanthropic foundations announcing major investments in postsecondary education include the Bill and Melinda Gates Foundation, based in Seattle, Washington; and Lumina Foundation for Education, based in Indianapolis, Indiana.

78. Derek Bok and William Bowen, *The Shape of the River: Long-Term Consequences of Considering Race in College and University Admissions* (Princeton University Press, 1998), p. xxi.

Labor Market Outcomes and the Transition to Adulthood

Sheldon Danziger and David Ratner

Summary

According to Sheldon Danziger and David Ratner, changes in the labor market over the past thirty-five years, such as labor-saving technological changes, increased globalization, declining unionization, and the failure of the minimum wage to keep up with inflation, have made it more difficult for young adults to attain the economic stability and self-sufficiency that are important markers of the transition to adulthood. Young men with no more than a high school degree have difficulty earning enough to support a family. Even though young women have achieved gains in earnings, employment, and schooling relative to men in recent decades, those without a college degree also struggle to achieve economic stability and self-sufficiency.

The authors begin by describing trends in labor market outcomes for young adults—median annual earnings, the extent of low-wage work, employment rates, job instability, and the returns to education. Then they examine how these outcomes may contribute to delays in other markers of the transition to adulthood—completing an education, establishing independent living arrangements, and marrying and having children. They conclude that adverse changes in labor market outcomes are related to those delays but have not been shown to be the primary cause.

Danziger and Ratner next consider several public policy reforms that might improve the economic outlook for young adults. They recommend policies that would increase the returns to work, especially for less-educated workers. They propose raising the federal minimum wage and adjusting it annually to maintain its value relative to the median wage. Expanding the Earned Income Tax Credit for childless low-wage workers, the authors say, could also raise the take-home pay of many young adult workers, with minimal adverse employment effects. New policies should also provide work opportunities for young adults who cannot find steady employment either because of poor economic conditions or because of physical and mental disabilities or criminal records that make it hard for them to work steadily even when the economy is strong. Finally, the authors recommend increasing federal Pell grants for college and improving access to credit for would-be college students to raise the educational attainment of young adults from low-income families.

www.futureofchildren.org

Sheldon Danziger is the Henry J. Meyer Distinguished University Professor of Public Policy and Director of the National Poverty Center at the Gerald R. Ford School of Public Policy, University of Michigan. David Ratner is a doctoral student in the Department of Economics and the Gerald R. Ford School of Public Policy, University of Michigan.

One key marker of the transition to adulthood is achieving success in the labor market—in particular, attaining economic stability and self-sufficiency.[1] Over the past thirty years, changes in the labor market have made it more difficult for young adults to achieve financial independence. The labor market prospects of young men have declined, and the gap between less- and more-educated young adults has widened. Young men, particularly those with no more than a high school degree, now find it more difficult to earn enough to support a family than they did during the mid-1970s. And although young women have made remarkable gains in earnings, employment, and educational attainment since the mid-1970s, those without a college degree now have, like their male counterparts, great difficulty achieving economic stability.

How have the labor market difficulties of today's less-educated young adults affected other milestones in the transition to adulthood? Certainly employment and earnings prospects can influence decisions about how much education to pursue, when to move out of the parental home, and when to marry and have children. Without a sufficient and steady income, a young adult might decide to delay marriage and might not be able to qualify for a home mortgage. The worsened economic prospects of young men with no more than a high school degree might lead young women to stay in school longer, to focus more on their own careers, and to delay family formation and childbearing. The empirical evidence assembled by researchers, however, does not support the view that young adults' delays in completing an education, in establishing independent living arrangements, and in marrying have been caused primarily by

the increased labor market difficulties of less-educated men.[2]

We begin by reviewing labor market changes since the end of World War II. Next we document how changes since the mid-1970s have affected the extent to which young adults have achieved economic stability and self-sufficiency. We then discuss how these changes may have contributed to delays in other markers of the transition to adulthood. We conclude that attaining economic self-sufficiency is necessary for a successful transition to adulthood even if it does not guarantee success on other markers of adulthood. Finally, we describe public policy reforms that might improve the labor market fortunes of young adults, especially those with no more than a high school degree, and facilitate the transition to economic stability and self-sufficiency.

Overview of Labor Market Changes

The quarter-century following World War II was a "golden age" for most workers and their families. Employment and earnings grew rapidly for workers in all educational groups, even for men with a high school degree or less.[3] Recessions were relatively short and mild. Well-paying manufacturing jobs allowed many men to support a family on a single income. The share of men holding jobs that provided pensions and subsidized health insurance increased. The era of steady economic growth, rising real wage rates, and improved living standards for most workers ended by the mid-1970s. Lisa Bell and several colleagues document that the United States and other industrial countries—Canada, the United Kingdom, and Germany among them—saw a worsening of labor market prospects for young adults from the mid-1970s to the end of the twentieth century.[4] In most of these countries, the share of young adults, particularly men, able to earn an income sufficient to support a family declined.

In that same period in the United States, inequality in earnings and family incomes grew, and some government safety net programs eroded. The share of jobless workers receiving unemployment insurance and the share of single mothers receiving cash welfare declined. A series of labor market changes—computerization and other forms of labor-saving technology that reduced employer demand for less-educated workers, declines in the inflation-adjusted minimum wage, declining shares of workers covered by union contracts, and increased globalization—created hardships for many workers, especially men with no more than a high school degree. Claudia Goldin and Lawrence Katz attribute almost two-thirds of the increased earnings inequality to technological innovation that favored skilled over unskilled workers.[5] Now, as a result, young men with no more than a high school degree have lower employment rates, lower real wages, and less access to private pensions and employer-subsidized health insurance than did similar young workers during the mid-1970s.

Most of the economic gains of the past several decades accrued to the wealthiest families and highest earners.[6] Figure 1 shows rising inequality in hourly wage rates from 1979 to 2007 among men and women aged twenty-five to thirty-four.[7] For both young men and women, wage growth at the 90th percentile of the distribution outpaced that at the median and the 20th percentile. Wages at the 90th percentile of female earners grew 35 percent, from $21.29 to $28.75 an hour, compared with 13.7 percent for the median female worker, from $12.31 to $14.00, and only 4 percent for the 20th percentile, from

$8.65 to $9.00. Among men, wages grew 10 percent for the highest earners, from $29.57 to $32.50 an hour, but fell 14.5 percent for the median worker, from $18.30 to $15.65, and fell 19 percent, from $12.38 to $10.00, at the 20th percentile.

As figure 1 shows, the labor market prospects of young women aged twenty-five to thirty-four improved between 1973 and 2007. More young women are now working, and their earnings have increased both relative to inflation and relative to those of young men. But women continue to earn less than men. In 2007, the median hourly wage of a young female worker was 89 percent that of a young male ($14.00 compared with $15.65).

The improvements in economic well-being in the quarter-century leading up to the mid-1970s affected the transition to adulthood in similar ways for most workers. By contrast, the employment and earnings changes of the past three decades have affected that transition in ways that vary sharply by gender and education. Young male high school graduates take longer now than they did in the mid-1970s to become self-sufficient and to earn enough to support a family by working steadily in a job with good wages and benefits. Young women, however, are more likely to attain self-sufficiency now than they were in the mid-1970s.

The severe recession that started in December 2007 and the simultaneous large declines in the value of homes and the net worth of families imply that the economic prospects of young adults in the next several years will be worse than the data presented here suggest. As workers with the least labor force experience, young adults are likely to be disproportionately hurt during recessions ("last hired, first fired"). And some young

Figure 1. Hourly Wages of Workers Aged Twenty-Five to Thirty-Four, by Gender and Percentile of the Earnings Distribution, 1979 and 2007

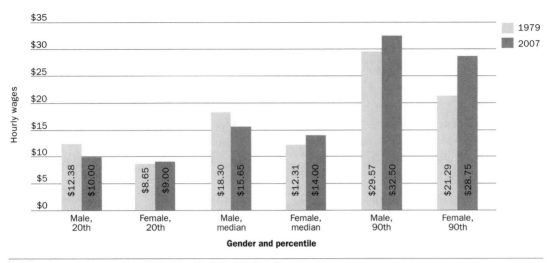

Note: Data are adjusted to 2009 dollars using CPI-U-RS. CPS ORG data.

adults may find that their parents' declining net worth will require them to rely more on their own earnings and less on parental support. Although the full negative labor market effects of this recession are not yet known, the employment rates and wage rates of young adults will likely be lower in 2010 than they were in 2007 (the last year of data available at this writing).

Labor Market Outcome Trends for Young Adults

As noted, a young adult's ability to work steadily and become economically self-sufficient is a primary, if not the most important, marker of a successful transition to adulthood. We next describe changes in young workers' median earnings, in the extent of low-wage work, in employment rates and job stability, and in educational attainment and the returns to schooling. We note how many of these changes differ by education, gender, and race and ethnicity.[8] Over the past three decades, the two primary labor market trends for young adults have

been the declining economic status of those with at most a high school degree relative to those with a college degree or more and the increasing economic status of women relative to men.[9]

We focus on "older" young adults, those aged twenty-five to thirty-four, most of whom have completed their education and are intent on establishing themselves in the labor market. Peter Edelman, Harry Holzer, and Paul Offner note that younger male high school graduates and dropouts have fared even worse economically than the age group on which we focus.[10] Updating their analysis of young men aged sixteen to twenty-four who are neither enrolled in school nor employed[11] (men they define as "idle," indicating extensive labor market problems), we find that the 2008 idleness rate for young men of that age group was 12 percent for whites, 21 percent for blacks, and 15 percent for Hispanics. Among women aged sixteen to twenty-four, that rate was 13 percent for whites, 21 percent for blacks, and 26 percent for Hispanics.

Figure 2. Median Annual Earnings of Employed High School Graduates, Aged Twenty-Five to Thirty-Four, by Race and Gender, 1973 and 2007

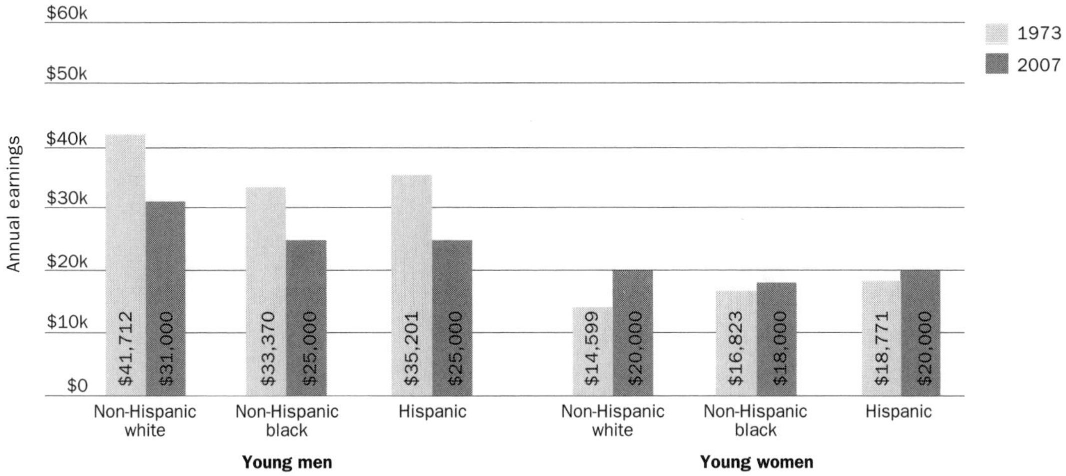

Note: Data are adjusted to 2007 dollars using the CPI-U-RS. Employed = worked at any time during year. March CPS.

As another indicator of labor market problems, Andrew Sum and several colleagues point out that teens have more trouble finding summer jobs now than they did three decades ago.[12] In July 1973, the summer employment rate for youth aged sixteen to nineteen was 52 percent for boys and 40 percent for girls.[13] By 2007, these rates had fallen to 34 percent and 36 percent. Thus, economic trends for younger workers are more negative than they are for twenty-five to thirty-four-year-olds, who are the focus here.

Median Annual Earnings by Education, Gender, and Race and Ethnicity

The median annual earnings (in constant 2007 dollars) of men aged twenty-five to thirty-four who worked at some time during the year fell by 21 percent between 1973 and 2007 (from $41,712 to $33,000); the median earnings of women workers of that age increased by 62 percent (from $16,685 to $27,000).[14] The large annual earnings increase for young women was attributable both to increased employment and to increased real wages (the latter shown in figure 1).

Figure 2 compares median annual earnings of employed high school graduates aged twenty-five to thirty-four, by race and ethnicity and by gender, in 1973 and 2007. For white non-Hispanics, black non-Hispanics, and Hispanics, the inflation-adjusted median earnings of male high school graduates fell by 26, 25, and 29 percent, respectively (left side of figure 2).[15] For women (right side of figure 2), the median for whites, blacks, and Hispanics rose by 37, 7, and 7 percent, respectively. Thus, for each race and ethnic group, the earnings of young women increased relative to those of young men. Figure 3 shows a similar pattern among college graduates. The earnings of young women increased relative to those of young men for each of the three race and ethnic groups. Median earnings increased for women, but were mostly unchanged for men.

A comparison of the left sides of figures 2 and 3 shows the widening educational differential

Figure 3. Median Annual Earnings of Employed College Graduates, Aged Twenty-Five to Thirty-Four, by Race and Gender, 1973 and 2007

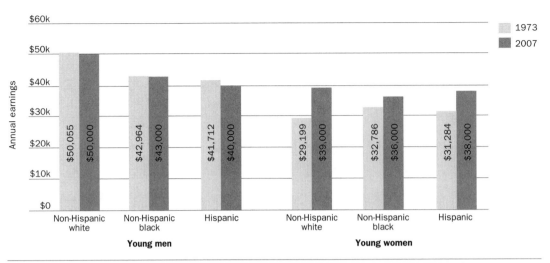

Note: Data are adjusted to 2007 dollars using the CPI-U-RS. Employed = worked at any time during year. March CPS.

for each race and ethnic group, holding gender constant. For example, in 1973, white male high school graduates earned 83 percent as much as white male college graduates ($41,712 compared with $50,055); by 2007, they earned only 62 percent as much ($31,000 compared with $50,000).

The Extent of Low-Wage Work

Trends in the median do not reveal how workers at other points in the wage distribution fared during a period of rising inequality. Thus, we examine changes in the share of young adults who are "low-wage workers," which we define as those earning less than $9 an hour in 2007 dollars. This wage exceeds the 2007 national minimum wage of $5.85 and corresponds to the 15th percentile of the 2007 wage distribution for all young adult workers. Working full-time, full-year (forty hours, fifty-two weeks) at this wage yields annual earnings of $18,720, which falls between the official poverty lines for a family of three persons and a family of four persons.[16]

Figure 4 shows that between 1979 and 2007, the percentage of young workers who earned less than $9 an hour increased for men in each of the race and ethnic groups and declined for women across the board. White men were 3 percentage points more likely to have low wages in 2007 than in 1979, whereas white women were 7 points less likely. Young Hispanic men were much more likely than white and black men to be low earners in 2007, and had the largest increase since 1979. Among young women, the declines were greatest for whites. In 2007 young women, especially the mothers of young children, had more education and more labor force experience and thus earned higher wages than their counterparts in 1979.[17]

Employment Rate Differences by Education, Race and Ethnicity, and Gender

The level and trends in the annual employment rate also differed by gender. Among all young men, the employment rate fell 6.6

Figure 4. Percentage of Workers, Aged Twenty-Five to Thirty-Four, Earning Less than $9 an Hour, by Gender and Race, 1979 and 2007

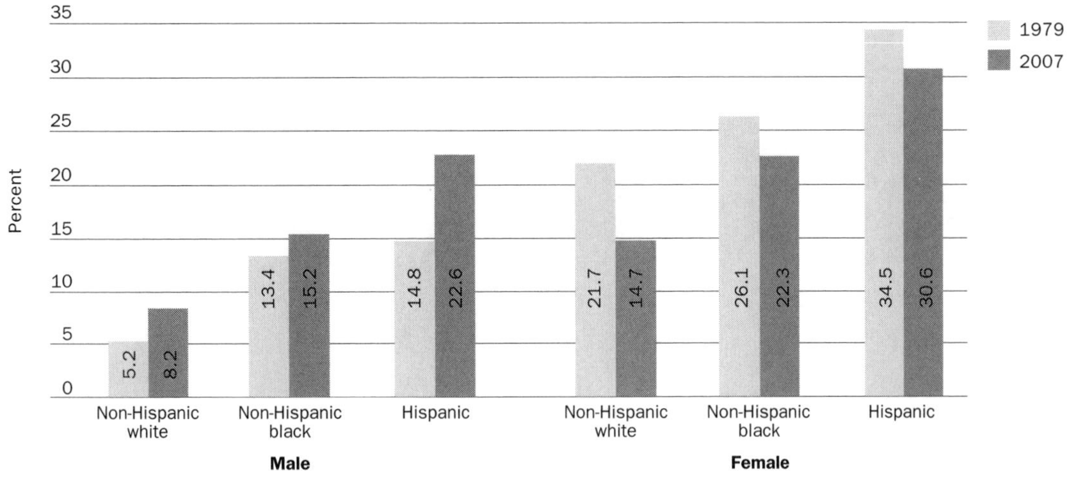

Note: Data are adjusted to 2007 dollars using the CPI-U-RS. Employed = worked at any time during year. CPS ORG data.

percentage points between 1973 and 2007, whereas for young women, the rate rose 16.1 points. The gender gap in employment, therefore, fell from 35.4 to 12.7 points over this period.

Chinhui Juhn, Kevin Murphy, and Robert Topel document an increase in the fraction of the year workers spend either unemployed or out of the labor force—the non-employment rate.[18] When we update their analysis for young adult men, the non-employment rate rose from 7.2 percent to 12.5 percent from 1973 to 2007. For women, the fraction of the year spent not working declined from 55 percent to 38 percent.[19] The rate increased the most for black male high school dropouts, who spent 49 percent of the year on average non-employed in 2007, up from 18 percent in 1973.[20]

Juhn, Murphy, and Topel attribute part of the rise in male non-employment to the lower real wages offered by employers who, in part because of labor-saving technological changes,

hired fewer less-educated men relative to more-educated ones. Michael Elsby and Matthew Shapiro suggest that choosing to work is analogous to getting on a "wage escalator," whereby workers earn higher wages with each year of labor force experience.[21] Because the "wage escalator" for the less-educated flattened after the mid-1970s, the payoff to work over a lifetime has fallen substantially.

Figure 5 compares the annual employment rates in 1973 and 2007 for high school graduates aged twenty-four to thirty-five, by gender and race.[22] Among men, the employment rate fell 23 percentage points for blacks, 7.3 points for whites, and 4.4 points for Hispanics, with the result that male Hispanic high school graduates in 2007 worked more than their white and black counterparts. Employment rates increased for each of the three groups of female high school graduates. Between 1973 and 2007, the male-female employment gap shrank for whites from 39.6 percentage points to 16.8 percentage points and for Hispanics from 31.7 points to 25.3

Figure 5. Employment Rate of High School Graduates, Aged Twenty-Five to Thirty-Four, by Gender and Race, 1973 and 2007

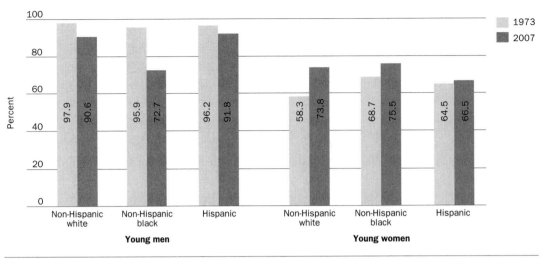

Note: Employed = worked at any time during year. March CPS.

points. For black high school graduates, the gender gap in employment had been essentially eliminated by 2007; employment rates were 75.5 and 72.7 percent, respectively for women and men.

One reason why employment declined more for young black men than for young white men is the dramatic rise in incarceration rates for black men over the past three decades and the negative effect of a criminal record on an employer's willingness to hire.[23] Steven Raphael reports that in 2001, among all adult men, 2.6 percent of non-Hispanic whites, 16.6 percent of non-Hispanic blacks, and 7.7 percent of Hispanics had served time in prison.[24] Among younger cohorts, incarceration rates are higher: more than two-thirds of black male high school dropouts, and one-third of those with less than a college education, had been incarcerated by the time they reached their early thirties.[25] Harry Holzer finds that increased incarceration accounts for an employment decline among black men of from 4 to 9 percentage points.[26]

William Julius Wilson offers several additional reasons for the more rapid decline in black employment—young black males' lower educational attainment (a "skills mismatch"), their residential concentration in the inner city during an era when jobs were moving to the suburbs (a "spatial mismatch"), and persisting employer racial discrimination, often reflected in how firms advertise for and recruit entry-level workers.[27]

Job Instability

Over the past thirty years the labor market has also seen increased "churning"—a term used by economists to refer to movements from employment to unemployment (involuntary job changes) as well as movements from one job to another (voluntary job changes), especially among younger workers.[28] Involuntary job changes tend to be associated with negative outcomes; voluntary changes, with positive outcomes.[29] Regardless of the subsequent wage changes associated with churning, job instability can lead young adults to postpone marriage or childbearing decisions and can reduce the likelihood of independent living. By making future employment and earnings more uncertain, increased churning makes purchasing a home or having a child a riskier decision.

The greater the extent of churning, the less time a worker spends with a single employer. Henry Farber analyzes the evolution of job tenure with a given firm for recent cohorts and finds that between 1973 and 2006, average private-sector job tenure for men, controlling for age differences, fell almost 25 percent, whereas female job tenure remained constant.[30] The proportion of men aged thirty-five to sixty-four in long-term jobs, defined as tenure of at least ten years, fell from about 50 percent to 35 percent between 1973 and 2006. Farber concludes that the "company man" who spent a lifetime with the same employer in earlier generations is no longer a staple of the labor market.

Farber also documents substantial job churning among young workers.[31] Between 1973 and 2006, about 34 percent of workers aged twenty to twenty-nine in private-sector jobs had held those jobs less than one year. Older workers are less likely to have job tenure of less than one year, suggesting that job churning has mainly affected the young over the past thirty years.

Although employment instability can delay the transition to adulthood, job churning in young adulthood might lead to better outcomes in later years. For example, making voluntary job changes from one firm to another can raise wages in the long run. By contrast, making many involuntary job changes can slow the acquisition of labor market skills and experience, which can reduce wages in the long run.

David Neumark documents the negative effects of job churning on future employment and earnings.[32] An additional year of job tenure in the first five years after leaving school, he finds, leads to an increase, on average, in adult wages of about 7 to 13 percent for men and 12 to 24 percent for women. One additional job held in the first five years after leaving school reduces wages by 8 percent for men. Holzer and Robert LaLonde also find that shorter job tenure and job instability for young workers reduce wage growth and employment opportunities in later adulthood.[33] The empirical evidence, therefore, suggests that the uncertain economic prospects faced by young adults may have long-lasting effects on employment and earnings.

Educational Attainment by Gender

Women's gains in relative earnings and employment over the past three decades are attributable in part to their increased access to jobs, particularly managerial and professional positions, and in part to their increased educational attainment, which in turn results in part from their improved labor market opportunities. Between 1973 and 2007, college completion rates more than doubled, from 16.4 percent to 35.9 percent, for women aged twenty-five to thirty-four, but increased only from 23.7 percent to 28.9 percent for men in the same age range. In 1973 young women were 7.3 percentage points less likely to have graduated from college than young men; by 2007, they were 7 points more likely to have graduated. College completion rates for women overtook those for men during the late 1980s.[34]

Some researchers have suggested that the improved economic status and educational attainment of young women relative to young men have contributed to delays in marriage and childbearing and to increases in divorce rates and single motherhood.[35] Claudia Goldin uses the term "the quiet revolution" to describe changes since the late 1970s in the way that women view employment, education, and family.[36] She suggests that thirty years ago women were secondary earners who worked if their families needed extra money, but that now they work because employment defines their "fundamental identity and societal worth."

Goldin notes that higher divorce rates and easier access to contraception have shortened the portion of their adulthood that women spend as wives. She contends that expectations of being married for fewer years have led women to invest more heavily in human capital, such as education in career-oriented subjects. Martha Bailey attributes women's increased investment in education to better access to contraception, particularly the birth control pill.[37] Like Goldin and Bailey, Maria Fitzpatrick and Sarah Turner attribute women's greater educational attainment both to economic changes and to shifting social norms about women's roles and labor market opportunities.[38]

Increasing Returns to Higher Education

Although college-educated young adults have always had more success in the labor market than those with high school degrees or less, differences between the two groups have grown in recent decades. In particular, the wage gap between high school and college graduates in their first seven years after entering the labor force has widened. In 1973, male college graduates in entry-level jobs earned 33 percent more than men with a high school degree or less; for women, the difference was 52 percent. By 2007, the educational premium had grown to 79 percent for men and 92 percent for women.[39] In addition, the gap in employment rates between

male college graduates and high school graduates widened from 0.2 to 5.8 percentage points between 1973 and 2007. College-educated workers are also less vulnerable to recessions, as they are not the marginal workers who are generally laid off.

James Heckman, Lance Lochner, and Petra Todd estimate that the rate of return to a college degree compared with a high school degree increased from 13 percent to 18 percent between 1970 and 2000 for all white workers and from 14 percent to 24 percent for all black workers.[40] David Card and Thomas Lemieux show that for workers aged twenty-six to thirty-five, college graduates earned 20 percent more than high school graduates in 1975, but 40 percent more in 1995.[41]

The Changing Labor Market and the Changing Transition to Adulthood

The labor market changes reviewed above have made it more difficult to achieve economic stability and self-sufficiency. We now review the social science evidence on the effect of labor market changes on changes in other aspects of the transition to adulthood.

Why Haven't the Growing Returns to College Led More Men to Complete College?

Economic theory predicts that the growing payoff to a college education should induce more young adults (especially men) to seek a college degree. Yet several studies all document the post-1970s slowdown in the growth rate of college graduates.[42] Claudia Goldin and Lawrence Katz argue that until the 1950s increasing educational attainment caused the supply of skilled labor to outpace demand; the declining growth in educational attainment, particularly among men, reversed this trend from the 1970s onward, leading to the widening wage gaps between less-educated and more-educated workers.[43]

Why haven't the widening wage and employment gaps led to a greater increase in male college graduation rates over the past three decades? Some analysts contend that rising tuition costs and reductions in grants have made college-going more difficult for young adults with parents of low socioeconomic status (SES). In 1988 the National Center for Education Statistics began tracking the educational attainment of a large sample of eighth graders; the study continued through 2000, by which time most youth in the sample were twenty-five and twenty-six years old.[44] Among those who scored in the bottom 25 percent on a mathematics test during high school, 30.3 percent from high-SES families completed a bachelor's degree or more, compared with only 2.9 percent from low-SES families.[45] Among the youth with the highest math scores, 28.8 percent from low-SES families completed college, compared with 74.1 percent from the most advantaged families.

Thomas Kane argues that increased tuition, smaller tuition subsidies, and lower borrowing limits for student loans explain why college attendance has not increased more in response to the increased returns to education.[46] He estimates that a $1,000 increase in college costs leads to about a 5 percentage point decline in college enrollment.

Research findings on the effects of federal Pell grants on college-going are mixed, but evidence shows that other public tuition subsidies substantially increase enrollment. Susan Dynarski finds that college enrollment fell 6 percentage points after Congress eliminated a tuition subsidy for students who were receiving Social Security benefits after a parental

death.[47] David Deming and Dynarski find that broad-based programs that have simple application procedures raise enrollment the most.[48] Expanding access to Pell grants and making it easier to apply for financial aid could thus increase college enrollment.

Over the past thirty years, changes in the labor market have made it more difficult for young adults to achieve financial independence. The labor market prospects of young men have declined, and the gap between less- and more-educated young adults has widened.

The most common source of college funding for students is their parents. But increasing inequality in parental income since the mid-1970s, particularly the declining real earnings of fathers with a high school education or less, has made it harder for some parents to afford college costs. Phillippe Belley and Lance Lochner highlight the increased link between family income and whether a young adult goes to college.[49] Test scores on the Armed Forces Qualification Test, the major correlate of educational attainment, remained equally important between 1979 and 1997. Family income, however, grew more important. In 1979 youth with family incomes in the highest quartile had a 9 percentage point higher rate of college enrollment than youth with family incomes in the lowest quartile, after controlling for test scores. That difference grew to 16 points in 1997.

One explanation for the increasing link between family background and education is that low-income young adults face impediments to borrowing, known as "credit constraints," meaning that some young adults who want to attend college either cannot find financing or are unwilling to borrow.[50] The evidence that more students are delaying college completion or continuing to work while they attend school, or both, is also consistent with binding credit constraints and may help to explain why enrollment has not increased more in response to the increased returns to education.

Maria Fitzpatrick and Sarah Turner conclude that credit constraints "prevent or delay students from earning degrees through a full-time, direct course of study."[51] They show that the fraction of students who combine work and college classes has increased, as has enrollment of "older" undergraduates. Among undergraduates aged twenty-four and older, almost 70 percent now combine work and classes. Belley and Lochner also find that college students from higher-income families are less likely to combine work with college than those from lower-income families. They find mixed evidence, however, on the connection between family background and a delay in college education.

In two papers, Pedro Carneiro and James Heckman reject the credit constraints hypothesis and attribute most of the positive link between college enrollment and family income during high school to differences in the cognitive ability of students, which is correlated with parental income during childhood and which is evident in early childhood.[52] To the extent that credit constraints operate, Heckman and Carneiro suggest that they mainly affect lower-ability students from low-income families who cannot secure financing for two-year colleges.

The American Council on Education reports that the proportion of college graduates who incurred college debt rose from 49 percent to 65 percent between 1993 and 2000, with much of the increase coming from students with high family incomes who now find it easier to borrow.[53] Although a larger proportion of college students now finance education through loans, Sandy Baum and Marie O'Malley find most graduates feel that the benefits of taking on the debt outweigh the debt burden.[54] If credit constraints do reduce educational investments with a high rate of return, then young adults should be willing to incur even greater college debt than is now the case if the constraints were removed. On the other hand, even if credit constraints are not binding, there may still be a role for public policy to encourage educational attainment through subsidized loans and grants, given the strong link between family SES and children's educational attainment.

The increased importance of parental income for college completion has implications for policies regarding student loans and tuition waivers. Most high-ability students enroll in college, regardless of family income. Some academically qualified students from low-income families, however, postpone or forgo college even though it would increase their future employment and earnings.

Why Are Women Going to School Longer, Working More, and Having Fewer Children?

Claudia Goldin suggests that women's changing economic expectations, along with changing social norms, have led to their increased educational attainment, increased their labor force participation, and delayed their age of first marriage and childbirth—all key changes associated with the lengthening transition to adulthood.[55] She does not consider these behavioral changes as being direct responses to the declining labor market prospects of young men, though the timing of both sets of changes is similar. Men's labor market prospects began declining during the mid-1970s. Goldin's "quiet revolution" in women's employment, education, and family behaviors began during the late 1970s.

According to Goldin, for the past three decades, young women have formed their adult identity before marriage, whereas previous generations of women married at an early age and formed their adult identity after marriage. Goldin argues that young women are now active economic actors "who bargain somewhat effectively in the household and labor market." Most are no longer passive actors who make their employment decisions after those of their husbands.

As more young women have come to expect that their own employment and earnings will be important in their own right, not secondary to those of their husbands, more have sought college and graduate degrees. According to Claudia Buchman, Thomas DiPrete, and Anne McDaniel, the share of all bachelor's degrees earned by women rose from 35 percent in 1960 to 58 percent in 2004.[56] During the late 1960s, women made up only 5 percent of entering law students; by the early 2000s, 50 percent. Women made similar gains in the field of medicine.[57]

Buchman and her colleagues suggest that higher educational attainment and declining gender discrimination in the labor market allow some women to delay or forgo marriage both because they have more difficulty finding a similarly educated husband and because they can achieve economic independence on their own. That view is similar to Goldin's argument that women's higher expectations about their abilities and opportunities have led them to seek more education, which has in turn led to greater labor force attachment over the life course and to delays in marriage and childbearing.

Have Declining Economic Prospects Reduced Young Men's Marriage Prospects?

As noted, the labor market prospects of less-educated men of all races and ethnic groups worsened between the mid-1970s and 2007. To what extent have these economic difficulties contributed to the family structure changes associated with the transition to adulthood? William Julius Wilson, in *The Truly Disadvantaged,* suggested that the decline in manufacturing jobs, the suburbanization of employment, and increased employer demand for educated workers reduced the probability that less-educated, inner-city males could find jobs that could support a family.[58] Wilson argued that their declining economic prospects made them less marriageable and contributed to reductions in marriage and increases in non-marital childbearing. But researchers investigating the correlation between increasing non-marital childbearing and male labor market problems have had a difficult time establishing a causal link.

David Ellwood and Christopher Jencks review the evidence and conclude that "no consensus has emerged about why American families changed or why the amount of change varied by race and education."[59] They conclude that though declines in men's economic opportunities are associated with reduced or delayed marriage, the earnings declines have not been large enough to explain the long delay in marriage and substantial increase in nonmarital childbearing, even among the least-educated. They also note that "marriage patterns have changed nearly as much for advantaged and employed males as for others."

> *The delay in marriage means that more young adults are living either with parents, with roommates, on their own, or with a partner, and that fewer are living with a spouse.*

Do Labor Market Changes Affect the Living Arrangements of Young Adults?

It seems reasonable to think that employment instability and low wages could influence young adults' decisions to move into or out of their parental homes, but evidence about this connection too is mixed. One reason for the difficulty in sorting out the causal effects of economic changes is that noneconomic factors also affect living arrangements. Changes in social norms have made it more acceptable to marry later, to cohabit with a partner of the same or opposite sex, and to be a single parent. The delay in marriage means that more young adults are living either with parents, with roommates, on their own, or with a partner, and that fewer are living with a spouse.

Jordan Matsudaira examines changes in living arrangements of young adults and finds that

the share living at home with parents has increased since the 1960s.[60] But the share living with neither parents nor spouse has increased even more. Between 1960 and 2000, among men aged twenty-five to twenty-nine, the share living with parents grew 3 percentage points (from 15.1 to 18.2 percent), while the share living without a parent or spouse grew 26.3 points (from 13.6 to 39.6 percent). The decline in the share of men who were married (from 71.3 to 42.3 percent) resulted in a greater share cohabiting, living with roommates, or living on their own.

Matsudaira examines the correlation, by region, between two labor market measures—the employment rate of adults aged thirty-five to forty-four and average wages—and the probability of living with at least one parent. He finds that a 1 percentage point increase in a region's employment rate of adults decreases the likelihood that men aged nineteen to twenty-four and those twenty-five to twenty-nine live with their parents by 1.28 and 0.61 percentage points, respectively. For women, the estimated effects are similar but smaller, with those aged nineteen to twenty-four and twenty-five to twenty-nine being 0.61 and 0.26 percentage points less likely to live at home, respectively. Thus, in a growing economy, young adults are more likely to leave home.

Carolyn Hill and Harry Holzer compare two cohorts of youth aged twenty to twenty-two and find a weaker relationship between economic conditions and living arrangements than does Matsudaira.[61] For all race, gender, and educational groups, youth of this age were less likely to be married, more likely to live at home, and more likely to cohabit in 2002 than they were in 1984. In both 1984 and 2002, youth from higher-income families were more likely to live at home than those from less-advantaged families, suggesting that living arrangement choices were not primarily determined by finances. Hill and Holzer conclude that declining male earnings and employment cannot explain the large declines in marriage rates and changes in living arrangements for young adults.

Greg Kaplan examines a sample of young adults who never attended college to determine the extent to which labor market fluctuations caused them to move into and out of their parental homes.[62] Less-educated young adults, he notes, have unstable labor market outcomes—the annual rate of employment separations is 30 percent, and earnings vary significantly from month to month. The young adults in his sample are 54 percent more likely to move back home if they are not working and 15 percent more likely to leave home if they are. Forty percent of those who move out of their parental home moved back in by the time they were twenty-two. In a period of increased labor market volatility, for the less-educated, the ability to live with parents offers some financial insurance against labor market risks.

Policies to Improve Labor Market Outcomes

The severe recession that began in December 2007 makes it unlikely that the labor market prospects of young workers will improve substantially in the near future.[63] Public policy reforms, however, can raise employment and earnings for young adults, thus increasing their likelihood of making a successful transition to adulthood.

Frank Levy and Peter Temin make the case that changes in the nation's economic policies since the 1980s have fostered both slow growth in earnings and rising inequality.[64] They argue that policies emanating from

the New Deal and World War II, such as a relatively high minimum wage, support for strong unions, and progressive taxes, helped constrain earnings inequality and promote broadly shared productivity. By contrast, policies since the mid-1980s have discouraged unionization, permitted a low and falling real minimum wage, and emphasized inflation-fighting and budgetary discipline. In so doing, they argue, these policies fostered wage stagnation and rising inequality.

Several public policy reforms can improve the economic prospects of today's young adults by making work pay and by expanding employment; other reforms can increase the educational attainment, and hence the earnings, of the next generation of young workers. The American Recovery and Reinvestment Act (ARRA) of 2009 and President Obama's budget proposals for fiscal year 2010 include several reforms that would raise the employment and earnings prospects of young adults struggling to achieve labor market success.

Making Work Pay for Low-Wage Workers

Making work pay requires changes in government regulations about wages and working conditions and increases in work-related income supplements for low-wage workers. Because the 1996 federal welfare reform greatly reduced access to cash welfare, new policies should provide work opportunities for those who are willing to work but cannot find steady employment either because of poor economic conditions or because of physical and mental disabilities or criminal records that make it hard for them to work steadily even when the economy is strong. Indeed, the experiences of young adults during the economic booms of the 1980s and 1990s showed that a growing economy on its own was necessary, but not sufficient, to raise the earnings of many less-educated workers.

One way to make work pay is to foster a labor market that rewards workers with the same skills equally, without regard to race, ethnicity, or gender. As noted, the labor market has seen substantial progress in reducing gender disparities in recent decades, as women's employment and earnings have increased relative to those of men. Racial and ethnic earnings disparities too have narrowed. Disparities in employment and wages between white non-Hispanics and racial and ethnic minorities remain large, however; some have even widened. Young black men face substantially worse labor market opportunities than similar white men, a gap that both reflects and contributes to high levels of incarceration.[65] Reducing labor market discrimination should become a higher priority for public policy than it has been in recent years.

Several other policy changes can raise the wages of less-educated workers. One involves the federal minimum wage. Between the early 1960s and early 1980s, the minimum wage (in 2009 dollars) ranged between about $6.50 and $8.00 an hour, roughly 40 to 50 percent of the average wage of non-supervisory workers.[66] Congress increased the minimum wage only a few times after the mid-1980s, and it ranged between $5.15 and $6.75 (in 2009 dollars) between the late 1980s and 2009. After holding the minimum wage constant in nominal terms at $5.15 an hour from 1997 to 2007, Congress passed a three-part increase to $5.85 in July 2007, to $6.55 in July 2008, and to $7.25 in July 2009. One study attributes between 30 and 60 percent of the increased inequality at the bottom of the wage distribution (and almost one-third of the total increase in male wage inequality) to the falling real value of the minimum wage.[67]

Despite a lack of consensus about the extent to which increasing the minimum wage reduces employment for low-skilled workers, the fact is that many young adults with no more than a high school degree will continue to struggle to attain self-sufficiency unless the minimum wage is raised more often during the next decade than it has been since the mid-1980s. A higher minimum wage would be an important step toward making work pay. One possibility is to set the minimum wage at 45 percent of the median wage of production workers and to adjust it annually as that median changes. In July 2009, such a minimum wage would have been about $8.00.

One study attributes between 30 and 60 percent of the increased inequality at the bottom of the wage distribution to the falling real value of the minimum wage.

Setting the minimum wage too high would significantly reduce employment for low-skilled workers. But empirical evidence on how moderate increases in the minimum wage affect employment is mixed.[68] A meta-analysis by David Neumark and William Wascher reports that most studies find that the minimum wage reduces employment.[69] In contrast, even though the disemployment effects are negative, David Autor and colleagues conclude that they are small.[70]

Other policies too could make work pay. Expanding income supplements for low-wage workers without children would raise the take-home pay of young adults without causing adverse employment effects. The Earned Income Tax Credit (EITC) provides substantial support for low-income families with children without reducing work incentives, but it provides only modest benefits to childless workers.[71] The maximum federal credit for a family with two or more children (in current dollars) was $400 in 1975, $550 in 1986, $953 in 1991, and $4,824 in 2008. For a single person or a married couple without children, however, the maximum EITC in 2008 was only $438.

Because most young adults are neither married nor parents, they do not benefit much from the EITC. Adam Carasso and several colleagues analyze proposals to expand the EITC for childless workers and note that expanded credits for single individuals can increase marriage disincentives.[72] Some proposals reduce marriage penalties, for example, by taxing spouses separately, but at a higher cost.[73] Despite the costs, the declines in the employment and earnings of young men since the mid-1970s make it necessary to expand the EITC for childless workers to facilitate the transition to adulthood.

Public policy changes can also help raise private-sector wage rates. Average wages of unionized workers, for example, are 15 percent higher than those of comparable non-union workers. David Card's finding that the union wage premium especially benefits the lowest quintile of the wage distribution suggests that the large decline over the past thirty years in the share of the workforce covered by a union contract has contributed to the increased extent of low-wage work among young workers.[74]

The Employee Free Choice Act, considered by Congress in 2009, is designed to facilitate increased unionization and raise private-

sector wages. Arguing that the current adversarial model of labor relations reduces the flexibility of firms to adapt in today's dynamic labor market, Barry Hirsch proposes, instead, a less-adversarial governance model with a default form of collective voice for workers, but without full collective bargaining rights.[75] Unlike current labor law, the new model would involve management closely in a firm's labor relations procedures.

Expanding Employment for Less-Educated Workers
The United States has not operated a large public-service employment program since the early 1980s, when the Comprehensive Employment and Training Act (CETA) was terminated. However, during recessions many less-skilled workers are willing to work, but unable to find steady employment. A transitional jobs-of-last-resort program could reduce their employment instability. Workers in last-resort jobs could perform socially beneficial tasks for which there is little effective labor demand, such as labor-intensive public services in disadvantaged communities—neighborhood maintenance, weatherizing homes, assisting the elderly. Jobs could be time-limited and offer wages just below the minimum wage, thereby giving workers an incentive to accept available private-sector jobs.

Investing over the Life Course to Increase Skills for Future Young Adults
Investing more in education and training over the life course could raise the employment and earnings of the next generation of young adults. The President's Council of Economic Advisors projects that many jobs in growing industries over the next five to ten years will require "non-routine" skills, though they are still expected to pay low wages.[76] The Council endorses government policies that

promote lifelong participation in educational programs and supports increased funding to promote access to such programs, particularly for young people from disadvantaged backgrounds.

More effective early childhood and K–12 educational policies would result in fewer high school dropouts and more college graduates in the next generation. Educational policies remain appealing to the public, but in the short term they are more expensive than policies that make work pay for today's young adults. And the payoffs from successful programs—increased schooling, employment, and earnings, and lower rates of incarceration and non-marital births when the children reach adulthood—require many years to materialize.

The best way to improve the economic prospects of the next generation of young adults is to raise high school graduation rates and skills and ensure that more earn community college degrees and certificates and four-year college degrees. The nation's education system falls well short of providing low-income students with the skills they need to succeed in the twenty-first century labor market. Studies by Brian Jacob and Jens Ludwig and by Kathryn Magnuson and Elizabeth Votruba-Drzal document the importance of expanding the scope of early childhood education for low-income children.[77] The ARRA expanded funding for Early Head Start and Head Start, and the Obama administration has also proposed increased funding for early childhood education and services.[78]

"Second-chance" workforce development programs seek to raise the skills and wages of disadvantaged young adults. Harry Holzer shows that federal funding for education and training programs for adult workers, typically young adults, has declined dramatically since the early 1980s, just as the labor market rewards for skills have been increasing. Holzer proposes additional workforce development spending to raise the employment and earnings of young adults.[79] Noting that the decline in federal funding is due in part to the weak effects on employment and earnings of many earlier such programs, Holzer argues that some programs have, in fact, produced modest, but cost-effective, results. And he cites promising new training programs that take into account the local labor market demand for certain types of workers, that coordinate worker training with employers or industries that offer well-paying jobs, and that provide work supports, such as subsidized child care or transportation.

Although the United States graduated a larger share of its young adults from college than any other country for most of the twentieth century, it has fallen behind a number of other countries in recent decades.[80] President Obama has proposed increased federal spending to make college more affordable. And as the article in this volume by Thomas Brock notes, the ARRA includes a new tax credit for college students and increases the annual amount of Pell grants. The fiscal year 2010 budget also proposes indexing Pell grants to inflation and making them an entitlement.

Summary

Since the mid-1970s, the labor market prospects of young men in the United States have improved, on average, much less than they did for young men who entered the labor market in the quarter-century following World War II. And the employment rates and inflation-adjusted wage rates of men with no more than a high school degree are lower now than they were thirty years ago.

Meanwhile, the labor market outcomes of young women have increased relative to those of young men for all race and ethnic and education groups.

Policies to improve the labor market prospects of young adults are necessary to facilitate successful transitions to adulthood, even if labor market success, on its own, is not sufficient to achieve the other markers of adulthood (living independently, marrying, and having children). Numerous public policy reforms can raise the employment and incomes of today's young adults and increase the educational attainment, and hence the labor market success, of the next generation.

Endnotes

1. Gordon Berlin, Mary Corcoran, Susan Dynarski, Harry Holzer, Bridget Lavelle, and Future of Children conference participants provided helpful comments on a prior draft; Bridget Lavelle provided excellent research assistance. This paper was supported, in part, by a grant from the Research Network on Transitions to Adulthood to the National Poverty Center and by funds provided to the National Poverty Center by the U.S. Department of Health and Human Services, Office of the Assistant Secretary for Planning and Evaluation, #1 U01 AE000002-02.

2. Sheldon Danziger and Cecilia Elena Rouse, *The Price of Independence: The Economics of the Transition to Adulthood* (New York: Russell Sage Foundation, 2007).

3. Sheldon Danziger and Peter Gottschalk, *America Unequal* (Harvard University Press, 1995).

4. Lisa Bell and others, "Failure to Launch: Cross-National Trends in the Transition to Economic Independence," in *The Price of Independence: The Economics of Early Adulthood*, edited by Sheldon Danziger and Cecilia Elena Rouse (New York: Russell Sage Foundation, 2007), pp. 56–83.

5. Claudia Goldin and Lawrence Katz, *The Race between Education and Technology* (Cambridge, Mass.: Belknap Press, 2008).

6. Congressional Budget Office, *Historical Effective Tax Rates, 1979 to 2005: Supplement with Additional Data on Sources of Income and High-Income Households* (Washington: Congressional Budget Office, 2008).

7. We computed these wage rates from the merged Outgoing Rotation Group (ORG) files of the Current Population Survey (CPS), available annually starting in 1979. All data in this paper are adjusted for inflation to 2007 dollars using the CPI-U-RS, which corrects (at least partially) for the overstatement of inflation in the standard inflation series, the CPI-U. In addition to being the first year of the ORG data, 1979 is near the business cycle peak (a recession started in early 1980). The most recent recession started in December 2007. Thus, a comparison between 1979 and 2007 reflects long-run trends between two business cycle peaks, not changes due to business cycle conditions.

8. We do not distinguish between native-born and foreign-born Hispanics. Differences between these two groups are discussed in the article in this volume by Rubén Rumbaut and Goldnaz Komaie on immigrant youth.

9. While ORG wage rates are first available in 1979, the March CPS has data on annual earnings from the mid-1960s onward. We analyze annual earnings beginning in 1973, as November 1973 was a business cycle peak; 1973 was also the year in which the lowest annual poverty rate was recorded by the Census Bureau. Our results would not differ qualitatively if we began the analysis for annual earnings in 1979.

10. Peter B. Edelman, Harry J. Holzer, and Paul Offner, *Reconnecting Disadvantaged Young Men* (Washington: Urban Institute Press, 2006).

11. School enrollment and employment are measured during the week before the March CPS interview.

12. Andrew Sum and others, "The Collapse of the 2008 Summer Teen Job Market," Working Paper (Boston: Northeastern University Center for Labor Market Studies, 2008).

13. Sum and colleagues focus on changes between 2000 and 2008. We computed the July employment rates for

1973 and 2007, two years near the business cycle peak, using their methodology and data from the Bureau of Labor Statistics.

14. There is disagreement about how best to adjust for inflation. As mentioned, we use the CPI-U-RS, a more conservative inflation index than the official CPI-U. Some economists contend that the CPI-U-RS also overstates inflation. If this were true, our analyses understate real wage and earnings growth, and would overstate negative growth in wages. Lerman suggests that real earnings changes of the less-educated would be less negative if the analysis accounted for increased immigration by comparing the earnings of immigrants in their country of origin with their earnings in the United States. Inflation adjustments do not affect comparisons by race, gender, and education. Robert Lerman, "U.S. Wage-Inequality Trends and Recent Immigration," *American Economic Review Papers and Proceedings* 89 (1999): 2; Robert Lerman, "U.S. Income Inequality Trends and Recent Immigration," in *Inequality, Welfare, and Poverty: Theory and Measurement,* vol. 9 of *Research on Income Inequality*, edited by John A. Bishop (Amsterdam: Elsevier Science Ltd., 2003), pp. 289–307.

15. Data in the figures refer to non-Hispanic blacks and non-Hispanic whites; for brevity, we use the terms blacks and whites. CPS sample sizes are too small to report trends for American Indians or Asian Americans.

16. Results were similar when we used an alternative measure of low-wage work—the percentage of workers who earn less than the poverty line for a family of four in each year (results available from the authors upon request).

17. Maria Cancian and Deborah Reed, "Changes in Family Structure, Childbearing, and Employment: Implications for the Level and Trend in Poverty," in *Changing Poverty, Changing Policies,* edited by Maria Cancian and Sheldon Danziger (New York: Russell Sage Foundation, 2009), pp. 92–121.

18. Chinhui Juhn, Kevin Murphy, and Robert Topel, "Why Has the Natural Rate of Unemployment Increased over Time?" *Brookings Papers on Economic Activity* 1991, no. 1: 2; Chinhui Juhn, Kevin Murphy, and Robert Topel, "Current Unemployment, Historically Contemplated," *Brookings Papers on Economic Activity* 2002, no. 1: 79.

19. Following Juhn, Murphy, and Topel, we define the employment rate as the fraction of weeks during the year in which a young adult was employed. The non-employment rate is the percent of the year, also in weeks, spent unemployed or out of the labor force. Data by detailed year and demographic groups are available upon request from the authors. For these analyses, Hispanics are included as whites or blacks.

20. Also see Corcoran and Matsudaira for analysis of non-employment by birth cohort and race. Mary Corcoran and Jordan Matsudaira, "Is Stable Employment Becoming More Elusive for Young Men?" in *The Transition from School to Work,* edited by Ingrid Schoon and Rainer Silbereisen (Cambridge University Press, 2011, forthcoming).

21. Michael Elsby and Matthew Shapiro, "Stepping off the Wage Escalator: The Effects of Wage Growth on Equilibrium Employment," NBER Working Paper 15117 (Cambridge, Mass.: National Bureau of Economic Research, 2009).

22. The annual employment rate is defined as the percentage who worked at any time in the calendar year.

23. Harry J. Holzer, Steven Raphael, and Michael A. Stoll, "Perceived Criminality, Criminal Background Checks, and the Racial Hiring Practices of Employers," *Journal of Law Economics* 49, no. 2 (2006): 451.

Incarcerated men are not surveyed in the CPS. If they were counted, the employment rate would be lower and the trends more negative.

24. Steven Raphael, "Early Incarceration Spells and the Transition to Adulthood," in *The Price of Independence: The Economics of Early Adulthood*, edited by Sheldon Danziger and Cecilia Elena Rouse (New York: Russell Sage Foundation, 2007): 278–305.

25. Bruce Western and Christopher Wildeman, "The Black Family and Mass Incarceration," *Annals of the American Academy of Political and Social Science* 621, no. 1 (2009): 221.

26. Harry Holzer, "Collateral Costs: The Effects of Incarceration on the Employment and Earnings of Young Workers," IZA Discussion Paper 3118 (Bonn, Germany, 2007).

27. William Julius Wilson, *The Truly Disadvantaged: The Inner City, The Underclass, and Public Policy* (University of Chicago Press, 1987); William Julius Wilson, *More Than Just Race: Being Black and Poor in the Inner City* (New York: Norton, 2009).

28. We concentrate on jobs instability rather than earnings instability. Fluctuations in earnings and income have also increased in recent decades. Karen Dynan, Doug Elmendorf, and Daniel Sichel, "The Evolution of Household Income Volatility," Finance and Economics Discussion Series 2007-61 (Washington: Federal Reserve Board, 2007).

29. In recent years, lower-wage workers have become more likely to secure larger wage increases when they move voluntarily from one firm to another than when they stay with the same employer. Rucker Johnson and Mary Corcoran, "The Road to Economic Self-Sufficiency: Job Quality and Job Transition Patterns after Welfare Reform," *Journal of Policy Analysis and Management* 41, no. 3 (2004): 615.

30. Henry Farber, "Is the Company Man an Anachronism? Trends in Long-Term Employment in the United States, 1973–2006," in *The Price of Independence: The Economics of Early Adulthood*, edited by Sheldon Danziger and Cecilia Elena Rouse (New York: Russell Sage Foundation, 2007), pp. 56–83; Henry Farber, "Employment Insecurity: The Decline of Worker-Firm Attachment in the United States," Working Paper 530 (Princeton University Industrial Relations Section, 2008). Ann Huff Stevens finds that the average tenure of the longest job held by male workers, ages fifty-eight to sixty-two, was constant at about twenty-two years in both 1969 and 2002. Her results are not inconsistent with the possibility that workers now experience substantial job churning in young adulthood, delaying the transition to adulthood, but eventually settle into a steady job. Also, the latest cohort she examines was aged twenty-five to thirty-four in the 1960s, a different labor market than the one now facing young men. Ann Huff Stevens, "The More Things Change, the More They Stay the Same: Trends in Long-Term Employment in the United States, 1969–2002," NBER Working Paper W11878 (Cambridge, Mass: National Bureau of Economic Research, 2005).

31. Farber, "Is the Company Man an Anachronism?" (see note 30).

32. David Neumark, "Youth Labor Markets in the United States: Shopping Around vs. Staying Put," *Review of Economics and Statistics* 84, no. 3 (August 2002).

33. Harry J. Holzer and Robert J. LaLonde, "Job Change and Job Stability among Less-Skilled Young Workers," Institute for Research on Poverty Discussion Paper no. 1191–99 (University of Wisconsin-Madison, 1999).

34. Thomas Kane, "Public Intervention in Post-Secondary Education," in *Handbook of the Economics of Education*, vol. 2, edited by Eric Hanushek and Finis Welch (Amsterdam: North Holland, 2006).

35. David T. Ellwood and Christopher Jencks, "The Uneven Spread of Single-Parent Families: What Do We Know? Where Do We Look for Answers?" in *Social Inequality,* edited by Kathryn M. Neckerman (New York: Russell Sage Foundation, 2004), pp. 3–77.

36. Claudia Goldin, "The Quiet Revolution That Transformed Women's Employment, Education, and Family," *American Economic Review* 96, no. 2 (2006): 1.

37. Martha Bailey, "More Power to the Pill: The Impact of Contraceptive Freedom on Women's Lifecycle Labor Supply," *Quarterly Journal of Economics* 121, no. 1 (February 2006): 289.

38. Maria Fitzpatrick and Sarah Turner, "Blurring the Boundary: Changes in the Transition from College Participation to Adulthood," in *The Price of Independence: The Economics of Early Adulthood*, edited by Sheldon Danziger and Cecilia Elena Rouse (New York: Russell Sage Foundation, 2007), pp. 107–37.

39. Lawrence Mishel, Jared Bernstein, and Heidi Shierholz, *The State of Working America 2008/2009* (Washington: Economic Policy Institute, 2008).

40. James J. Heckman, Lance J. Lochner, and Petra E. Todd, "Fifty Years of Mincer Earnings Regressions," NBER Working Paper 9732 (Cambridge, Mass.: National Bureau of Economic Research, 2003).

41. David Card and Thomas Lemieux, "Can Falling Supply Explain the Rising Return to College for Younger Men? A Cohort-Based Analysis," *Quarterly Journal of Economics* 116, no. 2 (2001): 705.

42. David Autor, Lawrence Katz, and Alan Krueger, "Computing Inequality: Have Computers Changed the Labor Market?" *Quarterly Journal of Economics* 113, no. 4 (1998): 1169; David T. Ellwood, "The Sputtering Labor Force of the 21st Century: Can Social Policy Help?" in *The Roaring Nineties: Can Full Employment Be Sustained?* edited by Alan Krueger and Robert Solow (New York: Russell Sage Foundation, 2001); Card and Lemieux, "Can Falling Supply Explain the Rising Return to College for Younger Men?" (see note 41).

43. Goldin and Katz, *The Race between Education and Technology* (see note 5).

44. National Center for Education Statistics, *Youth Indicators 2005: Trends in Well-Being of American Youth* (U.S. Department of Education, Institute of Education Sciences, NCES 2005-050, July 2005).

45. Low socioeconomic background is defined by the NCES as the bottom quartile of a composite index of family income, parents' education, and occupation; high SES is the top quartile.

46. Kane, "Public Intervention in Post-Secondary Education" (see note 34).

47. Susan Dynarski, "Does Aid Matter? Measuring the Effect of Student Aid on College Attendance and Completion," *American Economic Review* 93, no. 1 (2003): 279.

48. David Deming and Sue Dynarski, "College Aid," in *Targeting Investments in Children: Fighting Poverty When Resources Are Limited,* edited by Phil Levine and David Zimmerman, volume in preparation.

49. Phillippe Belley and Lance Lochner, "The Changing Role of Family Income and Ability in Determining Educational Achievement," Working Paper, London, Ontario, University of Western Ontario, 2008.

50. Brian Cadena and Benjamin Keys provide a behavioral explanation for why some college students do not want to incur debt and hence do not accept interest-free student loans. Brian Cadena and Benjamin Keys,

"Can Self-Control Explain Avoiding Free Money? Evidence from Interest-Free Student Loans," unpublished manuscript, University of Colorado, Boulder, Department of Economics, 2009.

51. Fitzpatrick and Turner, "Blurring the Boundary: Changes in the Transition from College Participation to Adulthood" (see note 38).

52. Pedro Carneiro and James J. Heckman, "The Evidence on Credit Constraints in Post-Secondary Schooling," *Economic Journal* 112, no. 482 (2002): 705; Pedro Carneiro and James J. Heckman, "Human Capital Policy," in *Inequality in America: What Role for Human Capital Policies?*, edited by James J. Heckman and Alan B. Krueger (MIT Press, 2005), pp. 79–239.

53. American Council on Education, *Debt Burden: Repaying Student Debt,* Issue Brief (Washington: ACE Center for Policy Analysis, 2004). The 1992 Higher Education Act allowed students, regardless of need, to access unsubsidized loans.

54. Sandy Baum and Marie O'Malley, "College on Credit: How Borrowers Perceive Their Education Debt," *Journal of Student Financial Aid* 33, no. 3 (2003): 7. This finding contradicts Tamara Draut, who argues that young adults are overburdened by debt. Even though a greater percentage of students are taking student loans, there is little evidence that recent graduates are overburdened by college debt. Tamara Draut, *Strapped: Why America's 20- and 30-Somethings Can't Get Ahead* (New York: Doubleday, 2006).

55. Goldin, "The Quiet Revolution" (see note 36).

56. Claudia Buchman, Thomas DiPrete, and Anne McDaniel, "Gender Inequalities in Education," *Annual Review of Sociology* 34 (2008): 319–37.

57. Goldin, "The Quiet Revolution" (see note 36).

58. Wilson, *The Truly Disadvantaged* (see note 27).

59. Ellwood and Jencks, "The Uneven Spread of Single-Parent Families: What Do We Know? Where Do We Look for Answers?" (see note 35), pp. 3, 60.

60. Jordan Matsudaira, "Economic Conditions and the Living Arrangements of Young Adults," unpublished manuscript, Cornell University, 2009.

61. Carolyn Hill and Harry J. Holzer, "Labor Market Experiences and Transition to Adulthood," in *The Price of Independence: The Economics of Early Adulthood*, edited by Sheldon Danziger and Cecilia Elena Rouse (New York: Russell Sage Foundation, 2007), pp. 107–37.

62. Greg Kaplan, "Moving Back Home: Insurance against Labor Market Risk," Job Market Paper, New York University, Department of Economics, 2009.

63. This section draws heavily from the introductory chapter in Maria Cancian and Sheldon Danziger, eds., *Changing Poverty, Changing Policies* (New York: Russell Sage Foundation, 2009).

64. Frank Levy and Peter Temin, "Inequality and Institutions in 20th-Century America," Working Paper 07-17 (Cambridge, Mass.: MIT, 2007).

65. Bruce Western and Christopher Wildeman, "The Black Family and Mass Incarceration" (see note 25).

66. Adjusted for inflation using the CPI-U-RS.

67. David Autor, Alan Manning, and Christopher Smith, "The Minimum Wage's Role in the Evolution of U.S. Wage Inequality over Three Decades: A Modest Re-Assessment," Working Paper (Cambridge, Mass: MIT Department of Economics, 2008).

68. Economic theory predicts that binding minimum wages reduce employment. David Lee and Emmanuel Saez, however, argue that minimum wages might be optimal even in competitive labor markets if redistribution toward low-skilled workers is valued. In that case, lost efficiency from unemployment is compensated, in a social welfare sense, by higher wages for low-skilled workers. Guillaume Rocheteau and Murat Tasci show that the effects of minimum wages are ambiguous if there are systemic problems in finding jobs (known as search frictions). David Lee and Emmanuel Saez, "Optimal Minimum Wage Policy in Competitive Labor Markets," NBER Working Paper 14320 (Cambridge, Mass.: National Bureau of Economic Research, 2008); Guillaume Rocheteau and Murat Tasci, "Positive and Normative Effects of a Minimum Wage," Federal Reserve Bank of Cleveland Working Paper 08-01 (2008).

69. David Neumark and William Wascher, "Minimum Wages and Employment," *Foundations and Trends in Microeconomics* (January 2007): 1–182.

70. Autor, Manning, and Smith, "The Minimum Wage's Role in the Evolution of U.S. Wage Inequality over Three Decades" (see note 67).

71. John Karl Scholz, Robert Moffitt, and Benjamin Cowan, "Trends in Income Support," in *Changing Poverty, Changing Policies,* edited by Maria Cancian and Sheldon Danziger (New York: Russell Sage Foundation, 2009), pp. 203–41.

72. Adam Carasso and others, "The Next Stage for Social Policy: Encouraging Work and Family Formation among Low-Income Men," Urban Institute Discussion Paper 28 (Washington: Urban Institute, 2008).

73. Gordon L. Berlin, "Rewarding the Work of Individuals: A Counterintuitive Approach to Reducing Poverty and Strengthening Families," *Future of Children* 17, no. 2 (2007): 17.

74. David Card, "The Effect of Unions on the Structure of Wages: A Longitudinal Analysis," *Econometrica* 64, no. 4 (1996): 957.

75. Barry T. Hirsch, "Sluggish Institutions in a Dynamic World: Can Unions and Industrial Competition Coexist?" *Journal of Economic Perspectives* 22, no. 1 (2008).

76. Executive Office of the President, Council of Economic Advisors, *Preparing the Workers of Today for the Jobs of Tomorrow* (2009) (www.whitehouse.gov/administration/EOP/CEA/Jobs-of-the-Future).

77. Brian Jacob and Jens Ludwig, "Improving Educational Outcomes for Poor Children," in *Changing Poverty, Changing Policies*, edited by Maria Cancian and Sheldon Danziger (New York: Russell Sage Foundation, 2009), pp. 266–300; Katherine Magnuson and Elizabeth Votruba-Drzal, "Enduring Influences of Childhood Poverty," in *Changing Poverty, Changing Policies,* edited by Maria Cancian and Sheldon Danziger (New York: Russell Sage Foundation, 2009), pp. 153–79.

78. See (www.whitehouse.gov/agenda/education/) and (www.whitehouse.gov/assets/Documents/Recovery_Plan_Metrics_Report_508.pdf).

79. Harry J. Holzer, "Workforce Development as an Antipoverty Strategy: What Do We Know? What Should We Do?" in *Changing Poverty, Changing Policies,* edited by Maria Cancian and Sheldon Danziger (New York: Russell Sage Foundation, 2009), pp. 301–29.

80. Robert H. Haveman and Timothy M. Smeeding, "The Role of Higher Education in Social Mobility," *Future of Children* 16, no. 2 (2006): 125.

Civic Engagement and the Transition to Adulthood

Constance Flanagan and Peter Levine

Summary

Constance Flanagan and Peter Levine survey research on civic engagement among U.S. adolescents and young adults. Civic engagement, they say, is important both for the functioning of democracies and for the growth and maturation it encourages in young adults, but opportunities for civic engagement are not evenly distributed by social class or race and ethnicity.

Today's young adults, note the authors, are less likely than those in earlier generations to exhibit many important characteristics of citizenship, raising the question of whether these differences represent a decline or simply a delay in traditional adult patterns of civic engagement. Flanagan and Levine also briefly discuss the civic and political lives of immigrant youth in the United States, noting that because these youth make up a significant share of the current generation of young adults, their civic engagement is an important barometer of the future of democracy.

The authors next survey differences in civic participation for youth from different social, racial, and ethnic backgrounds. They explore two sets of factors that contribute to a lower rate of civic engagement among low-income and minority young adults. The first is cumulative disadvantage—unequal opportunities and influences before adulthood, especially parental education. The second is different institutional opportunities for civic engagement among college and non-college youth during the young-adult years. Flanagan and Levine survey various settings where young adults spend time—schools and colleges, community organizations, faith-based institutions, community organizing and activism projects, and military and other voluntary service programs—and examine the opportunities for civic engagement that each affords.

As the transition to adulthood has lengthened, say the authors, colleges have become perhaps the central institution for civic incorporation of younger generations. But no comparable institution exists for young adults who do not attend college. Opportunities for sustained civic engagement by year-long programs such as City Year could provide an alternative opportunity for civic engagement for young adults from disadvantaged families, allowing them to stay connected to mainstream opportunities and to adults who could mentor and guide their way.

www.futureofchildren.org

Constance Flanagan is a professor of youth civic development in the College of Agricultural Sciences at Pennsylvania State University. Peter Levine is the director of CIRCLE (The Center for Information and Research on Civic Learning and Engagement) at the Tisch College of Citizenship and Public Service, Tufts University.

The civic engagement of young adults—whether in the form of joining community groups, volunteering to help neighbors, or leading grassroots efforts to gain civil rights—is important to the health and performance of democracy. It is also important for personal growth and identity formation during the transition to adulthood.

When younger Americans have a voice in community affairs, they can contribute their insights to public debates and their energies to addressing public problems. Issues that centrally involve adolescents and young adults—such as the high-school dropout crisis, the costs of higher education, or youth violence—especially benefit from youth input. Young adults who identify with, have a stake in, and want to contribute to their communities can help to stabilize democratic societies by directing their discontent into constructive channels. They can also be a force for political change, by bringing new perspectives on political issues and offering fresh solutions.

During late adolescence and young adulthood, people chart a course for their future and "take stock" of the values they live by and the kind of world they want to be part of.

The personal and psychological benefits of civic engagement for young adults include fulfillment of the human need to belong and to feel that life has a purpose beyond the pursuit of individual gain. Whether through voting, working in community-based organizations to address local problems, or volunteering time or money to a social cause, civic activities raise issues involving connection to others, public goods and values, and the collective nature of solving problems. Engaging with fellow members of a community-based group also helps youth form social networks, build social capital, and connect to educational and occupational opportunities.

Civic Engagement and the Changing Transition to Adulthood

Like other markers of adulthood such as finishing school and starting a family, civic engagement is a key part of the transition between adolescence and mature adulthood. During childhood and adolescence people become aware of political institutions, social issues, and larger communities; learn facts and concepts related to politics; and begin to practice active citizenship by volunteering, belonging to groups, consuming news media, and discussing issues. The opportunities and choices of these years shape interests and pathways.[1] During late adolescence and young adulthood, people chart a course for their future and "take stock" of the values they live by and the kind of world they want to be part of. Moral and political issues become salient concerns. Exploring alternative political perspectives, working with people from different social backgrounds, and wrestling with a range of perspectives on social issues provide opportunities to reflect on one's own views and decide where one stands.

According to life-cycle theories, stable patterns of civic engagement take hold once individuals have settled into adult roles, such as steady jobs, marriage, and parenting, that build up their stake in community affairs. These adult roles give a predictable structure to life that makes regular engagement in community affairs more likely and increases the probability of being recruited into civic affairs.[2] By contrast, the lives of young adults are unsettled and in flux as they move into and out of institutional settings such as school or work. Although they are more likely to take part in civic life when they are in such settings, their involvement tends to be episodic. Nonetheless, opportunities to explore civic issues and to wrangle with others who have different perspectives help young adults to crystallize their values and political stands. Political identities formed in the early-adult years are highly predictive of the positions individuals will hold in middle and even late adulthood. Political views as well as levels and forms of engagement will vary within every generation, but the politics of a generation takes shape in the context of the political climate, issues, and range of tenable solutions circulating when a cohort comes of age.

In this article, we summarize research findings on civic engagement in late adolescence and early adulthood and on how patterns of engagement today may differ from those in earlier generations. As the transition to adulthood lengthens, is it taking longer for persistent patterns of civic engagement to take hold? We discuss how civic participation varies for youth from different social, racial, and ethnic backgrounds and for new immigrants. In particular, we assess two sets of factors that may contribute to a civic divide. The first is cumulative disadvantage (unequal opportunities and influences before adulthood); the second is differing institutional opportunities during the young-adult years themselves. Next we focus on a variety of institutional settings where young adults spend time—schools and colleges, community organizations, faith-based groups, community activist groups, the military, and year-long

programs such as AmeriCorps—and examine the opportunities for civic engagement that each affords. We conclude with a discussion of policy directions.

Decline or Delay? Trends in Young Adults' Civic Engagement

Young adults today are less likely than their counterparts in the 1970s were to exhibit nine out of ten important characteristics of citizenship: belonging to at least one group, attending religious services at least monthly, belonging to a union, reading newspapers at least once a week, voting, being contacted by a political party, working on a community project, attending club meetings, and believing that people are trustworthy.[3] Only in a tenth form of citizenship—volunteering—are they more likely to participate, probably as a result of deliberate efforts over the past several decades by schools, colleges, and community groups to encourage volunteering. For several of these ten types of engagement—notably voting—rates have risen in the 2000s compared with the 1990s, but not enough to compensate for thirty years of decline.

These changes invite us to ask whether the nation's younger generations have permanently weaker connections to civic life than their predecessors or whether the lengthening transition to adulthood means that young people today take longer to begin to forge those connections (much as they take longer to get married or finish their education).

Trends in voting provide evidence that at least some of the change is a matter of delay, not a permanent generational decline. During any era, young adults are less likely than their elders to vote. Since 1972, when eighteen-year-old Americans were first eligible to vote, the voting gap between youth aged eighteen to twenty-five and their elders has fluctuated

Figure 1. Voting Turnout over the Life Course

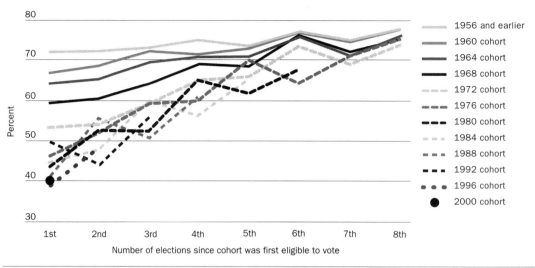

Source: Census Current Population Supplement.

in presidential election years between 16 percent and 27 percent, with the smallest margin in 1972 and the largest in 2000.[4]

Figure 1 shows voting rates over the life course for twelve different cohorts (each born within a different four-year period) that became eligible to vote in time for presidential elections from 1956 to 2000. The overall pattern is that each generation moves toward the same high level of turnout over the life course. For instance, the cohorts that are old enough to have voted in five elections are all voting at rates above 60 percent. But the earlier generations start at a higher rate and rise less to reach the 60 percent level or above. Every successive cohort has had a lower starting point, but has also become substantially more engaged during their twenties and into their thirties, narrowing the gap.

This interpretation is consistent with a political life-cycle model that holds that political engagement increases as one's life, roles, and institutional connections in the community

become more stable. Delays in role changes (stable jobs, marriage, and family formation) associated with the increasingly protracted transition to adulthood have been accompanied by delays in the voting patterns of successive cohorts of young adults. These trends in voting patterns tell a story of delay rather than one of decline.

But a protracted developmental period and delayed civic engagement cannot explain all the changes in forms of engagement. First, certain civic activities have become *more* common for young adults than they once were. As noted, the volunteering rate for young adults rose during the 1990s and is higher today than it was during the 1970s and 1980s. Today young adults are about as likely as their contemporary elders to volunteer, raise funds for causes, and say they have worked on local projects with other people in their communities. Youth today are more likely than their contemporary elders to engage in global activism, to use the Internet for political information and action (which was impossible thirty years ago), and to engage in lifestyle and consumer politics.[5]

Second, in some forms of civic engagement that have declined substantially, younger generations do not catch up with their elders as they move through their twenties. Newspaper readership is one example: recent generations have not narrowed the gap with their parents as they have aged.[6] Social trust reflected generational declines through the 1990s but showed some recovery in the new millennium and, across cohorts, increased through the third decade of life.[7] For some other forms of engagement (such as meeting attendance and working on community projects), we lack sufficient long-term data to be able to tell whether downward trends represent declines or delays.

For several decades, both forms and patterns of young adult civic engagement have been changing. For example, panel studies indicate that patterns of civic engagement in young adulthood have become increasingly episodic over the past several generations. Even the civic engagement of the baby boom generation (1965 high school graduating cohort) was more episodic than that of their parents at similar ages. Consequently, it is more challenging to predict lifelong patterns of conventional engagement based on adolescent activity. For the baby boom generation, levels of civic engagement in high school were a poor predictor of engagement in their mid-twenties. As the boomers settled into adult roles in their thirties and forties, however, patterns of civic engagement became more predictable.[8] These trends across generations have led to speculation that the character of American civic life is changing toward more short-term and episodic engagement and away from enduring memberships in associations and community organizations.

Nonetheless, the young adult years are a formative period when civic values and political ideologies crystallize. Opportunities for engaging with others to address civic concerns make it more likely that in the long run people will identify with and contribute to the common good.

Immigrant Youth and Undocumented Youth

The nature of the civic and political lives of immigrant youth in the United States is an important barometer for the future of democracy, if for no other reason than that these youth make up a significant share of the younger generation (see the article by Rubén Rumbaut in this volume for more detail on immigrant youth). Examining the ways in which society includes or excludes these groups, the forms their political engagement takes, and the opportunities they have to exercise their political voice and develop civic competencies begin to yield a picture of tomorrow's political landscape. Besides sheer numbers, immigrant youth provide unique insights into the social contract and the ties of rights and responsibilities that bind us as Americans. Only immigrants, after all, choose to become U.S. citizens. That decision may be instrumental—a path to other ends—or it may be motivated by more lofty (patriotic) goals. In either case, choosing to become a citizen and accepting the rights and responsibilities of that decision is a form of civic engagement unique to immigrants. Newcomers who lack legal permanent residency, of course, do not have that choice.

For many immigrants, especially the undocumented, citizenship itself is contested, and everyday life raises political issues. It is estimated that roughly half of immigrant children live in families where at least one adult is not an American citizen. In 2005, it was estimated that 11 percent of children in immigrant families were unauthorized and 18 percent were born in the United States to an unauthorized parent.[9] Many of the mainstream institutions that engage most Americans are not open to the undocumented. One exception is the public school, from which undocumented children cannot legally be excluded. Passages into adulthood (jobs or postsecondary education) after school, however, are severely constrained, because the undocumented cannot legally work and are denied access to most publicly funded programs, including ones with explicit civic missions, such as Conservation Corps. Even applying for a library card or driver's license is off limits for those without the proper identity papers. Furthermore, because the undocumented are ineligible for most college financial aid programs, they face enormous barriers to higher education.

It is thus not surprising that working to change systemic barriers and legalizing access to higher education are meaningful forms of civic engagement that unite immigrant communities. In a national survey of youth conducted in the spring of 2006—a time when major protests were being organized in most large American cities against restrictions on immigration—23 percent of immigrant youth and 18 percent of children of immigrant parents reported that they had protested in the past twelve months.[10] In contrast, young people who were born in the United States to native-born parents reported a protest rate of just 10 percent. Student activist groups such as California's Orange County Immigrant Student Group (OCISG) have coalesced around the shared goal of educational access. Group members, who come from California's postsecondary public education system, include both documented and undocumented immigrants and current,

former, and aspiring students. Organizing is now focused on the DREAM (Development, Relief and Education for Alien Minors) Act, a bill under consideration in Washington to legalize qualified young immigrants who came to the United States as children. Past organizing targeted California's Assembly Bill 540, which was signed into law in 2001 and which now guarantees in-state tuition for undocumented residents. That achievement is marked by some student leaders who refer to themselves as "AB 540 students." But their civic engagement extends beyond campus as they reach out to explain issues of access to high school students and their parents.[11]

Immigrant youth engage in a wide array of civic activities, working in faith-based groups and using their bilingual skills to assist fellow immigrants as translators and tutors. Comparisons of nationally representative studies of foreign-born, second-generation, and native-born seventh through twelfth graders reveal that new immigrants are just as likely as any of their contemporaries to embrace core American political values and to engage in volunteerism. Further, once socioeconomic differences are taken into account, immigrant youth are as likely, or almost as likely, as their native-born peers to be engaged in most conventional forms of civic participation.[12]

Social Class and Civic Participation
The long-recognized and stubborn relationship in the United States between social class and political participation has been referred to as the "best-documented finding in American political behavior research."[13] The class divide in political participation takes many forms. The self-reported volunteering rate is 25 percent for young adults (ages eighteen to twenty-nine) who have attended college even briefly, but only 11

percent for those who have never attended college—about half the youth population.[14] In 2008, the voter turnout rate for young people without college experience was 36 percent, compared with 62 percent for those with college experience.[15] These gaps tend to be larger in the United States than in many European nations, where labor unions play a major role in political recruitment. Trends over the past several decades suggest that the U.S. class divide in civic participation has widened (although the verdict is still out).

Young people are most likely to become civically engaged when they are in settings, such as faith-based institutions, workplaces, schools, and community organizations, where they become knowledgeable about issues and about how to take action on them, where they are asked by someone to join an organization or attend a meeting, or where normative pressures encourage them to participate in civic affairs.[16] Young adults from advantaged and disadvantaged backgrounds, however, do not have equal access to such opportunities.

Inequalities in political participation among young Americans are rooted in the differing education and political involvement of their parents. Parents of high socioeconomic status pass on to their children such advantages as political awareness, access to community and educational resources, and, ultimately, the child's own educational attainment. Parental education is a more powerful predictor of a young adult child's voting than is parental profession or income, though, not surprisingly, its influence diminishes over time as a child's adult roles and the normative pressures associated with them begin to shape habits of civic participation. Voting in young adulthood entails certain "costs," such as learning about political parties and about the registration and voting process; in addition, peers of

young adults are more likely to be non-voters. Having better educated parents overcomes many of these costs and also increases normative pressures to be engaged.[17]

The class divide in civic participation is thus attributable, in part, to cumulative disadvantage over the course of childhood and adolescence. But it also results from a lack of institutional opportunities for civic activities for young adults who do not attend college. In years past, non-college-bound youth had alternative sites for civic learning and recruitment. During the 1970s, for example, almost 14 percent of young adults without college experience belonged to unions, which promoted voting, leadership skills, and issue discussion among their members. And about 40 percent of young adults who had not gone to college attended weekly religious services, where they could be recruited for civic and political activities and consequently develop civic and organizational skills. More than two-thirds of this group also read a newspaper at least a "few times" a week to keep up with social issues and civic affairs. Today, however, according to the self-reports of eighteen- to twenty-nine-year-olds who have not attended college, union membership has dropped by more than half (to just 6 percent), newspaper readership is down by more than one-third (to 45 percent), and regular religious attendance is down 5 points to about 41 percent.[18] These forms of engagement have declined for college-educated young people as well, but their situation is less isolating. Not only do they have college itself as a civic opportunity, but the alternative institutions appear to serve them better. They are, for example, more likely to belong to unions than their non-college-educated contemporaries. Thus even institutions traditionally understood as resources for the working class are now more likely to serve young members of the middle class.

The importance of "being there" in institutional settings (such as school or work) where one can be recruited into civic activities is illustrated by estimates by the Independent Sector that 71 percent of volunteers and 61 percent of charitable contributors take part in these activities at someone's request.[19] A disconcerting report by Child Trends reveals that many of the nation's young adults aged eighteen to twenty-four have no access to such settings: about 14 percent are not in school or the military, have no degree beyond high school, and are not in the work force. And that share has been growing.[20] Community-based programs like City Year provide one alternative institutional setting for youth who are not going to college, but funding for these programs falls far short of their needs.

Students' engagement in extracurricular activities in high school and their feelings of social connectedness to community institutions predict voting and other forms of civic engagement in young adulthood.

Inequalities before the Transition to Adulthood

The civic skills, habits, and motivations of young adults result, in part, from the accumulation of engagement opportunities in the child and adolescent years. Long-term studies have shown that, controlling for background factors, both students' engagement in extracurricular activities in high school and their feelings of social connectedness to community institutions predict voting and other forms of civic engagement in young adulthood.[21] Social incorporation into the body politic begins in the formative years through the opportunities that children and teens have as members of local organizations, exercising the rights and assuming the responsibilities associated with membership. In short, becoming a stakeholder in one's society develops through the accumulated opportunities to be involved in groups that build civic identities and skills.

Social class disparities in civic participation that begin in the pre-adult years are exacerbated by unequal opportunities for gaining civic practice. Schools with more privileged student bodies, for example, provide more and better opportunities. Civic opportunity disparities also exist within schools; a student's race or family background makes it more or less likely that he will engage in civically relevant activities such as studying the Constitution and engaging in mock trials or in community voluntary service.[22] Besides disparities in opportunities between and within schools, providing civic practice for children growing up in disadvantaged communities offers numerous challenges. For example, many volunteering and civic engagement opportunities take place in the context of community-based youth organizations. Those groups rely on adult volunteers to carry out programming, making it difficult for some low-income communities with very high ratios of children to adults to muster enough adult volunteers.[23]

Two specific events during a young person's life are associated with reduced rates of adult civic engagement: dropping out of high school and being arrested. Long-term studies following eighth graders into early adulthood show that, controlling for the effects of growing up in disadvantaged families and neighborhoods, dropping out of high school decreases voting turnout by 19 percent for whites, 11 percent for blacks, and 10 percent for Hispanics. Youths' reports of being arrested in the tenth or twelfth grade reduced voter turnout by 7 percent for whites and 21 percent for blacks.[24]

A felony conviction is a profound barrier to civic engagement. Current prisoners or former felons (or both) are forbidden to vote in forty-eight states, to hold public office in forty states, and to serve on juries in forty-seven states. Some "five million citizens—mostly poor people and people of color—… are currently locked out of the democratic process."[25] Not all of the five million are young adults, but felons and former felons are predominantly young, male, poor, and unsuccessful in school. Although the argument for not allowing felons who are in prison to vote is clear, the rationale for continuing to disenfranchise former felons who have served their time and paid their debt to society and who are now attempting to reintegrate into community life raises more difficult questions for society. Christopher Uggen and Sara Wakefield found that former felons "viewed disenfranchisement as a clear indicator that they were unwanted or unaccepted as full citizens in their communities"—a message that "may inhibit the assumption of other adult roles and undermine the reintegrative goal of encouraging offenders to empathize with or identify with other citizens."[26]

Institutionalized Opportunities for Civic Engagement

Several leading American institutions already engage substantial numbers of people under the age of thirty in civic activities. These settings, though, could provide more effective

and equitable civic opportunities. We explore the most common forms of institutionalized engagement in the following sections.

Community Volunteer Work

Organized volunteering activities—typically arranged by schools, colleges, religious congregations, or nonprofit organizations—represent common institutionally supported opportunities for civic engagement and learning. Today's young adults grew up during a period when community service was becoming almost a normal part of growing up. Since the early 1990s, a steadily increasing number of middle and, especially, high schools have been offering some type of community service or service-learning courses as an option or, in some cases, a mandate for high school graduation. Trends in the Monitoring the Future study of high school seniors show that volunteering in the community has become more common. Between 1976 and 1990, rates were fairly steady, with 22 percent of young people reporting that they had participated in community affairs or volunteer work at least once or twice a month or more. Between 1990 and 2000 there was a steady increase, with 35 percent in 2000 reporting such involvement, and the trend has held steady since that time.[27]

According to the Corporation for National and Community Service's national study of public school principals, between 1999 and 2008 the share of middle and high schools offering opportunities for students to serve rose from 64 to 68 percent, with the share of high schools growing from 83 to 86 percent. Schools in low-income areas, however, were 26 percent less likely to have opportunities for service learning.[28]

Adolescents also get engaged in community service through community-based youth organizations and religious congregations. According to a national survey of youth aged twelve to eighteen, those who regularly attend religious services are nearly twice as likely to volunteer as are those who never attend services. Of the 49 percent who attend weekly services, 64 percent report that they regularly volunteer in their community, although not necessarily with their congregation. The religious congregation is the main avenue through which youth from disadvantaged backgrounds volunteer.[29]

Colleges and universities are also offering more opportunities for, and expecting more students to engage in, community volunteer work. A comparison of a large student cohort attending more than a hundred universities between 1985 and 1989 and another cohort attending those same universities between 1994 and 1998 showed substantial increases in community service across time.[30] Population-based studies of American adults also show that the share of college students who have done some kind of volunteer work rose from 27.1 percent in 2002 to 30.2 percent in 2005, surpassing the 28.8 percent rate for the general adult population.[31]

Although only 11 percent of non-college young adults reported volunteering in 2008, that figure nevertheless represents millions of volunteers, most of whom served through institutions. Thirty-seven percent of young-adult volunteers without college experience reported serving through churches or other religious congregations; 27 percent, through children's educational, sports, or recreational programs. In both cases, volunteers without college experience were more likely than their college-educated peers to have named these organizations as their main site of volunteering. About half of non-college youth who volunteered reported being asked

to serve by someone in the organization.[32] Although institutionalized opportunities for community service are fairly rare for young adults who do not attend college, about 5 percent of this population reports serving as a result of being recruited by someone in a service organization. This institutional infrastructure could be expanded.

The benefits to the volunteer in terms of motivations and skills depend on the quality of the service project itself. But some evidence suggests that engaging in volunteer work generally during the high school years causes young people to pause and reconsider their vocational priorities. For example, one panel study of a representative community sample found that taking part in community service strengthens intrinsic work values, leads youth to rethink their vocational priorities, and encourages a less individualistic focus on careers.[33] The potential civic benefits of time spent in community work during the late adolescent and young-adult years may be especially important because trends over the past three decades indicate that youth may be adapting to an unpredictable labor market by considering stable paid work less central to their identities.[34] As the transition to adulthood lengthens, community volunteer work may allow youth to become more relaxed about finding the "right job," at least "right away," and may help them to reevaluate what they are looking for in a job.

Youth Organizing and Activism Projects

Over the past twenty years, scholars have begun paying closer attention to youth organizing and activism projects.

Activism as a form of civic engagement is distinct from service or volunteer work and from political advocacy on behalf of youth in that young activists themselves define the political targets and lead the projects. Adults are involved as partners and train the younger generation in community organizing, analyzing power, developing skills, and devising strategies for institutional change. But the young people are the agents of change. And, typically, youth organizing and activism attract young people in marginalized communities who, collectively, are addressing issues that concern them. Prominent themes in youth activist projects include reform of public education and the poor quality of urban schools, community development projects to include marginalized youth and challenge gentrification, the criminal justice system, police brutality and racial profiling, and gender and sexual equality.

Youth activism also differs from service-learning and mainstream youth development programs in that it empowers young people to redress perceived injustice rather than to provide a community service. The model borrows heavily from community organizing, typically involves a critical analysis of social, political, and economic power, and emphasizes collective concerns identified by and actions led by young people to improve their everyday lives. Many projects draw from youth culture and educate the young people about the history of civil rights activism of their racial/ethnic group.

Both the practice and the study of youth organizing and activism have grown over the past several decades and focus on issues of school reform, incarceration, and community safety. Youth activism offers unique opportunities for political growth for youth whose interests and needs are too often marginalized by traditional youth organizations.[35] According to a two-year study of twelve community organizations—as part of the Youth Leadership for Development Initiative

of the Ford Foundation—activism tends to engage late adolescents and young adults, reframes "personal" problems of everyday life into "political" issues shared by a community, and provides challenge, leadership, and personal support comparable to or greater than that provided by conventional youth organizations.[36]

Higher Education

As noted, young adults with college experience are much more civically engaged than their peers who do not attend college. This gap reflects the differing advantages and opportunities that accumulate from childhood on, but colleges and universities also directly strengthen the civic skills, motivations, and knowledge of their students through the courses and extracurricular opportunities that they offer. After all, the mission statements of most colleges and universities contain some reference to the civic preparation of younger generations.

Higher education is increasingly committed to a civic mission. One form that commitment takes is organized volunteering, already mentioned above, but it also includes community-based research, durable partnerships between colleges or universities and nearby community organizations, political discussion and debate on campus, courses that impart civic skills, student-produced news media, internships and study-abroad opportunities, and events and exhibitions meant to serve communities. Among the groups endorsing a broad civic mission are Campus Compact (a consortium of more than one thousand colleges and universities that have adopted principles of civic engagement), the American Association of State Colleges and Universities' American Democracy Project, the Association of American Colleges and Universities' Core Commitments program, and the American Association of State Colleges and Universities' Civic Indicators project, to name a few. Likewise, over the past several decades, higher education has moved toward a public and outreach scholarship model of undergraduate education, one that integrates public and civic issues with courses in an undergraduate major. As the transition to adulthood grows more protracted, this model of higher education may offer psychological benefits by helping students find purpose in roles other than the (often unpredictable) world of work and by helping them see that citizenship is not a part-time enterprise.[37]

Several of the forms of civic education offered on campuses have not been evaluated for their impact on students. But research does show that engaging in diversity workshops and socializing with diverse groups of peers, discussing social and political issues with fellow students, joining student organizations, and participating in learning communities and collaborative learning strengthen students' community orientation and commitments.[38] Service-learning courses that tie service to course content support students' commitment to social activism, their awareness of social and economic inequality and systemic causes of those inequities, and their personal feelings of social responsibility. In-depth studies using long-term data show that ambitious courses in which students analyze and address social problems increase civic knowledge and narrow gaps in civic engagement among students.[39]

The opportunities colleges offer for civic learning vary widely, with most of the variations reflecting differences in endowments and prestige. A study of 400 randomly recruited undergraduates at Ivy League universities, flagship state universities, and selective liberal arts colleges found student experiences with civic engagement virtually universal and popular. By contrast, at non-selective public universities and poorly endowed private colleges, many students reported no civic engagement and low efficacy.[40]

The most affordable, most accessible, and most egalitarian institutions of higher education in the nation are community colleges. In 2005, these two-year colleges enrolled nearly 40 percent of all college students, including more than half of all minority and first-generation college students. Rough estimates are that 80 percent of community college students are the first in their families to attend college. Community colleges serve a far more diverse population than do four-year colleges. According to the American Association of Community Colleges, minority students account for 30 percent of enrollment. English as a Second Language courses are typical, reflecting the recent immigrant status of many of their students. Community colleges are thus a key institutional setting for recruiting into political life members of groups who now participate at lower levels.

Long-term analyses following eighth graders into young adulthood find very significant effects of attending two-year colleges on voting. According to Juliana Pacheco and Eric Plutzer, full-time enrollment in a four-year college would increase voting rates by 10 percent for whites, 10 percent for blacks, and 14 percent for Hispanics. But for African Americans, attending a two-year college half time would increase voting rates more than attending a four-year school full time.[41] A recent experimental study in Louisiana described in more detail in the article by Tom Brock in this volume provides a clue to potential mechanisms. This incentive scholarship program combined with counseling for low-income, largely African American mothers in their mid-twenties raised the likelihood of registering to vote and of donating time or money to a political campaign. Students improved their course attendance and earned more credits; they also enjoyed other psychosocial benefits, such as feeling able to set and pursue personal goals, feeling a sense of purpose in life, and feeling that they have something positive to contribute.[42]

Community colleges are a key institutional setting for recruiting into political life members of groups who now participate at lower levels.

The Military

Given its potential personal costs, some would argue that military service is the highest form of civic engagement. Patriotism ranks high among the reasons recruits give for signing up, and time in the military may further imbue them with an ethic of civic participation and provide skills that can be used in peacetime service at home.

Studies indicate that, with the possible exception of veterans from the war in Vietnam, veterans are more likely than non-veterans to vote. Analyses of the 2005 Current Population Survey show that volunteering is higher among African American and Hispanic veterans than among the general public, but not among veterans overall.[43] Of those veterans who have served since the terrorist attacks on September 11, 2001, on New York and

Washington, 25.1 percent reported volunteering in the United States in 2008.[44] Military training emphasizes group solidarity and works to overcome inter-group hostilities.

Military service in foreign wars since 2001 has provided both opportunities and challenges for the civic engagement of those who served. On one hand, the usual civic benefits of military service (such as socialization into norms of service and solidarity, and experiences of diversity) apply; and some military personnel abroad were involved in activities like planning reconstruction and relief programs and canvassing residents' needs that could provide useful civic skills back home. Veterans of the wars in Iraq and Afghanistan who spent most of their time on planning and reconstruction were slightly more likely to volunteer back home than those who took part in combat or medical assistance. They were especially involved with serving military families upon return.[45]

On the other hand, many returning veterans suffer from trauma or otherwise face challenges in reintegrating with civic communities. Veterans under the age of thirty are having a more difficult time transitioning back to civilian life than those who are thirty and older; 46.5 percent of veterans aged twenty-nine and younger agree or strongly agree that their transition is going well, as compared with 57 percent of veterans thirty and older. Younger veterans are slightly less likely than older veterans to have volunteered in civilian contexts.

Sources of support and civic incorporation for returning veterans include veterans' organizations and the military itself. More than half of current volunteering veterans have been asked to serve by a veterans' organization, and 78 percent of those who had been asked to serve by a veterans' organization have volunteered since their return.[46]

AmeriCorps Programs

AmeriCorps, created in 1993, is a federal funding stream for several large programs, including City Year, whose members devote a year to service through local community organizations and institutions. Participants, the vast majority of whom are under age thirty, provide service in exchange for a modest living stipend (enough to cover living expenses for most participants) and an educational award.

The intersection of developmental timing and institutional opportunities for service is evidenced by the upticks in program enrollment at ages eighteen and twenty-two, when youth typically finish high school or college. Contrary to popular stereotypes of corps members as college graduates, a sizable number of AmeriCorps members come from disadvantaged backgrounds: 36 percent of participants report having received public assistance or lived in public housing before their service work, indicating that national programs can provide opportunities for disadvantaged youth to connect with their communities. More analyses are needed, but AmeriCorps may be one route through which youth from disadvantaged circumstances can be empowered to improve their own lives through education and training and to improve their communities through their service work.

Does a year of service in AmeriCorps programs have civic benefit? A recent study by the Corporation for National and Community Service compared AmeriCorps participants with individuals who looked into but did not enroll in AmeriCorps and followed the two groups for eight years.[47] Findings from the study are suggestive, not definitive, because the groups were not randomly assigned and the comparison group inquired about AmeriCorps but ultimately did not apply. The comparison group may have had alternative options that they pursued or the motivations of the two groups may have differed, or both.

AmeriCorps may be one route through which youth from disadvantaged circumstances can be empowered to improve their own lives through education and training and to improve their communities through their service work.

Nonetheless, the study identified several differences in civic involvement between the groups eight years after baseline. AmeriCorps participants felt more connected to their communities, had more identification with and understanding of problems within their communities, were more confident in their ability to work with the local government and lead a community-based movement, and participated more in community affairs. They were also more likely to be working in the public sector after completing their service, and they reported higher life satisfaction. Even eight years after joining the program, the civic outcomes of the AmeriCorps program persisted. Furthermore, subgroup analyses revealed that ethnic minority corps members and those from disadvantaged backgrounds were more likely than their counterparts in the comparison group to be in careers in public service or the public sector. Other work shows positive relationships between civic engagement and educational gains for youth in both the program and comparison groups. An evaluation of Youth Corps has also identified civic benefits for African American men. Besides positive benefits in education and employment, the evaluation also found increases in social and personal responsibility and in intentions to vote. Connecting with a supportive, caring adult and with better-educated individuals were among the explanations offered for the effects.[48]

The Internet

The National Conference on Citizenship's 2008 Civic Health Index survey revealed gaps in civic engagement between young adults with and without college experience. Gaps in certain forms of *online* engagement, however, were smaller. For example, 57 percent of young adults with college experience, and 52 percent of young adults without college experience, said that they had used social networking sites such as MySpace or Facebook to address social issues.[49] On six measures of online engagement, college youth were ahead of non-college youth, but these gaps were notably smaller than the gaps in traditional forms of engagement that were observed in the same survey.

According to the Civic Health Index, non-college youth who used various types of digital media (such as e-mail, Facebook or MySpace, posting videos online, text messaging other people, or watching a video of a presidential candidate) were between 10 and 40 percent more likely to volunteer than non-college youth who did not use these media.[50] To be sure, this correlation does not show that digital media cause volunteering rates to rise. But future research should investigate the potential of digital media to engage young people. In principle, the new

electronic media have several advantages. Barriers to entry are low, communities of interest are diverse and numerous, and peers can recruit one another for political or service activities even if they are physically dispersed.

Conclusion and Directions for Policy

Civic engagement of young adults is important both for the functioning of a democratic society and for individual development. As generational replacement theories suggest, democracies depend on the social integration of successive younger generations into the body politic. For individual youth, civic engagement fulfills a need to belong and provides opportunities to work in concert with fellow citizens to realize shared ends. Through civic activities young generations come to appreciate their identities as members of the public. New generations get recruited into civic life by being in settings that offer opportunities to get engaged, to develop civic competencies, and to connect their lives with the lot of others.

But opportunities for civic engagement are not evenly distributed by social class or by racial and ethnic group, and wide disparities in political participation exist. As the transition to adulthood has lengthened, four-year colleges have become perhaps the central institution for civic incorporation of younger generations. They are heavily subsidized by public dollars, and no comparable institution exists for young adults who complete their education with a high school diploma or less. Institutions, such as unions, that once attempted to involve these youth in public affairs have diminished in reach.

Opportunities for sustained engagement by programs such as City Year could provide an alternative developmental path during the prolonged transition to adulthood. When youth aged eighteen to twenty-five are asked what it means to them to be an adult, they cite responsibility for one's actions and awareness of others.[51] Their journey into adulthood could be more meaningful if society were to provide institutional opportunities for responsible civic engagement. Such opportunities could also compensate for the lack of occupational outlets, especially for forming careers, that many young adults face today.

Opportunities for sustained community engagement also could provide new norms or markers of mature adult behavior that young adults could use as a gauge for their own maturation. (Even without a steady job or life partner, it is still possible to be a responsible and committed member of one's community.) Society could also use civic activity as a new benchmark for assessing how this age group is faring. Finally, such "sustained civic activity" programs could be a new institutional model that would enable young adults from disadvantaged families to stay connected to mainstream opportunities and to adults who could mentor and guide their way.

The Edward M. Kennedy Serve America Act (P.L. 111–13), signed by President Barack Obama in April 2009, responds to several issues concerning civic engagement and the prolonged transition to adulthood. First, it increases the number of slots in AmeriCorps programs and adds new corps to address America's most pressing needs in health care, education, the environment, emergency preparedness, and public service. These new opportunities will enable corps members to work on civic issues and, at the same time, explore career options in expanding occupations. A year in an AmeriCorps program could become a pathway into adulthood and transform the episodic style of much of the

current youth engagement into a more sustained form.

Second, the legislation adds flexibility to ways that young people can get engaged in service and so is attuned to the balancing act that characterizes young adulthood today. For example, the National Civilian Conservation Corps will now have a non-residential component, which means that youth could focus on such things as disaster relief or energy conservation in the community where they grew up and still rely on the support of family and friends. Third, the education award, which has been a key element of AmeriCorps, is increased to $5,350 (the amount of Pell grants) and can be applied to a wider range of institutions. Although the award remains small compared with the rising costs of education, these changes should make the program more attractive to youth at different stages in their educational career.

Fourth, and perhaps most important in our view, is that the legislation not only targets the needs of low-income communities but also makes the inclusion of marginalized youth a priority. For example, at least 50 percent of the participants in the National Civilian Conservation Corps must be youth from economically disadvantaged backgrounds (including youth in foster care) or represent the ethnic diversity of America. With respect to K–12 service learning, the law encourages a semester of service in high school, urges schools to tie service to local community needs, and also extends to sixth to twelfth graders the opportunity to earn income for a summer of community service. Although these efforts would hardly put a dent in the cumulative disadvantage that leads to inequalities in civic participation, they are steps in the right direction.

Accountability and innovation are integral to the goal of building the nation's volunteer infrastructure. Toward this end, the law includes a ten-year study of the benefits of service learning and directs the Census Bureau to conduct a national Civic Health Index. The law also includes capacity building for nonprofits, a social innovation fund, and training and technical assistance, especially for programs that mix youth with older adults.

The Kennedy Act represents an important investment but could be improved in several ways in the future. It forbids corps members from engaging in political activity of any sort. Thus, youth who become engaged in sustained efforts to address national needs as outlined in the legislation (safeguarding the environment, strengthening schools, improving health care in low-income communities) may not use the knowledge and experience gained in their service to work for policies that could potentially improve the very problems they are addressing in their volunteer service.

Further, the legislation provides nothing like a common curriculum or set of learning standards and objectives for AmeriCorps programs. The emphasis is on generating service hours and addressing social problems, but not making sure that participants obtain any specified set of civic skills or motivations. AmeriCorps would be more effective as a tool for civic engagement if, like the Civilian Conservation Corps of the 1930s, it aimed to teach democratic skills and was assessed on those terms.[52]

Overall, the evidence supports providing alternative civic learning opportunities for young adults not in college. AmeriCorps, especially if modified to become more educative and more open to politics, would be an important step, but would by no means suffice to close the civic engagement gap or to reverse declines since the 1970s.

Endnotes

1. Constance Flanagan and Lonnie R. Sherrod, "Youth Political Development: An Introduction," *Journal of Social Issues* 54, no. 3 (1998): 447–56; David O. Sears and Sheri Levy, "Childhood and Adult Political Development," in the *Oxford Handbook of Political Pyschology*, edited by David Sears, Leonie Huddy, and Robert Jervis (Oxford University Press, 2003), pp. 60–109; and Richard Niemi and Mary Hepburn, "The Rebirth of Political Socialization," *Perspectives on Political Science* 24 (1995): 7–16.

2. Donald Kinder, "Politics and the Life Cycle," *Science* 312 (2006): 1905–08; M. Kent Jennings and Laura Stoker, "Social Trust and Civic Engagement across Time and Generations," *Acta Politica* 39 (2004): 342–79; and U.S. Bureau of the Census, *Voting and Registration in the Election of November 2000* (Washington: U.S. Bureau of the Census, 2002).

3. Constance A. Flanagan, Peter Levine, and Richard Settersten, *Civic Engagement and the Changing Transition to Adulthood*, CIRCLE monograph, January 2009, using General Social Survey (GSS) for trust, group membership, religious attendance, union membership, and reading newspapers. Self-reported voting and being contacted by a party come from the American National Election Study. Volunteering, working on a community project, and attending club meetings come from the DDB Life Styles Surveys.

4. Census Current Population Voting Supplements, 1972–2006, tabulated by CIRCLE (The Center for Information and Research on Civic Learning and Engagement).

5. Dietlind Stolle in collaboration with Michele Micheletti and Marc Hooghe, "Reconceptualization of Political Participation and Responsibility-Taking," in *Youth Civic Engagement: An Institutional Turn*, edited by Peter Levine and James Youniss, CIRCLE Working Paper 45 (2006), pp. 44–46, www.civicyouth.org; and Pippa Norris, ed., *Critical Citizens: Global Support for Democratic Governance* (Oxford University Press, 1999).

6. David T. Z. Mindich, *Tuned Out: Why Americans under 40 Don't Follow the News* (Oxford University Press, 2005).

7. Laine Briddell and others, *Role Transitions and Social Trust: A Study of Late Adolescence*, paper presented at the Society for Research on Child Development meetings, Denver, Colo., April 2009.

8. Jennings and Stoker, "Social Trust and Civic Engagement" (see note 2).

9. Donald J. Hernandez, Nancy A. Denton, and Suzanne E. Macartney, "Children in Immigrant Families: Key to America's Future," *Society for Research in Child Development Social Policy Report* 22, no. 3 (2008).

10. Mark Hugo Lopez and others, *The 2006 Civic and Political Health of the Nation: A Detailed Look at How Youth Participate in Politics and Communities*, CIRCLE monograph, www.civicyouth.org.

11. Roberto G. Gonzales, "Born in the Shadows: The Uncertain Futures of the Children of Unauthorized Mexican Migrants" Ph.D. dissertation, Department of Sociology, University of California–Irvine, 2008; and Hinda Seif, "The Civic Education and Engagement of Latina/o Immigrant Youth: Challenging Boundaries and Creating Safe Spaces," in *Handbook of Research on Civic Engagement in Youth*, edited by Lonnie Sherrod and others (Hoboken, N.J.: Wiley, forthcoming).

12. Mark Hugo Lopez and Karlo Barrios Marcelo, "The Civic Engagement of Immigrant Youth: New Evidence from the 2006 Civic and Political Health of the Nation Survey," *Applied Developmental Science* 12, no. 2

(2008): 66–73; Carola Suárez-Orozco, Marcelo M. Suárez-Orozco, and Irina Todorova, *Learning a New Land: Immigrant Students in American Society* (Cambridge, Mass.: Harvard University Press, 2008); and Kei Kawashima-Ginsberg and Emily Hoban Kirby, "Volunteering among Youth of Immigrant Origin," CIRCLE Fact Sheet, July 2009, www.civicyouth.org.

13. Norman H. Nie, Jane Junn, and Kenneth Stehlik-Barry, *Education and Democratic Citizenship in America* (University of Chicago Press, 1996), p. 31.

14. Emily Hoban Kirby, Karlo Barrios Marcelo, and Kei Kawashima-Ginsberg, "Volunteering and College Experience," CIRCLE Fact Sheet, August 2009, www.civicyouth.org.

15. Emily Hoban Kirby and Kei Kawashima-Ginsberg, "The Youth Vote in 2008," CIRCLE Fact Sheet, June 2009, www.civicyouth.org.

16. Sidney Verba, Kay Lehman Schlozman, and Henry Brady, *Voice and Equality: Civic Voluntarism in American Politics* (Harvard University Press, 1995).

17. Eric Plutzer, "Becoming a Habitual Voter: Inertia, Resources, and Growth in Young Adulthood," *American Political Science Review* 96, no. 1 (2002): 41–56; Sidney Verba, Nancy Burns, and Kay Lehman Schlozman, "Unequal at the Starting Line: Creating Participatory Inequalities across Generations and among Groups," *American Sociologist* 34, no. 1–2 (2003): 45–69.

18. General Social Survey data, aggregated from the surveys of 1972, 1973, 1974, 1975, 1976, 1977, 1978, 2000, 2002, 2004, and 2006.

19. Verba, Schlozman, and Brady, *Voice and Equality* (see note 16).

20. Susan Jekielek and Brett Brown, *The Transition to Adulthood: Characteristics of Young Adults Ages 18 to 24 in America* (Washington: Child Trends, 2005).

21. Daniel A. McFarland and R. Jack Thomas, "Bowling Young: How Youth Voluntary Associations Influence Adult Political Participation," *American Sociological Review* 71, no. 3 (2006): 401–25; Naomi Duke and others, "From Adolescent Connections to Social Capital: Predictors of Civic Engagement in Young Adulthood," *Journal of Adolescent Health* 44, no. 2 (2009): 161–68; and Elizabeth S. Smith, "Effects of Investment in the Social Capital of Youth on Political and Civic Behavior in Young Adulthood: A Longitudinal Analysis," *Political Psychology* 20, no. 3 (1999): 553–80.

22. Joseph E. Kahne and Ellen Middaugh, "Democracy for Some: The Civic Opportunity Gap in High School," in *Policies for Youth Civic Engagement*, edited by James Youniss and Peter Levine (Vanderbilt University Press, 2009), pp. 29–58.

23. Daniel Hart and Robert Atkins, "Civic Competence in Urban Youth," *Applied Developmental Science* 6 (2002): 227–36.

24. Julianna Sandell Pacheco and Eric Plutzer, "Political Participation and Cumulative Disadvantage: The Impact of Economic and Social Hardship on Young Citizens," *Journal of Social Issues* 64 (2008): 571–93.

25. Christopher Uggen, Jeff Manza, and Melissa Thompson, "Citizenship, Democracy, and the Civic Reintegration of Criminal Offenders," *The ANNALS of the American Academy of Political and Social Science* 605 (2006): 297–98.

26. Christopher Uggen and Sara Wakefield, "Young Adults Reentering the Community from the Criminal Justice System: The Challenge of Becoming an Adult," *On Your Own without a Net: The Transition to Adulthood for Vulnerable Populations*, edited by D. Wayne Osgood and others (Chicago: University of Chicago Press, 2007), pp. 132–33.

27 Amy Syvertsen and others, "Thirty-Year Trends in American Adolescents' Civic Engagement: A Story of Changing Participation and Educational Differences," manuscript under review.

28. Corporation for National and Community Service, Office of Research and Policy Development, *Community Service and Service-Learning in America's Schools, 2008* (Washington: 2008).

29. Corporation for National and Community Service, *Building Active Citizens: The Role of Social Institutions in Teen Volunteering*, Brief 1 in the Youth Helping America Series (Washington: 2005).

30. Alexander W. Astin, Jennifer R. Keup, and Jennifer A. Lindholm, "A Decade of Change in Undergraduate Education: A National Study of System 'Transformation,'" *Review of Higher Education* 25, no. 2 (2002): 141–62.

31. Corporation for National and Community Service, *College Students Helping America,* Research Report (Washington: Corporation for National and Community Service, 2006).

32. Kirby, Marcelo, and Kawashima-Ginsberg, "Volunteering and College Experience" (see note 14), pp. 4–6.

33. Monica Kirkpatrick Johnson and others, "Volunteerism in Adolescence: A Process Perspective," *Journal of Research on Adolescence* 8 (1998): 309–32.

34. Laura Wray-Lake and others, "Exploring the Meaning of Work for High School Seniors from 1976 to 2005" *Youth & Society* (forthcoming).

35. Daniel Hart and Ben Kirshner, "Civic Participation and Development in Urban Adolescents," in *Engaging Young People in Civic Life*, edited by James Youniss and Peter Levine (Vanderbilt University Press, 2009), pp. 102–20; Shawn Ginwright, *Black Youth Rising: Activism and Radical Healing in Urban America* (Teachers College Press, 2009).

36. Heather Lewis-Charp and others, *Extending the Reach of Youth Development through Civic Activism: Outcomes of the Youth Leadership for Development Initiative* (Social Policy Research Associates, 2003); Hart and Kirshner, "Civic Participation and Development in Urban Adolescents" (see note 35), pp. 102–20.

37. Ann Colby and others, *Educating Citizens: Preparing America's Undergraduates for Lives of Moral and Civic Responsibility* (San Francisco: Jossey-Bass, 2003); and Constance Flanagan, "Public Scholarship and Youth at the Transition to Adulthood," *New Directions for Teaching and Learning* 105 (San Francisco: Jossey-Bass, 2006).

38. For evaluations with control groups, see, for example, Ratnesh Biren and others, "Evaluating Intergroup Dialogue: Engaging Diversity for Personal and Social Responsibility," *Diversity & Democracy* 12, no. 1 (January 2009); Kary Harriger and Jill J. McMillan, *Speaking of Politics: Preparing College Students for Democratic Citizenship through Deliberative Dialogue* (Dayton, Ohio: Kettering Foundation Press, 2007); and Greg Markus, J. Howard, and D. King, "Integrating Community Service and Classroom Instruction Enhances Learning: Results from an Experiment," *Educational Evaluation and Policy Analysis* 15 (1993): 410–19.

39. Elizabeth Beaumont, Thomas Ehrlich, and Josh Corngold, *Educating for Democracy: Preparing Undergraduates for Responsible Political Engagement* (San Francisco: Jossey-Bass, 2007).

40. Abby Kiesa, Alexander P. Orlowski, and others, *College Students Talk Politics: A Study of College Student Civic Engagement*, CIRCLE monograph, 2007, www.civicyouth.org.

41. Pacheco and Plutzer, "Political Participation and Cumulative Disadvantage" (see note 24).

42. Lashawn Richburg-Hayes and others, *Rewarding Persistence: Effects of a Performance-Based Scholarship Program for Low-Income Parents* (New York: MDRC, January 2009). See page 124 of this volume for Thomas Brock's description of the program.

43. D. L. Leal, "It's Not Just a Job: Military Service and Latino Political Participation," in *Political Behavior* 21, no. 2 (1999): 153–74; Charles C. Moskos and J. S. Butler, *All That We Can Be: Black Leadership and Racial Integration in the Army Way* (New York: Basic Books, 1996); Rebecca Nesbit and David A. Reingold, "Soldiers to Citizens: The Link between Miliary Service and Volunteering" paper presented at the Minnowbrook III research conference, September 5–7, 2008; and Jeremy M. Teigen, "Enduring Effects of the Uniform: Previous Military Experience and Voting Turnout," *Political Research Quarterly* 59 (2006): 601–07.

44. Kei Kawashima-Ginsberg, Surbhi Godsay, and Amanda Nover, "Volunteering and Civic Engagement among Veterans," CIRCLE Fact Sheet, July 2009, www.civicyouth.org.

45. Ibid. Using data from a 2009 Civic Enterprises survey of returning veterans. The sample was constructed using a snowball strategy (non-random) and then weighted to reflect national data.

46. Ibid.

47. Corporation for National and Community Service, *Still Serving: Measuring the Eight-Year Impact of AmeriCorps on Alumni* (Washington: Corporation for National and Community Service, 2008).

48. JoAnn Jastrzab and others, *Youth Corps: Promising Strategies for Young People and Their Communities*, no. 1-97 (Cambridge, Mass.: Abt Associates Inc., 1999); Susan Jekielek, Stephanie Cochran, and Elizabeth Hair, *Employment Programs and Youth Development: A Synthesis*, no. 1-82 (Washington: Child Trends, 2002); and Andrea Finlay and Constance Flanagan, "Making Educational Progress: Links to Civic Engagement during the Transition to Adulthood," CIRCLE Working Paper 67, www.civicyouth.org.

49. National Conference on Citizenship, "2008 Civic Health Index: Beyond the Vote," www.ncoc.net.

50. Kirby, Marcelo, and Kawashima-Ginsberg, "Volunteering and College Experience" (see note 14), pp. 7–8.

51. Jeffrey J. Arnett, *Emerging Adulthood: The Winding Road from the Late Teens through the Twenties* (Oxford University Press, 2004).

52. Melissa Bass, "Civic Education through National Service: Lessons from American History," CIRCLE Working Paper 12, March 2004, www.civicyouth.org.

The Military and the Transition to Adulthood

Ryan Kelty, Meredith Kleykamp, and David R. Segal

Summary

Ryan Kelty, Meredith Kleykamp, and David Segal examine the effect of military service on the transition to adulthood. They highlight changes since World War II in the role of the military in the lives of young adults, focusing especially on how the move from a conscription to an all-volunteer military has changed the way military service affects youths' approach to adult responsibilities.

The authors note that today's all-volunteer military is both career-oriented and family-oriented, and they show how the material and social support the military provides to young servicemen and women promotes responsible membership in family relationships and the wider community. As a result, they argue, the transition to adulthood, including economic independence from parents, is more stable and orderly for military personnel than for their civilian peers. At the same time, they stress that serving in the military in a time of war holds dangers for young adults.

The authors examine four broad areas of military service, focusing in each on how men and women in uniform today make the transition to adulthood. They begin by looking at the social characteristics of those who serve, especially at differences in access to the military and its benefits by socio-demographic characteristics, such as age, gender, race and ethnicity, social class, and sexual orientation.

Military service also has important effects on family formation, including the timing of marriage and parenthood, family structure, and the influence of military culture on families. Family formation among servicemen and women, the authors observe, is earlier and more stable than among civilians of the same age. The authors then consider the educational and employment consequences of service. Finally, they scrutinize the dangers of military service during times of war and examine the physical and psychological effects of wartime military service. They also note the sexual trauma endured both by male and female military personnel and the physical and symbolic violence women can experience in a male-dominated institution.

Kelty, Kleykamp, and Segal conclude by seeking policy lessons from the military's success in facilitating the transition to adulthood for young men and women in uniform.

www.futureofchildren.org

Ryan Kelty is an assistant professor of sociology at Washington College. Meredith Kleykamp is an assistant professor of sociology at the University of Kansas. David R. Segal is a professor of sociology at the University of Maryland.

Military service has been characterized as a "moratorium" in the transition to adulthood, a period during which young men and women can defer such adult responsibilities as marriage, childbearing, establishing a household, and acquiring a full-time career.[1] Indeed, for past generations of American conscripts, military service has typically been a pause in the life course, lasting only a few years. But since 1973, as the all-volunteer force has evolved, military service has become less a hiatus in the transition to adulthood and more an experience through which youth become adults. Unlike the nation's armed forces from World War II through the end of the Vietnam War, today's military is staffed not by conscripts, but by volunteers, many of whom intend to make military service a career.[2] Not all who volunteer expect to serve for a twenty-year career; many enlist to gain training, skills, or educational benefits to use for college. For them, military service represents a means to achieve future goals.

Military service affects a young man's or young woman's transition into adulthood in a wide variety of ways, depending, among other things, on the race, gender, class, and sexual orientation of the service member. Although the military's extensive social support system facilitates the transition for many, the unique risks of military service can also make that transition seriously problematic. In this article we highlight key ways in which military experience both reflects and influences changes in the transition for these various groups, and we seek policy lessons from how the military facilitates the transition for those who serve. We highlight changes since World War II in the role of the military in the lives of young adults, and we examine changes in

the structure and policies of the armed forces that have contributed to such differences.

In the remainder of this article we examine four broad areas of military service, focusing in each on how men and women in uniform today make the transition to adulthood. First, we look at the social characteristics of those who serve, especially at differences in access to the military and its benefits by socio-demographic characteristics, such as age, gender, race and ethnicity, social class, and sexual orientation. Then we explore the effect of military service on family formation, including the timing of marriage and parenthood, family structure, and the influence of military culture on families. Third, we consider the consequences of military service on workforce participation through examining the influence of service on educational and employment outcomes. Finally, we scrutinize the dangers of military service during times of war and examine how the physical and psychological effects of wartime military service and the sexual trauma endured both by male and female military personnel can affect the transition to adulthood. We conclude by considering lessons to be learned from the military approach in facilitating the transition to adulthood.

Who Serves in the Volunteer Military?

During the era of America's conscripted military, those who served were (theoretically) a representative sample of the country's age-eligible, male youth. While there were constraints on who could serve historically, there was always a sense that those who served reflected the society from which they came. The current all-volunteer force relies on market dynamics in conjunction with individuals' call to service to fill its ranks. Several social-structural characteristics are important in determining not only who serves, but the

Figure 1. Age Distribution of the Military Population, by Gender, 2007

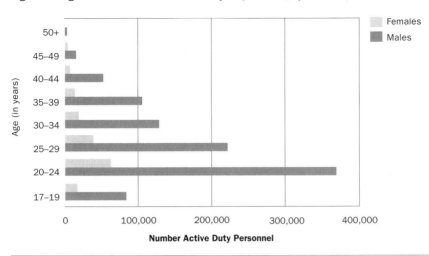

Department of Defense, "Population Representation in the Military Services FY2007" (www.defenselink.mil/prhome/PopRep2007/index.html [June 22, 2009]).

experiences they have while in service. In particular, the characteristics of age, gender, race and ethnicity, sexual orientation, and social class are important in determining who enlists, what they do, and the experiences they have—all of which influence one's transition to adulthood in the military context.

Age

Because of its hierarchical nature, its reliance on up-or-out promotion systems with little to no lateral entry, and its demands for physical fitness, military service is often a mission for the young. The age composition of the nation's armed force is far different from that of the civilian labor force. Across all military services, nearly 50 percent of the force is between seventeen and twenty-four years old, as shown in figure 1. The age distribution of men and women in the force is similar, but there is an obvious gender disparity. Although 50 percent of both the men and women serving are under twenty-five, among all service members under twenty-five, roughly 15 percent are women.

This overall portrait of the age distribution obscures differences across the individual services, most notably the Marine Corps' emphasis on maintaining a young, non-career force.[3] As figure 1 also shows, there are slightly more women at the younger ages, and more men at older ages, largely because of gender differences in retention: women leave the military at earlier ages than men, perhaps for family reasons (an issue discussed in greater detail below).

The rigorous and all-encompassing military socialization and training process is not uniquely aimed at young adults, but it is well suited to facilitate economic independence from parents and to promote responsible membership in intimate relationships and communities. The military emphasizes personal responsibility, health, constant training and self-improvement, and community and civic engagement—all key components of a successful transition to adulthood—and it holds all members to the same codes of conduct. Personal growth thus takes place

Table 1. Distribution of Military Experience, by Age and Gender, 2005–07

Percent	No military service	Veteran	National Guard/ reserves only	Active duty
Women				
17–19	99.13	0.13	0.51	0.23
20–24	98.26	0.77	0.51	0.43
25–29	98.00	1.28	0.46	0.26
30–34	97.91	1.40	0.54	0.16
35–39	97.71	1.57	0.58	0.13
40–44	97.48	1.76	0.68	0.08
45–49	97.41	1.83	0.72	0.04
50+	97.52	1.73	0.72	0.03
Total	97.89	1.35	0.58	0.18
Men				
17–19	97.61	0.39	0.91	1.08
20–24	93.80	2.85	0.97	2.37
25–29	92.21	5.42	0.88	1.50
30–34	90.21	7.44	1.17	1.18
35–39	87.63	9.90	1.45	1.02
40–44	85.97	11.73	1.61	0.69
45–49	84.82	13.43	1.44	0.31
50+	83.37	15.23	1.25	0.15
Total	89.63	8.02	1.23	1.13

Source: Authors' calculations from the American Community Survey (ACS) 2005–2007 Datafile.

in a highly structured setting. Within that setting, service members are also secure in knowing that their basic material needs are provided—reasonable wages, generous in-kind transfers, free medical care, housing, educational benefits, and training that may be highly transferable to civilian work.

Although about half of the men and women in the military are between seventeen and twenty-four years of age, only a small fraction of U.S. young adults in that age range has any military experience. Table 1 shows the percentage of the population with military experience, by age and gender. Although men serve at higher rates than women, among both men and women few aged seventeen to twenty-four have either current or past military experience. Higher rates among older men largely reflect higher service rates among older cohorts, who were at risk of being drafted into the military. Military experience, rare among today's young adults, was more common in earlier generations.

Gender

Military service has historically been a masculine role, though the share of young women serving in the armed forces has risen significantly since the advent of the all-volunteer force. Legal reforms in 1967, and more recent legal reforms associated with the initiation of the all-volunteer force, lifted official ceilings on women's service (once capped at 2 percent of the force).[4] In 1973, at the birth of the volunteer force, women made up 1.6 percent of active duty personnel; by 2005, that share had grown to some 15 percent.[5] By September 2008, 20 percent of enlisted personnel and officers in the Air Force were women. The Navy and Army had 15 percent and 14 percent, respectively; the Marine Corps had a significantly smaller share of women—only 6 percent.[6]

Over the past twenty years, women in uniform have increasingly chosen military service as their adult occupation. Their representation in the senior enlisted and officer ranks has grown and now accounts for nearly 12 percent of senior enlisted personnel and officers in all services except the Marine Corps, which is much lower at just over 3 percent.[7]

The military is the only major social institution in the nation that may legally discriminate in employment on the basis of gender. By Army regulation, women may serve "in any… specialty or position except those in battalion size or smaller units which are assigned a primary mission to engage in direct ground combat or which collocate routinely with units assigned a direct ground combat mission."[8] Women have access to more than 90 percent of the *occupations* in the Army, but are excluded from a number of occupational fields (for example, infantry, armor, special forces), which amount to a third of all Army jobs.[9]

The Navy restricts women from serving aboard submarines, on some small combat-oriented ships, and in support positions with Marine Corps ground combat units.[10] As with the Army, more than 90 percent of Navy positions are open to women.[11] The ability to provide separate berthing on ships by

gender affects the number of women in the fleet; typically, ships have berthing to accommodate women as 20 percent of the crew.[12] In the Marine Corps, more than 90 percent of occupations are open to women—again with exclusions for direct combat-related occupations. However, because the Marines are highly combat-focused, the exclusion of females in these occupations means women are ineligible to serve in 38 percent of all Marine Corps jobs.[13] The Air Force is the least restrictive, with 99 percent of occupational specialties and positions open to women.[14]

Although, as suggested by many of the articles in this volume, women appear to be making more successful transitions to adulthood in many areas than men, the military remains one area where structural and cultural impediments to their advancement remain. The differential treatment of military women at the institutional and interpersonal level affects their transitions to adulthood and the pursuit of military careers in several important ways. First, the exclusions on occupational specialty limit the number of women who can serve and preclude female officers and enlisted personnel from the most prestigious units and jobs in the military. These limits affect service entry and both the rate and height of their ascent in the organization should they choose to remain for a career.[15]

Second, the hyper-masculine culture of the military devalues feminine qualities and characteristics.[16] This devaluation often leads to both physical and symbolic violence against women, a significant source of motivation for women's leaving military service.[17] Experiences of harassment have led to increased turnover among female service members.[18] Even within the officer corps, sexual harassment has been identified as a significant motivation for separating from service, though incidences of reported sexual harassment are lower among female officers than among female enlisted personnel.[19] This harassment can escalate to more serious sexual assault, a point we take up later.

Gender as social capital within the military is expressed in assumptions about and direct challenges to women. For example, having particular qualifications (badges and tabs) readily visible on one's uniform is limiting for women, who have fewer opportunities for earning such awards or distinctions. Women have to resort to "pulling rank" more than men to gain compliance from subordinates.[20] Women endure numerous kinds of "tests" (for example, sabotage, constant scrutiny, and indirect threats) that men do not necessarily experience to prove they are capable of serving in the military. Differential treatment of women may be due to the possible Catch-22 of being accused of discrimination on the one hand or being insensitive to real differences in the needs or limitations of women on the other.[21] The result, however, is that different standards can be perceived as inequitable, leading to negative social and professional consequences for female service members. Although career military service is not for everyone, many choose it, and these systematic barriers facing women limit or impede their ability to achieve their military career goals. Because retirement with benefits is possible only after twenty years of service (unless one is injured in the line of duty), the additional stressors placed on women in the military may cause them to leave the service prematurely, with real consequences to the development of their own human capital through schooling, training, and leadership experience and also through potential forfeiture of benefits tied to career service.

Third, mentorship is important in fostering maturation of young professionals. The significant increase in more senior women in both the officer corps and enlisted ranks provides many more role models and mentors to share important social and cultural experiences. Despite persistent challenges, young female service members today have a more supportive and positive environment in the military than at any time in our nation's history. On balance, the challenges mean that more women than men who enter the service will leave after a short period of service; for these women, their service functions as a transition into other adult occupational, familial, and educational roles rather than a transition to a military career. As we will show, these choices vary by race and ethnicity as well as gender.

Race and Ethnicity

During the debates on the end of conscription, critics of the volunteer force concept argued that a force recruited through labor market dynamics would place the burden of service disproportionately on the shoulders of economically disadvantaged groups: the poor and racial and ethnic minorities.[22]

The architects of the volunteer force had expected that the end of conscription would not affect the racial composition of the force. However, African American participation in the military increased dramatically during the 1970s and remained around 22 percent from 1980 through 2001. Since the advent of the war on terror, African American participation has declined, dipping below 20 percent in 2006 for the first time in more than a quarter of a century. By contrast, African American participation in the civilian labor force since the late 1970s has remained constant between 11 and 13 percent.[23] Through the 1990s, including the first Persian Gulf War, the military was consistently able to draw highly capable African American youth. Research on high school graduates shows that blacks are more likely to enlist than whites and that blacks see the military as a viable alternative to the civilian labor force. Highly qualified black youths may prefer the immediate benefits of the military, including its more rigorous meritocratic structure relative to civilian employment options, to advanced education and civilian labor force participation.[24] During the all-volunteer force era, African Americans have consistently been over-represented in the military compared with their presence in the civilian labor force, but that over-representation has been decreasing since the United States began military operations in Afghanistan and Iraq. Nonetheless, for many young African Americans, joining the military is a transition to an adult military role, rather than a step taken before assuming alternative adult roles.

Hispanic participation in the military has risen sharply since the early 1990s. From the inception of the all-volunteer force until 1994, Hispanics made up less than 6 percent of military personnel. Since the late 1980s, Hispanics have increased their share of the military; by 2006, nearly 13 percent of the military identified as Hispanic, more than double the share in 1991.[25] In contrast to African American trends, Hispanic participation in the military mirrors an increase in civilian labor force participation during this time period. When adjusted for those who qualify for military service on the basis of education, Hispanics are actually slightly over-represented in the military compared with the civilian labor force. Latinos are most likely to enlist in the Marine Corps and least likely to enlist in the Air Force, whereas the Army has the highest share of African American service members and the Marine Corps the lowest.[26]

This difference among branches is consequential for whether military service represents a transition to a military career, or a step toward alternative careers. The Marine Corps has the smallest career force; the Air Force, the largest. The concentration of Hispanics in the former suggests that service will represent a transition to alternate adult roles for young Hispanic men and women.

Immigrants are allowed to serve in the armed forces, and more than 65,000 (both non-citizens and naturalized citizens) do; 11,000 of them are women.[27] Immigrants make up roughly 5 percent of the active duty force. Serving in the military makes immigrants eligible for expedited citizenship, and since 2001 more than 37,000 have become citizens.[28] Some lawmakers have suggested military service as a path to gaining legal status, and the Development, Relief, and Education for Alien Minors (DREAM) Act introduced in Congress in March 2009 contains provisions allowing illegal immigrants who arrived in the United States before age sixteen a path to citizenship in exchange for two years of military service.[29] Recently, the military has opened opportunities for immigrants on short-term visas, who earlier were not eligible without legal permanent resident status.[30]

Race and gender intersect in important ways in the military. African Americans generally are over-represented, but African American women are more over-represented than men by nearly a 2:1 margin as a share of enlisted soldiers and by more than 2:1 in both officer and warrant officer ranks.[31] Half of the women serving in the military are minority women, with African Americans accounting for 30 percent of all military women.[32] Among Hispanic soldiers, men have historically outnumbered women. In 2006, however, Latinas surpassed Latinos in their representation in the military in both the enlisted (11.0 percent men, 12.2 percent women) and officer ranks (4.8 percent men, 5.3 percent women).[33]

In 2005, blacks and Hispanics composed 19.9 percent and 9.8 percent of the enlisted ranks, respectively, across all branches of service. Their shares in the officer corps were significantly lower (8.7 percent black, 4.8 percent Hispanic),[34] but reflect the representation of African Americans among the college graduate population, from which officers are drawn. The number of officers of color has increased since the 1990s.[35] Even so, at the highest levels of leadership in the military, racial and ethnic minorities continue to be under-represented. Of the 893 general officers across the four service branches in 2005, only 48 (5.4 percent) were black, and only 11 (1.2 percent) were Hispanic.[36]

Much of the early criticism of the over-representation of minorities in the military was based on their concentration in the combat arms, where, in a conventional war, they would be over-represented among fatalities and casualties. As recently as the 1980s, African Americans were over-represented in units like the 82nd and 101st Airborne Divisions—among the first units to deploy in wartime. But by 1990, blacks were no longer going disproportionately into combat units.[37] They are now under-represented in combat arms, electronic repair, and electrical and mechanical crafts occupations. By contrast, they are disproportionately serving in functional support, administrative, service, and supply specialties. Although combat occupations may be valued in making a military career, experience in support specialties is highly transferable to the civilian labor market. A recent study found that black men in support occupations had a hiring advantage over civilians, whereas those with combat

experience had minimal success applying for civilian positions.[38] Hispanics more closely resemble whites than they do blacks in their distribution in military specialties. Their highest representation is in the electrical specialty area, followed closely by equal proportions in combat arms and administration. They are more likely than whites to be in medical and dental and other allied health fields, administration, and supply occupations.[39]

Sexual Orientation

Homosexuals have served in the U.S. military since the Revolutionary War, though they have faced discrimination for much of that time. Gays were prohibited from service from 1950 until January 1993, when President Clinton signed the "Don't Ask, Don't Tell, Don't Pursue" policy on sexual orientation in the military.[40] Thus the gay community did not have the same access to service either as an adult role or as a gateway to other roles as did the straight community. Public opinion does not support banning homosexuals from serving openly in the military. Between 58 and 91 percent of people disapprove of the continued ban.[41]

These shifts in general public opinion are reflected to a lesser degree among military personnel. Military opinions on homosexuals serving openly in uniform have changed dramatically since the early 1990s. Upwards of 40 percent now support such service. Younger service members (both enlisted personnel and officers) offer considerably greater support, suggesting a generation gap in attitudes.[42] Even with marked increases in support for homosexuals among those in and around the military, well over a third of service members report being aware of fellow service members being harassed based on sexual orientation.[43]

Although military service might be playing a larger role in the transition to adulthood for women and for racial and ethnic minorities than it did in the past, and might do so in the future for homosexuals, it is less inclusive across the socioeconomic spectrum than it was during periods of wartime conscription.

From the early 1980s until 1994, the numbers of discharges for homosexual-related reasons fell. After the passing of the Don't Ask, Don't Tell policy, such discharges rose from 1994, peaking at 1,227 in 2001 (less than 1 percent of the active duty force). Beginning in 2002, the first full year of military operations in the war on terror, discharges under this policy have steadily declined, with 612 service members dismissed in 2006. Since the passing of the Don't Ask, Don't Tell policy, the vast majority of discharges have been triggered by service members' voluntarily admitting being homosexual.[44] Many observers question the equity of the policy's enforcement, arguing that in times of crisis, such as the war on terror, the military is much less likely to discharge for homosexuality because of manpower needs. Even so, there has been considerable public debate over the dismissal of homosexual service members, especially Arabic linguists, in recent years. Those who oppose the policy argue that it violates human rights and the

U.S. Constitution and that it defines homosexuals as second-class citizens—the latter a claim made in the past by African Americans and currently by women. During the 2008 presidential election campaign, Barack Obama promised to lift the ban on gays openly serving in the American military. Such a step would help pave the way for more young gays and lesbians to serve in the armed forces either as a career or as a transition to other adult roles.

Social Class

According to data from the National Longitudinal Study of the high school graduating class of 1972, men and women serving in the volunteer military did not come from the underclass of American society, but did come from somewhat lower socioeconomic backgrounds, and had somewhat lower academic performance, than their peers who did not serve. Officers performed better in high school and came from higher-status socioeconomic backgrounds than did enlisted personnel. African Americans were over-represented among those who served, primarily because they are over-represented in less affluent social strata.[45] The bottom quartile of the socioeconomic distribution was under-represented in the military, largely because of the educational, physical, mental aptitude, and moral[46] requirements for service. The top quartile was under-represented primarily because of self-selection. The force was thus manned by the middle range of the socioeconomic distribution, with a mean somewhat below that of the broader society. According to the University of Michigan's Monitoring the Future project, these patterns continued at least through the first two decades of the volunteer force among high school graduates. Enlistment was higher among blacks and Hispanics than among whites, among men from single-parent households, among those whose parents had lower levels of education, and among those who did not plan to attend college.[47] High school students with C grade averages were found to be approximately two times as likely to enter military service as their peers with A grade averages.[48] Thus, although military service might be playing a larger role in the transition to adulthood for women and for racial and ethnic minorities than it did in the past, and might do so in the future for homosexuals, it is less inclusive across the socioeconomic spectrum than it was during periods of wartime conscription.

The Transition to Family Roles

During the conscription era, the military was composed primarily of single young men. Men tended to postpone marriage and fatherhood until after their military service or, at times, to get married to avoid conscription. In either case, military service was decoupled from family roles. To the extent that the transition to adulthood in the past involved family formation, then military service often delayed that transition. Indeed, into the 1980s, it was still common for Army personnel managers to note, "If the Army wanted you to have a wife, it would have issued you one." Today's volunteer force is older, more career-oriented, and more family-oriented. Policy makers have recognized that the modern military still recruits individuals for the most part, but it retains—or fails to retain—families. Military roles and familial roles are now more closely coupled, and the military and its policies have evolved in response.

Marriage

The number of service members who are married increased after the advent of the all-volunteer force, as did the number of dual-service couples with both partners serving in uniform. The growth in marriage rates has

not been linear. The share of enlisted soldiers who are married climbed from 40 percent in 1973 to its height at 57 percent in 1994. After declining and then rising again over the next ten years, the share married in 2005 was 52 percent.[49]

In 2002, nearly 12 percent of marriages among service members involved dual-service unions. Although only 7 percent of married enlisted men were married to women who also served, 49 percent of married enlisted women were married to men in uniform. Proportions are similar among officers for both genders.[50] The significant difference in dual-service marriage rates by sex is due in part to the under-representation of women in the military.

Military personnel are slightly more likely than their civilian peers to be married, though they are less likely than their age peers to be married when they enter the military.[51] They enter single, but marry young. Military service is more closely coupled to the husband and father role than to the wife and mother role. Women (enlisted and officers) are less likely to be married than their male counterparts.[52] Data from 2002 suggest that men in the junior enlisted ranks are nearly twice as likely to be married as civilians aged eighteen to twenty-four years.[53] Interestingly, racial differences in family formation in the civilian population are absent in the military; the tremendous black-white gap in marriage among civilians is virtually non-existent within the military.[54]

Military divorce rates differ by gender, race, and rank. In 2005, marital dissolution rates (per 100, per annum) among men were nearly twice as high for enlisted (2.8) as for officers (1.5). Among women, that rate was more than twice as high for enlisted (7.3) as for officers (3.6). In both cases, the rates among women are significantly higher than among men, but especially among enlisted personnel.[55] Starting and maintaining a marriage appears to be most challenging for military women.

During the early years of the volunteer force, the divorce rate was higher among enlisted military personnel than among their civilian counterparts—in part because military personnel marry at an earlier age.[56] Relationships between race and divorce rates also ran counter to civilian patterns. Although African American civilians have higher divorce rates than white civilians, the pattern was reversed in the military. White enlistees were half-again as likely as white civilians to divorce, while black enlistees were more than 10 percent less likely to divorce than black civilians were. Jennifer Lundquist attributes the closing of the racial gap in marital dissolution within the military to an equalizing of the constraints faced by families in the military.[57] Military men are less likely to be divorced than their age-matched civilian counterparts, while women in uniform are significantly more likely to be divorced than their civilian counterparts.[58] Among service members older than twenty-five, there are large proportional differences for women versus men in first marriages. The share of military women in their first marriage is consistently lower than their civilian age-matched peers—the reverse pattern of that found among military and civilian men. In particular, older service women (ages forty to forty-nine) are approximately half as likely to be in their first marriage (27.2 percent) as are civilian women of the same age group (49.2 percent).[59]

Despite the stressors associated with deployments, there was no strong evidence before the ongoing wars in Iraq and Afghanistan that deployments negatively affect marriage. Current research based on deployments in Iraq and Afghanistan shows that deployments may actually strengthen military marriages while the military member is on active duty.[60] Recent findings show that once service members leave the military, their divorce rates are higher than those of their civilian peers. The military appears able to buffer against the stressors on marriages while individuals remain in service, but once the structures and support of the military are removed, veterans' marriages suffer.[61]

Many stressors experienced by military families may contribute to the observed marital patterns: financial stress, spouse employment, housing and neighborhood quality (off-post), access to services, separation from the social support networks of family and friends, frequent relocations, and risk of death and injury.[62]

Military service also has potential benefits for marriage. Supportive family policies, a supportive community, and professional development opportunities to improve human capital through training, education, and leadership opportunities can improve financial opportunities (through promotions and post-service work), as well as personal growth. Each of these outcomes may improve the resilience of marriages and family solidarity more generally.[63] Evidence also suggests that the suite of benefits available to military personnel and their families buffers against some of the stressors known to increase marital dissolution in the civilian population.[64] The Army provides marriage enrichment programs, often run by Army chaplains as well as "exceptional family member" programs to provide additional assistance (often in the form of preference in desired duty location and housing) to families with special-needs members. Military housing policy is especially favorable to married couples and families with children. Single service members may be required to live in common facilities like barracks, while married soldiers may reside in apartments or houses with their spouses, on or off military installations. Ironically, marriage may provide more freedoms to service members by allowing them independent households as opposed to remaining single and living in barracks or dormitories, and housing policies may in fact encourage early marriage and childbearing behaviors.

Childbearing

Nearly three-quarters of married military personnel have dependent children, though women in uniform are less likely than are men to have children.[65] The Department of Health and Human Services found that military and civilian men had nearly identical mean ages at the birth of their first child (25.0 and 25.1 years, respectively). However, mean age at the birth of first child was 1.5 years younger for military women than for civilian women (23.6 and 25.1 years, respectively).[66] This difference in part reflects the earlier age at first marriage among military women, perhaps because of the volunteer force's family-friendly policies.[67] Couples in dual-service marriages are less likely than single-service couples to have children.[68] Among all active-duty personnel regardless of marital status, 44 percent of the servicemen and women have dependent children. Comparable proportions of black men (53 percent) and women (52 percent) in uniform have children. White men (44 percent) are more likely to have children than white women (33 percent), matched by similar shares of Hispanic men (42 percent) and women (34 percent).[69]

Although deployments and frequent absences might suggest an unfriendly climate for childbearing and rearing, military policies are relatively pro-natal. Free medical care, housing policies based on family size, good schools on military installations, robust systems of organized youth sports and activities, and available and affordable child care support early childbearing and larger families. They also support single parents; more than 13 percent of Army women and roughly 6 percent of Army men are single parents. While custodial single parents are prohibited from enlisting, men and women who become single parents after joining can remain in the service.[70]

A key support for raising children in military families is the military child care system. Nearly all Child Development Centers are accredited, compared with only 8 percent of civilian providers.[71] Although the program is the largest employer-provided child care program in the nation, the capacity to serve all those needing care is still limited. In 2000, the military system covered only 58 percent of the need for child care spots.[72] And although more spouses prefer to use military child care, those using civilian services were more satisfied.[73]

The Influence of Military Culture on Families

If the military recruits individuals but retains families, then family members are important stakeholders affected by military policies and culture. Military culture pressures family members to conform because the actions of one's family reflect on the service member. The pressure is felt by spouses and children, but especially by officers' wives, who engage in a variety of volunteer activities, such as family readiness groups, youth activities, and unit social events, to support the community, in particular their husbands' units.[74] The military has a long history of hyper-masculine traditions that manifest themselves in both overt and subtle ways. Nevertheless, its adoption of family-friendly policies seems to have encouraged and supported family formation and growth, perhaps at the expense of spousal employment or educational advancement. Working military spouses have lower employment rates and lower wages than comparable non-military spouses.[75] Ironically, progress made by the military toward gender equality in some senses has outpaced gender equality in families. That the military allows women to do most of the things that men do, while society (and the military) still expects women to play the major role in childrearing, makes it difficult for women on active military duty to meet the demands at the intersection of the roles. Thus, military women are more likely to divorce or to leave active duty.

Children in military families are exposed to the lifestyle and culture of their respective service branch, especially if they live on military installations surrounded by other military families. These children learn to cope with parental absence and frequent moves, and most adapt successfully to the demands of military life, but parent absence and frequent moves have been shown to hamper children's academic achievement.[76]

One characteristic of military culture is relative race-neutrality. The race-friendly environment leads to less racial segregation in housing, education, and socializing, which in turn contributes to lower racial gaps in test scores among military children than in civilian society. Black-white gaps in SAT scores are 30 percent lower in Department of Defense schools, and gaps in elementary reading and writing test scores are half those found in civilian schools.[77]

Military culture pressures family members to conform because the actions of one's family reflect on the service member. The pressure is felt by spouses and children, but especially by officers' wives.

Finally, the constant exposure to military life often leads to an intergenerational transmission of service; children of service members disproportionately serve in the military. The rate of voluntary military service from the high school graduating class of 1972 was twice as high among sons of career military fathers as among sons of civilian families, and these military sons had double the rate of interest in a military career for themselves.[78] More recently, scholars have found that children with a parent currently serving in the military were more likely to join the military.[79]

Education, Civilian Labor Force Participation, and Military Service

Educational benefits from various forms of the GI Bill are a hallmark of the benefits package for those who serve in the armed forces. The GI Bill is available to all service members who are honorably discharged, though service members may opt out of this benefit. Only a small number of service members choose to opt out, and many who do contribute from their paycheck to GI benefits do not end up using the educational benefits they accrue. An updated version of the GI Bill, the "Post 9/11 GI Bill," provides those who served on or after September 11,

2001, with an enhanced educational benefits package. The new package provides more money toward tuition and books, as well as a living allowance; for the first time it allows service members to transfer unused educational benefits to their spouse or children.[80] Since the inception in 1944 of the GI Bill, the educational benefits tied to military service have channeled large numbers of veterans into higher education. Because military service and higher education are typically pursued at similar points in the life course, young military veterans may have lower levels of educational attainment than peers who go straight into college. Access to military educational benefits from the GI Bill provides some veterans with an opportunity to attend college after military service.

Veterans of World War II, Korea, and the post-Korea cold war attained higher educational levels than comparable non-veterans, facilitated by their access to generous educational benefits provided by the first GI Bill of Rights. Because of the scale of those wars and the support they received from the American public, relatively high numbers of men served who were not only well positioned to attend college, but also were well received on college campuses following their service. However, male veterans of the Vietnam era, the last conscription-based war, achieved lower levels of education than their peers who did not serve.[81] The discrepancy may partly stem from draft policies exempting college students from military service. These policies generated more college-educated non-veterans than veterans and may have induced some to enroll in college to avoid being drafted.[82] At the same time, educational benefits for the non-military population were expanded and became more widely available.[83] Further, antiwar sentiment on the home front during the 1960s and 1970s, especially among the youth

and those in academia, made many campuses a hostile environment for Vietnam veterans. The Vietnam-era pattern persisted, according to the National Longitudinal Survey, at least through the first decade of the volunteer force. Veterans of the volunteer force lagged educationally behind their peers who did not serve.[84] Although veterans earn benefits to attend college after their service, they may not be able to take full advantage of their benefits to attain the same levels of education as their peers who immediately pursue higher education. It is difficult to serve in the military and pursue higher education at the same time, and the longer they served, the more they fell behind their peers' attainment. Those who serve longer are also more likely to be married and have children, which may constrain the decision to return to school post-service.

The education gap observed during the 1970s between veterans and those who did not serve existed for both black and white veterans and for both genders.[85] Although black veterans showed increased educational attainment over the life course, the gains were not sufficiently strong to meet or exceed the educational attainment of blacks who did not serve. At the intersection of race and gender, African American women veterans did not differ significantly from white women veterans in terms of years of education or the share earning a college degree, although among non-veterans, white women are more likely to earn college degrees than are black women.[86] The better schooling of civilian men may have been due in part to increases during the 1960s in federal aid for higher education not tied to military service, or it may be a function of the disruptive effect of military service on educational pursuits and stagnation (or reduction) in veterans' educational benefits in the 1970s and early 1980s.

Most people who join the military do not make it a career. For them, military service is a transition between high school and higher education or the civilian workforce. Even for the minority who choose the military as an opportunity for extended service or a career, the military retirement system, which vests benefits after twenty years of service, and the premium placed on youth by the traditional military culture, mean that virtually all military personnel will leave the service too young and with too small a pension to retire fully. They are thus likely, also, to transition to civilian work roles.

The military offers its most junior enlisted personnel higher pay and better benefits than are available to civilian age-matched peers. Once individuals leave the military, these relative benefits decrease over time. Non-white men maintain slightly higher earnings than their civilian peers over time, but white veterans eventually earn less in their subsequent civilian lives than their counterparts who did not serve.[87] By contrast, as veterans, officers earn a 10 percent wage premium over their non-veteran peers.[88]

The military's pay and benefits structure, which is based on rank and years in service, is a much fairer employment environment than the civilian labor market in terms of monetary and non-monetary compensation. The pay gap between white and African American service members is significantly smaller than that between white and black civilians.[89] This relative pay equity is a major reason why African American women are disproportionately represented in the armed services. Not only does the military promote and compensate racial minorities more fairly than the civilian sector, it also compensates men and women much more evenly. Differences in pay by race and gender do exist, but the gap is considerably narrower than it is in the civilian labor market.

According to contemporary studies of the civilian workforce outcomes of veterans from the all-volunteer force that examine differences by race and gender, the share of women veterans with a bachelor's degree (14 percent) in 1990 was approximately one-third that of women who had never served in uniform.[90] Women veterans, both whites and blacks, also had higher jobless rates than non-serving women in 1990.[91] Women veterans were estimated to have 12.5 percent less in earnings and 11.7 percent less in family income than comparable women with no military service. These negative effects on women's earnings and family income are the unique contribution of military service once the effects of education and race have been accounted for.

By 2005, however, women veterans were earning approximately $7,000 more each year than female non-veterans. Much of the difference in earnings between female veterans and non-veterans is attributable to the fact that female veterans work more during the year than their non-serving female peers. Although women of both veteran and non-veteran status are equally likely to work year-round, female veterans are nearly one and a half times as likely to work full-time as non-veteran women.

Male veterans in 2005 also outperformed their civilian counterparts on earnings, but only by $3,000 a year.[92] White veterans' earnings, however, lag behind those of their non-serving peers for the first few years after separation from service.[93] African American and Hispanic veterans consistently fare better than white veterans relative to each group's non-serving counterparts.[94] Thus, the later life income benefit to military service is greatest for racial and ethnic minorities.

The Risks of Military Service

Although the military provides numerous supports for a successful transition to adulthood, the physical and psychological risks of service, which are amplified during wartime, may harm interpersonal relationships and diminish independence, thus imperiling the transition. In addition, many military women face sexual harassment and sexual abuse during their service. Indeed, the post-traumatic stress experiences that men (and women) face from combat parallel the pervasive traumatic sexual experiences of women, even in peacetime. These risks may carry over to military families, and spouses and children likely suffer poorer outcomes when their family member experiences any of these negative events.

Extrapolation of these findings produces an estimate that 300,000 of the service members deployed in support of Iraq and Afghanistan suffer from PTSD or major depression and that another 320,000 suffer probable traumatic brain injury.

Physical and Mental Health Effects of Service

The nature of military service, especially during war, exposes those who serve to potential physical and mental health disabilities. Through January 3, 2009, the Department

of Defense had reported 30,934 wounded in Iraq and another 2,627 in Afghanistan.[95] The most likely causes of physical injury are improvised explosive devices (IEDs), followed by artillery and gunshot.[96] Two of the major physical injuries suffered by personnel in current engagements are traumatic amputations and burns. As of August 1, 2008, more than 1,200 service members had suffered amputations—nearly three-quarters of which were major limb amputations.[97] Several hundred more had suffered serious burn wounds.[98]

The "invisible wounds" of cognitive and psychological trauma among service members are also major health outcome concerns. Traumatic brain injury had been diagnosed in more than 8,000 service members as of January 2009. The vast majority (88 percent) of these traumatic brain injuries were classified as "mild," and most were the result of exposure to blasts such as improvised explosive devices.[99]

Depression, post-traumatic stress disorder (PTSD), and suicide are three of the biggest mental health concerns. A recent report found that 14 percent of service members returning from Iraq and Afghanistan screened positive for major depression, and the same share screened positive for PTSD.[100] Similar data are reported from those working with the office of the Army Surgeon General—an estimated 12 percent of soldiers with anxiety and depression disorders after first deployment, rising to an estimated 27 percent after a third deployment.[101] Ground troops (soldiers and Marines) are more likely to report PTSD and depression than are sailors and airmen; women, enlisted personnel, Hispanics, and those not on active duty (Guard, Reserve, retired) are the most likely to report PTSD and depression.[102] Among 300,000 service members surveyed, 19 percent reported suffering a probable traumatic brain injury. Extrapolation of these findings produces an estimate that 300,000 of the service members deployed in support of Iraq and Afghanistan suffer from PTSD or major depression and that another 320,000 suffer probable traumatic brain injury.[103]

Suicide rates among military personnel are typically lower than civilian rates. In 2008, for the first time since Vietnam, the rate of suicides in the Army (128 deaths, or about 20 deaths per 100,000 soldiers) surpassed the rate among the civilian population.[104] Male veterans are twice as likely as their non-veteran peers to die by suicide. White veterans are more likely than blacks to die by suicide.[105] Suicide among service members and veterans is strongly related to PTSD, major depression, traumatic brain injury, and limitations in daily activities.[106] The cognitive and psychological wounds suffered by service members in Iraq and Afghanistan may produce psychological mortality surpassing the number of combat deaths in the war on terror.[107] The cognitive injuries suffered by service members are likely to impair their transitions to civilian work, their relationships with family and friends, and their broader life trajectories.

Service members report alarming failures to receive treatment for their cognitive and psychological disorders. Nearly half report seeking psychological treatment or counseling help for PTSD or major depression. Forty three percent of those who suspected that they had a traumatic brain injury were never seen by medical professionals for that condition.[108] The culture of the military (an extension of civilian culture in America) discourages people from seeking medical help for cognitive and psychological disorders.

Fear of negative effects on careers, personal stigmatization, and potential loss of peers' confidence are cited as major reasons to avoid professional help.[109] The negative implications for future health (including substance abuse and suicide), work outcomes, and relationship success (especially in families) of these high incidences of non-treatment for cognitive and psychological trauma cannot be overstated.[110]

Sexual Harassment and Sexual Assault

Sexual harassment and sexual assault affect many men and women in the United States, both within the military and in the civilian population. The issue has been given much more attention in the military in recent decades. Comparing sexual harassment and assault among civilians and military groups is challenging because reporting requirements differ between the two populations. Comparisons over time within the military are also complicated because the military has changed its reporting format several times in recent years. Still, it is possible to reach a fairly clear understanding of the extent and impact of such events on current military personnel and veterans.

Although both men and women in the military experience sexual harassment and sexual assault—referred to as military sexual trauma (MST)—rates are much higher among women. In 2006, one-third of women and 6 percent of men in uniform reported being sexually harassed, and 6.8 percent of military women and 1.8 percent of military men reported being sexually assaulted. Junior enlisted personnel were most likely to report military sexual trauma. Of the four branches, service members in the Army were most likely, and those in the Air Force least likely, to report such trauma.[111] The rate of sexual trauma among female veterans is estimated in the range of low 20 percent to low 30 percent.[112] The rate among male veterans is estimated at between 2 and 4 percent.[113]

Military sexual trauma impairs both physical and mental health. In 2007, the Veterans Health Administration found that women veterans who reported sexual trauma also presented with symptoms of PTSD, dissociative disorders, eating disorders, and personality disorders. Male veterans who reported sexual trauma had high rates of dissociative and personality disorders. Men were significantly more likely than women to be diagnosed with adjustment disorders. Both male and female victims of sexual trauma are more likely to be diagnosed with alcohol and anxiety disorders than are their same-sex veteran peers who did not experience such trauma; for both disorders, the association was stronger among women.[114]

The risk of developing PTSD from sexual trauma is at least as high as, if not higher than, the risk of developing PTSD from exposure to combat.[115] Among veterans, sexually traumatized women are nearly three times more likely than men to be diagnosed with PTSD. Women veterans who experience military sexual trauma are also up to five times more likely to develop PTSD than women who experience civilian sexual trauma.[116]

Behaviors associated with sexual trauma, such as substance abuse and risky behavior, expose these veterans to such physical health risks as liver disease, chronic lung disease, weight-related disorders, and HIV/AIDS. In addition, veterans who are sexually harassed or assaulted while in uniform attempt suicide or intentionally harm themselves at more than twice the rate of veterans without exposure to sexual trauma.[117]

For those who experience injury, either mental or physical, as a result of their service, or for those who suffer military sexual trauma, there is a high probability that their military service will be a serious interruption in the transition to adulthood. Personal relationships, careers, education, and in some cases physical independence are likely to suffer as a direct result of their military service. The wars in Iraq and Afghanistan have highlighted the physical and emotional risks of combat service, and the pervasive sexual harassment and assault military women experience also places them at particular risk of interrupted or unsuccessful transitions to adulthood.

Lessons for Civilian Policy

Do the military policies that contribute to a successful transition to adulthood hold lessons for civilian policy makers? Because the institutional structure of the military, including the Uniform Code of Military Justice, which codifies behavioral expectations, does not translate to civilian life, many military policies are not directly applicable in the civilian world. But some aspects of the military's approach may be successfully adapted for use in civilian policy making.

Those who choose a military career enjoy almost ideal employment relations—generous benefits, job security with regulated promotion rules, and a generous pension after twenty years of service. In exchange for long hours, dangerous conditions, and frequent deployment from home, career men and women in service receive child care, health benefits, and housing—supports that minimize but do not eliminate the challenges of raising a family in the military. By contrast, young adults pursuing civilian work face uncertain employment and wages, eroding benefits, and volatile housing markets, all of which likely delay family formation and challenge childrearing during these early years. The military benefits do not come without a cost or without risk, but they clearly provide an integrated web of institutional support for service members and their families.

Even though the all-volunteer force has become more a career force than the military was before the early 1970s, most who join still serve only a short time, typically four years. Those who serve for a limited period often do so to gain training, experience, discipline, or to earn the now-generous GI Bill educational benefits. For these youth, service represents an active transition to adulthood—a means to acquire an adult role—rather than a mere pause between adolescence and adulthood. Earlier generations of young adults who served may indeed have used military service as a "time out," moratorium, or pause in the transition to adulthood because their service was involuntary. Being conscripted into the military interrupted the plans and trajectories of these young people. But voluntary military service is part of a planned course into adulthood. The same institutional supports for marriage, childbearing, occupational attainment, and education that are available to career service members are also available to those who serve for shorter periods. These supports far exceed those available in the world of college or of work.

Sometimes the military is seen as one of a handful of "second-chance" institutions poised to help disadvantaged youth get back on track to a successful transition to adulthood. Fairly stringent enlistment criteria disqualify many who need a second chance— those with criminal records, those in poor health, and those who drop out of high school. Some policy researchers have suggested using military service as the equivalent of a

jobs or welfare program, but early experiments admitting into the military individuals who did not meet standard enlistment criteria were not successful, because they were implemented in a way that made these soldiers easy to identify and targets of differential treatment.[118] In recent years, changing force sizes have led to varying enlistment standards. Although these variations provide a natural experiment on how military service affects men and women accepted under relaxed standards, such analyses have yet to be conducted. An earlier natural experiment resulting from the misnorming of the Armed Forces Qualifying Test (AFQT) in 1976–80 found that the 400,000 individuals inadvertently admitted during the misnorming period performed more poorly than higher-aptitude peers.[119] Indeed, these low-aptitude recruits partly contributed to the characterization of the military at that time as a "hollow force."[120] In short, although military service does have the capacity to change those who serve, some of the positive outcomes are attributable to the selection process that screens out those least likely to succeed, a key lesson for policy makers interested in appropriating military models.

Quasi-military programs, public military academies, and JROTC programs in schools have recently become popular, especially in areas with large populations of vulnerable youth, and they appear to be successful. In an evaluation focusing on JROTC Career Academies (programs within traditional schools), students participating in the JROTC programs had higher grade point averages, lower absenteeism, and higher high school graduation rates than those not participating.[121] A recent ethnographic study of a public military academy suggests that such a model (where all students are cadets) may hold promise largely because of the military-like solidarity it promotes.[122] The National Guard Youth ChalleNGe program focuses on high school dropouts, also using a military-inspired model. The program provides an initial socialization phase similar to boot camp, a residential program of life skills, academic work, and physical fitness, followed by a post-residential placement into a job or further education.[123] After tough initial socialization, the residential phase emphasizes isolation from negative peer influences and focuses on discipline, leadership and followership, fitness and health, and academic, civic, and social education. Early results from a random-assignment demonstration show positive outcomes: the treatment group was more likely to have earned a GED (46 percent of the program group versus 10 percent of the control group earned a diploma or GED), to be working or attending college (30 percent versus 21 percent working full time, 11 percent vs. 3 percent in college), and less likely to report being arrested (14 percent versus 20 percent). The program evaluation is ongoing, but initial findings suggest the military model is helping high school dropouts in the transition to adulthood.

Military service plays a key role in the transition to adulthood for those who do serve, but two aspects of military service in the contemporary environment will likely be increasingly relevant. First, because of the occupational heritability of military service, the trends in military family policies we discuss have implications for the transition to adulthood of the next generation. Children growing up in today's military are exposed to the relatively pro-family policies and social environment of the military that may intensify the intergenerational transmission of military service. Second, military-connected trauma and disability can generate long-lasting effects on the life trajectories of those affected. There is often a substantial delay in the diagnosis of a service-related trauma or disability as well, implying yet more individuals whose lives may be negatively affected by their service in years to come. Thus, the health sequelae, like the educational and employment consequences of service, will be with veterans for the duration of their life course, not just during the transition to adulthood.

Endnotes

1. Michael J. Shanahan, "Pathways to Adulthood in Changing Societies: Variability and Mechanisms in the Life Course Perspective," *Annual Review of Sociology* 26 (2000): 667–92; Glen H. Elder Jr., "Military Times and Turning Points in Men's Lives," *Developmental Psychology* 22, no. 2 (1986): 233–45; Glen H. Elder Jr., "War Mobilization and the Life Course: A Cohort of World War II Veterans," *Sociological Forum* 2, no. 3 (1987): 449–72.

2. David R. Segal and Mady Wechsler Segal, "America's Military Population," *Population Bulletin* 59, no. 4 (2004).

3. Department of Defense, "Population Representation in the Military Services FY2007" (www.defenselink. mil/prhome/PopRep2007/index.html [June 22, 2009]).

4. Lori Manning, *Women in the Military: Where They Stand,* 5th edition (Washington: Women's Research and Education Institute, 2005).

5. Ibid.

6. Department of Defense, Statistical Information Analysis Division, "Military Personnel Statistics" (http:// siadapp.dmdc.osd.mil/personnel/MMIDHOME.HTM [January 9, 2009]).

7. Manning, *Women in the Military* (see note 4).

8. Headquarters, U.S. Department of the Army, "Army Regulation 600-13, Army Policy for the Assignment of Female Soldiers" (March 27, 1992).

9. Manning, *Women in the Military* (see note 4); Segal and Segal, "America's Military Population" (see note 2).

10. Manning, *Women in the Military* (see note 4).

11. Manning, *Women in the Military* (see note 4); Segal and Segal, "America's Military Population" (see note 2).

12. Segal and Segal, "America's Military Population" (see note 2).

13. Manning, *Women in the Military* (see note 4).

14. Segal and Segal, "America's Military Population" (see note 2).

15. James B. Stewart and Juanita M. Firestone, "Looking for a Few Good Men: Predicting Patterns of Retention, Promotion, and Accession of Minority and Women Officers," in *Managing Diversity in the Military,* edited by Mickey R. Dansby and others (New Brunswick, N.J.: Transaction Publishers, 2001), pp. 257–76.

16. Claire Snyder, "The Citizen-Soldier Tradition and Gender Integration of the U.S. Military," *Armed Forces & Society* 29, no. 2 (2003): 185–204; Laura Miller, "Not Just Weapons of the Weak: Gender Harassment as a Form of Protest for Army Men," *Social Psychology Quarterly* 60 (1997): 32–51.

17. Miller, "Not Just Weapons of the Weak" (see note 16).

18. Carra S. Sims, Fritz Drasgow, and Louise F. Fitzgerald, "The Effects of Sexual Harassment on Turnover in the Military: Time-Dependent Modeling," *Journal of Applied Psychology* 90, no. 6 (2005): 1141–52.

19. NiCole T. Buchanan, Isis H. Settles, and Krystle C. Woods, "Comparing Sexual Harassment Subtypes among Black and White Women by Military Rank: Double Jeopardy, the Jezebel, and the Cult of True Womanhood," *Psychology of Women Quarterly* 32, no. 4 (2008): 347–61.

20. Miller, "Not Just Weapons of the Weak" (see note 16).

21. Ibid.

22. Harry A. Marmion, *The Case against an All-Volunteer Army* (Chicago: Quadrangle Books, 1971); Morris Janowitz and Charles C. Moskos, "Racial Composition in the All-Volunteer Force," *Armed Forces & Society* 1 (1974): 109–24.

23. Mady W. Segal, Meridith H. Thanner, and David R. Segal, "Hispanic and African American Men and Women in the U.S. Military: Trends in Representation," *Race, Gender & Class* 14, no. 3-4 (2007): 48–64.

24. Jay D. Teachman, Vaughn R. A. Call, and Mady Wechsler Segal, "The Selectivity of Military Enlistment," *Journal of Political & Military Sociology* 21, no. 2 (1993): 287–309.

25. Segal, Thanner, and Segal, "Hispanic and African American Men and Women in the U.S. Military" (see note 23).

26. Ibid.

27. Jeanne Batolova, "Immigrants in the U.S. Armed Forces" (2008) (www.migrationinformation.org/USFocus/display.cfm?id=683 [June 23, 2009]).

28. Ibid.

29. Development, Relief, and Education for Alien Minors (DREAM) Act of 2009, 111th Cong. § 5 (2009).

30. Miriam Jordan, "A Korean Invasion Blinds the U.S. Army—But in a Good Way," *Wall Street Journal*, May 29, 2009, p.1.

31. Segal, Thanner, and Segal, "Hispanic and African American Men and Women in the U.S. Military" (see note 23).

32. Manning, *Women in the Military* (see note 4); Segal and Segal, "America's Military Population" (see note 2).

33. Segal, Thanner, and Segal, "Hispanic and African American Men and Women in the U.S. Military" (see note 23).

34. Department of Defense, "Population Representation in the Military Services FY2005: Executive Summary" (2005).

35. Segal, Thanner, and Segal, "Hispanic and African American Men and Women in the U.S. Military" (see note 23).

36. Department of Defense, "Population Representation in the Military Services FY2005" (see note 34).

37. David R. Segal and Naomi Verdugo, "Demographic Trends and Personnel Policies as Determinants of the Racial Composition of the Volunteer Army," *Armed Forces & Society* 20 (1994): 619–32.

38. Meredith Kleykamp, "A Great Place to Start? The Effect of Prior Military Service on Hiring," *Armed Forces & Society* 35, no. 2 (2009): 266–85.

39. Department of Defense, "Population Representation in the Military Services FY2005" (see note 34).

40. Kirby L. Bowling, Juanita M. Firestone, and Richard J. Harris, "Analyzing Questions That Cannot Be Asked of Respondents Who Cannot Respond," *Armed Forces & Society* 31, no. 3 (2005): 411–37; Mady W. Segal and Chris Bourg, "Professional Leadership and Diversity in the Army," in *The Future of the Army Profession*, edited by Lloyd J. Matthews (New York: McGraw-Hill, 2002), pp. 505–20.

41. Aaron Belkin, "Don't Ask, Don't Tell: Is the Gay Ban Based on Military Necessity?" *Parameters* 33 (2003): 108–19.

42. Ibid.

43. Bowling, Firestone, and Harris, "Analyzing Questions That Cannot Be Asked of Respondents Who Cannot Respond" (see note 40).

44. David F. Burrelli and Jody Feder, "Homosexuals and the U.S. Military: Current Issues," CRS Report for Congress (July 18, 2008) (http://assets.opencrs.com/rpts/RL30113_20080718.pdf [January 11, 2009]).

45. David R. Segal and others, "The All-Volunteer Force in the 1970s," *Social Science Quarterly* 79 (1998): 390–411.

46. The moral requirement for military service is generally oriented toward lawfulness—that is, does one have a criminal record?

47. Jerald G. Bachman and others, "Who Chooses Military Service? Correlates of Propensity and Enlistment in the U.S. Armed Forces," *Military Psychology* 12 (2000): 1–30.

48. Ibid.

49. Department of Defense, "Population Representation in the Military Services FY2005" (see note 34).

50. Segal and Segal, "America's Military Population" (see note 2).

51. Ibid.

52. Department of Defense, "Population Representation in the Military Services FY2005" (see note 34).

53. Francesca Adler-Baeder and others, "Marital Transitions in Military Families: Their Prevalence and Their Relevance for Adaptation to the Military" (Military Family Research Institute, Purdue University, 2005) (www.cfs.purdue.edu/mfri/pages/research/marital_transitions_in_military_families.pdf [February 20, 2009]); Segal and Segal, "America's Military Population" (see note 2).

54. Jennifer Hickes Lundquist, "When Race Makes No Difference: Marriage and the Military," *Social Forces* 83, no. 2 (2004): 731–57.

55. Benjamin R. Karney and John A. Crown, "Families under Stress: An Assessment of Data, Theory, and Research on Marriage and Divorce in the Military" (Arlington, Va.: RAND Corporation, MG-599-OSD, 2007).

56. Jennifer Hickes Lundquist, "A Comparison of Civilian and Enlisted Divorce Rates during the Early All-Volunteer Force Era," *Journal of Political and Military Sociology* 35, no. 2 (2007): 199–217.

57. Jennifer Hickes Lundquist, "The Black-White Gap in Marital Dissolution among Young Adults: What Can a Counterfactual Scenario Tell Us?" *Social Problems* 53, no. 3 (2006): 421–41.

58. Karney and Crown, "Families under Stress" (see note 55); Michael Pollard, Benjamin Karney, and David Loughran, "Comparing Rates of Marriage and Divorce in Civilian, Military, and Veteran Populations," paper presented at the Population Association of America annual meeting, New Orleans, La., April 2008.

59. Adler-Baeder and others, "Marital Transitions in Military Families" (see note 53).

60. Karney and Crown, "Families under Stress" (see note 55).

61. Pollard, Karney, and Loughran, "Comparing Rates of Marriage and Divorce in Civilian, Military, and Veteran Populations" (see note 58).

62. Richard T. Cooney Jr., "Moving with the Military: Race, Class, and Gender Differences in the Employment Consequences of Tied Migration," Ph.D. dissertation, Department of Sociology, University of Maryland, 2003; Karney and Crown, "Families under Stress" (see note 55); Mady W. Segal, "The Military and the Family as Greedy Institutions," *Armed Forces & Society* 13, no. 1 (1986): 9–38.

63. Karney and Crown, "Families under Stress" (see note 55).

64. H. R. Watanabe and others, "Soldier Functioning under Chronic Stress—Effects of Family Member Illness," *Military Medicine* 160, no. 9 (1995): 457–61.

65. Segal and Segal, "America's Military Population" (see note 2).

66. U.S. Department of Health and Human Services, Administration for Children and Families, Office of Family Assistance, *Responsible Fatherhood Spotlight* (www.fatherhood.gov/documents/nrfcspotlightmilitary.pdf [February 22, 2009]).

67. Jennifer Hickes Lundquist and Herbert L. Smith, "Family Formation among Women in the U.S. Military," *Journal of Marriage and the Family* 67, no. 1 (2005): 1–23.

68. Segal and Segal, "America's Military Population" (see note 2).

69. Jay Teachman, "Military Service and Educational Attainment in the All-Volunteer Era," *Sociology of Education* 80, no. 4 (2007): 359–74.

70. Bradford Booth, Mady Wechsler Segal, and D. Bruce Bell, "What We Know about Army Families 2007 Update" (www.army.mil/fmwrc/documents/research/whatweknow2007.pdf [June 23, 2009]).

71. Ibid.

72. Ibid.

73. Ibid.

74. Margaret C. Harrell, "Army Officers' Spouses: Have the White Gloves Been Mothballed?" *Armed Forces & Society* 28, no. 1 (2001): 55–75.

75. James Hosek and others, "Married to the Military: The Employment and Earnings of Military Wives Compared with Those of Civilian Wives" (Santa Monica, Calif.: RAND Corporation, MR-1565-OSD, 2002) (www.rand.org/pubs/monograph_reports/2009/MR1565.pdf [June 24, 2009]); Margaret C. Harrell

and others, "Working around the Military: Challenges to Military Spouse Employment and Education" (Santa Monica, Calif.: RAND Corporation, MG-169-OSD, 2004) (www.rand.org/pubs/monographs/2007/RAND_MG566.pdf [June 24, 2009]).

76. David S. Lyle, "Using Military Deployments and Job Assignments to Estimate the Effect of Parental Absences and Household Relocations on Children's Academic Achievement," *Journal of Labor Economics* 24, no. 2 (2004): 319–50.

77. Charles C. Moskos and John Sibley Butler, *All That We Can Be* (New York: Basic Books, 1996); Leslie R. Hinkson, "Schools of the Nation: Department of Defense Schools and the Black-White Test Score Gap," Ph.D. dissertation, Department of Sociology, Princeton University, 2007.

78. John H. Faris, "The All-Volunteer Force: Recruitment from Military Families," *Armed Forces & Society* 7, no. 4 (1981): 545–59.

79. Meredith Kleykamp, "College, Jobs, or the Military? Enlistment during a Time of War," *Social Science Quarterly* 87, no. 2 (2006): 272–90.

80. U.S. Department of Veterans Affairs, www.gibill.va.gov/GI_Bill_Info/CH33/Post-911.htm (October 30, 2009).

81. Jere Cohen, David R. Segal, and Lloyd V. Temme, "The Educational Cost of Military Service in the 1960s," *Journal of Political and Military Sociology* 14 (1986): 303–19.

82. J. Peter Matilla, "Determinants of Male School Enrollments: A Time-Series Analysis," *Review of Economics and Statistics* 64, no. 2 (1982): 242–51.

83. David R. Segal, *Recruiting for Uncle Sam: Citizenship and Military Manpower Policy* (University Press of Kansas, 1989).

84. Jere Cohen, Rebecca L. Warner, and David R. Segal, "Military Service and Educational Attainment in the All-Volunteer Force," *Social Science Quarterly* 76, no. 1 (1995): 88–104.

85. Ibid.

86. Richard T. Cooney Jr. and others, "Racial Differences in the Impact of Military Service on the Socioeconomic Status of Women Veterans," *Armed Forces & Society* 30, no. 1: 53–85.

87. Joshua D. Angrist, "Estimating the Labor Market Impact of Voluntary Military Service Using Social Security Data on Military Applicants," *Econometrica* 66 (1998): 249–88.

88. Barry T. Hirsch and Stephen L. Mehay, "Evaluating the Labor Market Performance of Veterans Using a Matched Comparison Group Design," *Journal of Human Resources* XXXVIII, no. 3 (2003): 673–700.

89. Bradford Booth and David R. Segal, "Bringing the Soldiers Back in: Implications of Inclusion of Military Personnel for Labor Market Research on Race, Class, and Gender," *Race, Gender & Class* 12, no. 1 (2005): 34–37.

90. Cooney and others, "Racial Differences in the Impact of Military Service on the Socioeconomic Status of Women Veterans" (see note 86).

91. Ibid.

92. Kelly A. Holder, "Exploring the Veteran-Nonveteran Earnings Differential in the 2005 American Community Survey," conference paper, American Sociological Association annual meeting, 2007.

93. Robert L. Phillips and others, "The Economic Returns to Military Service: Race-Ethnic Differences," *Social Science Quarterly* 73, no. 2 (1992): 340–59.

94. Cooney and others, "Racial Differences in the Impact of Military Service on the Socioeconomic Status of Women Veterans" (see note 86); Holder, "Exploring the Veteran-Nonveteran Earnings Differential in the 2005 American Community Survey" (see note 92); Phillips and others, "The Economic Returns to Military Service" (see note 93).

95. Department of Defense, Statistical Information Analysis Division, "Military Personnel Statistics" (see note 6).

96. Department of Defense, Statistical Information Analysis Division, "Casualty Summary by Reason Code" (2009) (http://siadapp.dmdc.osd.mil/personnel/CASUALTY/gwot_reason.pdf [February 5, 2009]).

97. Hannah Fischer, "United States Military Casualty Statistics: Operation Iraqi Freedom and Operation Enduring Freedom," Congressional Research Service: CRS Report for Congress (2008) (www.fas.org/sgp/crs/natsec/RS22452.pdf [February 4, 2009]).

98. B. S. Atiyeh, S. W. A. Gunn, and S. N. Hayek, "Military and Civilian Burn Injuries during Armed Conflicts," *Annals of Burns and Fire Disasters* 20, no. 4 (2007) (www.medbc.com/annals/review/vol_20/num_4/text/vol20n4p203.asp [February 5, 2009]).

99. Fischer, "United States Military Casualty Statistics" (see note 97).

100. Terri Tanielian and Lisa H. Jaycox, "Invisible Wounds of War: Psychological and Cognitive Injuries, Their Consequences, and Services to Assist Recovery" (Arlington, Va.: RAND Corporation, RC552.P67T34, 2008) (www.rand.org/pubs/monographs/2008/RAND_MG720.pdf [February 4, 2009]).

101. Arline Kaplan, "Untreated Vets: A 'Gathering Storm' of PTSD/Depression," *Psychiatric Times* 25, no. 12 (2008) (www.psychiatrictimes.com/depression/article/10168/1342040 [February 5, 2009]).

102. Ibid.

103. Tanielian and Jaycox, "Invisible Wounds of War" (see note 100).

104. Julia Ritchey, "US Army, Mental Health Experts Team Up to Fight Rising Suicide Rate," Voice of America News (2009) (www.voanews.com/english/2009-01-30-voa59.cfm?renderforprint=1 [February 5, 2009]).

105. Tanielian and Jaycox, "Invisible Wounds of War" (see note 100).

106. Ibid.

107. Ibid.

108. Ibid.

109. Ibid; Ritchey, "US Army, Mental Health Experts Team Up to Fight Rising Suicide Rate" (see note 104).

110. Tanielian and Jaycox, "Invisible Wounds of War" (see note 100).

111. Rachel N. Lipari and others, "2006 Gender Relations Survey of Active Duty Members," Defense Manpower Data Center (DMDC) Report No. 2007-022, March 2008. (www.sapr.mil/contents/references/WGRA_OverviewReport.pdf [February 26, 2009]).

112. Estimates for male and female veterans' rates of MST are obtained from studies of veterans applying for benefits through Veterans Affairs hospitals. These estimates should be viewed cautiously since they are not necessarily reflective of all veterans' experiences. For a summary of MST rates among veterans see: Naomi Himmelfarb, Deborah Yaeger, and Jim Mintz, "Posttraumatic Stress Disorder in Female Veterans with Military and Civilian Sexual Trauma," *Journal of Traumatic Stress* 19, no. 6 (2006): 837–46.

113. Antonette M. Zeiss, "Veterans Health Administration Care for Mental Health Problems Related to Military Sexual Trauma," unpublished data from Office of Mental Health Services, Department of Veterans Affairs (www.militarysexualtrauma.org/files/Veterans_Administration_Care_for_Mental_Health_Problems_Related_to_Military_Sexual_Trauma_DTFSAM.ppt. [February 26, 2009]); Melissa A. Polusny and Maureen Murdoch, "Sexual Assault among Male Veterans," *Psychiatric Times* 22, no. 4 (2005): 34–38.

114. Rachel Kimerling and others, "The Veterans Health Administration and Military Sexual Trauma," *American Journal of Public Health* 97, no. 12 (2007): 2160–66.

115. Himmelfarb, Yaeger, and Mintz, "Posttraumatic Stress Disorder in Female Veterans with Military and Civilian Sexual Trauma" (see note 112); Jessica Wolfe and others, "Sexual Harassment and Assault as Predictors of PTSD Symptomotology among US Female Persian Gulf War Military Personnel," *Journal of Interpersonal Violence* 13, no. 1 (1998): 40–57; Han Kang and others, "The Role of Sexual Assault on the Risk of PTSD among Gulf War Veterans," *Annals of Epidemiology* 15, no. 1 (2005): 191–95.

116. Himmelfarb, Yaeger, and Mintz, "Posttraumatic Stress Disorder in Female Veterans with Military and Civilian Sexual Trauma" (see note 112); A. Suris and others, "Sexual Assault in Women Veterans: An Examination of PTSD Risk, Health Care Utilization, and Cost of Care," *Psychosomatic Medicine* 66, no. 5 (2004): 749–56.

117. Kimerling and others, "The Veterans Health Administration and Military Sexual Trauma" (see note 114).

118. Janice Laurence and Peter F. Ramsberger, *Low Aptitude Men in the Military* (New York: Praeger, 1991).

119. Ibid.

120. Ibid.

121. Marc N. Elliott, Lawrence M. Hanser, and Curtis L. Gilroy, "Evidence of Positive Student Outcomes in JROTC Career Academies" (www.rand.org/publications/MR/MR1200/MR1200.pdf [June 23, 2009]).

122. Remi Hajjar, "The Public Military High School: A Powerful Educational Possibility," *Armed Forces & Society* 32, no. 1 (2005): 44–62.

123. Dan Bloom, Alissa Gardenhire-Crooks, and Conrad Mandsager, "Reengaging High School Dropouts: Early Results of the National Guard Youth ChalleNGe Program Evaluation" (www.mdrc.org/publications/512/full.pdf [June 23, 2009]).

Vulnerable Populations and the Transition to Adulthood

D. Wayne Osgood, E. Michael Foster, and Mark E. Courtney

Summary

D. Wayne Osgood, E. Michael Foster, and Mark E. Courtney examine the transition to adulthood for youth involved in social service and justice systems during childhood and adolescence. They survey the challenges faced by youth in the mental health system, the foster care system, the juvenile justice system, the criminal justice system, and special education, and by youth with physical disabilities and chronic illness, as well as runaway and homeless youth.

One problem is that the services these vulnerable populations receive from these systems as children and adolescents often end abruptly as they transition to adulthood, even though the need for them continues. Youth must leave systems tailored for clients their age and, if they are eligible for further services at all, enter adult systems that are not equipped to address their needs. One exception is the special education system, whose services extend into early adulthood and are designed for individuals' needs.

The authors review current public policies directed toward vulnerable youth in transition and find problems in four areas: eligibility criteria that exclude youth from services that might benefit them, inadequate funding for transition services, a lack of coordination across service systems, and inadequate training about young-adult developmental issues for service professionals.

The authors then discuss policy options that can help create a developmentally appropriate and socially inclusive system of support for vulnerable youth. Among the options are strengthening all programs for youth in transition, improving the existing systems of care for children and adolescents, addressing the loss of access to services at the age of majority, and coordinating today's multiple systems into a single coherent system. The authors see heightened governmental interest in better supports for vulnerable young adults, both through expanding the federal role in their lives and through improving coordination of the systems that serve them. The Fostering Connections Act of 2008, for example, extended services to adolescents in foster care from the age of eighteen to the age of twenty-one.

www.futureofchildren.org

D. Wayne Osgood is a professor of crime, law, and justice and sociology at Pennsylvania State University. E. Michael Foster is a professor at the Gillings School of Global Public Health, University of North Carolina–Chapel Hill. Mark E. Courtney is a professor at the School of Social Work, University of Washington.

How an adolescent fares during the transition to adulthood has long-term repercussions. Earning a college degree leads to a higher-paying and more prestigious job, while early parenthood, unsuccessful marriage at a young age, and involvement in crime or problematic substance use all foretell difficulties in finances, family relationships, and beyond.[1] More than twenty years ago, the William T. Grant Foundation's influential report on *The Forgotten Half* demonstrated that non-college-bound youth have much poorer prospects for successful and satisfying adult lives than do college-bound youth.[2] In this article we focus on what the transition to adulthood means for youth who are considerably more vulnerable, as evidenced by their involvement in social service and justice systems during childhood and adolescence.[3] If the transition to adulthood is likely to be smooth for college-bound middle-class youth, but is often rough sledding for working-class non-college-bound youth, then it can be a minefield for such vulnerable populations.[4]

As Rick Settersten and Barbara Ray make clear in their article in this issue, moving into adulthood involves a long and often difficult transition in the United States and other industrialized nations in the West. The period after high school and well into the twenties has become a time of semi-autonomy during which youth typically remain dependent on their parents in many ways, not only financially, but also for help ranging from a place to live to extended child care. If the transition to adulthood is slow and arduous for a large share of the general population, how much harder must it be for young people who have spent years in the mental health or juvenile justice system or in foster care? The problems facing these groups as they transition to adulthood are critically important, to these youths and their families of course, but also to the public institutions that have evolved over time to address their special needs, and to the nation as a whole.

These vulnerable youth populations can be described in terms of the specific challenges they confront—their disabilities, for example, or their trauma histories—over and above those faced by young people generally. They can also be described with respect to the public systems that provide services to them, and often constrain their opportunities, before and during the transition to adulthood. Because vulnerable youth often face multiple challenges and are often served by multiple public systems, it is difficult to estimate precisely the size of the population as a whole, as well as to identify clear policy directions. We have chosen here to describe these youth in terms of the public systems with which they are involved. Although this approach has its limits, its strength is that it illuminates the challenge of how policy reform can help vulnerable youth move successfully into adulthood. We consider the transition to adulthood for seven populations, distinguished by their involvement in specific government systems: the mental health system, the foster care system, the juvenile justice system, the criminal justice system, special education, the health care system (for youth with physical disabilities and chronic illness), and (though these youth really have no comprehensive system of care) runaway and homeless youth.

At the outset, it is important to recognize that the diverse missions of the systems that provide services for vulnerable youth complicate the task of assisting the transition to adulthood. Some of the systems, notably foster care and juvenile justice, are custodial in nature, while others generally provide support to young people but do not take over parental responsibility. The foster care and juvenile justice systems are held legally accountable for the overall safety and well-being (for example, education and health) of youth in their care, though they often rely on other systems for assistance in carrying out these roles. In contrast, although they can provide crucial support to vulnerable youth, the health and special education systems are responsible for more specialized services targeting particular needs of young people. And although the juvenile and adult justice systems are responsible for meeting the needs of the populations they serve, they are also expected to play a role in ensuring public safety. The different missions of these custodial and non-custodial systems are not, at least in principle, in conflict with each other, but their distinct goals can get in the way of close collaboration.

Even if the transition to adulthood had not become so demanding, members of these vulnerable groups would face exceptional challenges finding employment, attending college, and marrying and starting a family. Many struggle with emotional or behavioral problems; many have histories of problems in school and the community. Often their families are unable or unwilling to provide the support that most families provide to their children during this transition—funding for college, child care that permits work or schooling for young parents, a place to live when times are hard. Some of these young adults are hampered by limited capacities and difficulty acquiring skills. The day-to-day tasks of achieving financial and residential independence can be daunting because of physical disabilities, chronic illness, or mental illness. And it has long been thought that involvement in the justice and foster care

systems may exacerbate the problems of some youth or carry a stigma that makes success less likely.[5]

It is important to recognize that the diverse missions of the systems that provide services for vulnerable youth complicate the task of assisting the transition to adulthood.

The difficulties that members of these groups encounter as children and adolescents lead all of them to depend on (or be entangled in) public systems, often for many years. But the transition to adulthood changes their established relationships with these systems, typically in dramatic ways. Reaching the age of eighteen or twenty-one may end eligibility for services, sometimes abruptly. The eligibility cutoffs are increasingly problematic because most other young people their age continue to depend on others and need support and training, often for many years. Only rarely, as with special education services and foster care, are programs already in place to smooth the transition to adulthood. More often, youth leave systems tailored for clients their age and, if they are eligible for further services at all, enter new systems that serve much older people and that are not equipped to address the special issues of young adulthood. Such changes in eligibility and in service systems pose important and complex issues for public policy.

The Challenges They Face
As noted, one reason to pay closer attention to these vulnerable populations is that the

lengthening transition to adulthood poses an even greater challenge for them than for other youth. Some of these vulnerable youth must accomplish tasks that other youth do not face. Whereas most young people begin the transition to adulthood from the security of their family's home, runaway and homeless youth and youth leaving foster care may have to find their own housing. Youth entangled with the juvenile or adult justice system may have to pay restitution or follow rules of probation or parole that restrict their activities. Physically disabled youth often must arrange medical services or assistive devices. Taking on these extra burdens makes it that much more difficult to get a college education or develop a strong romantic relationship that may lead to marriage.

Some of these populations have only limited ability to perform everyday tasks. Those with physical disabilities, for example, may have reduced strength and range of movement; youth in special education may have learning disabilities or cognitive impairments. Such limitations could preclude certain occupations or even rule out independent living without special assistance. Young adults with mental illness and behavioral problems could find it hard to meet the expectations of employers, friends, or romantic partners.

Deficiencies in family support—a common challenge for most of these vulnerable populations—are increasingly significant in the context of the lengthening transition to adulthood. Youth in the general population typically receive valuable support from their families, and even when they do not, they know it would be forthcoming were a special need to arise. Family financial support—in the form, say, of funding for a college education—is essential to the ability of middle-class families to put their children on a professional career track. Vulnerable youth often have poor relationships with their families, who themselves have limited economic resources. Youth in the juvenile justice system and in special education often come from poor, single-parent families.[6] Most problematic of course, are the limited (even absent) or negative relations with family commonly experienced by runaway and homeless youth and youth who have been living in foster care. The difficulty is not always a family's lack of motivation. In many cases parents and extended family of these youth strive to be supportive, but the cumulative demands of the long journey through childhood can sap parents' ability to take on the burdens of a longer transition to adulthood.

Changing and Narrowly Defined Eligibility for Service Systems

The services these vulnerable populations receive as children and adolescents often come to an end during the transition to adulthood, even if the need for them continues and even if current life circumstances present obvious difficulties. The government assumes different relationships with children than with adults and offers separate sets of service systems for the two groups. Because the government sees children as being dependent, it makes more services available to them and puts less restrictive eligibility criteria on them.

As adolescents move into adulthood, their program eligibility ends, sometimes abruptly and sometimes in phases. State-supported foster care, for instance, stops between ages eighteen and twenty-one, depending on the state, reflecting an outdated notion that the step from childhood dependence to adult independence is a simple one. Independence is, indeed, the appropriate goal, but the modern transition to adulthood is long and complex, and chances of success are much enhanced by continued support. More than ever, adolescents benefit from assuming responsibility gradually, while receiving continued guidance from concerned adults. After the difficulties that youth in foster care have faced earlier in life, their need for continuing assistance from adults is no doubt greater than that of most other youth. It is deeply problematic that, having assumed the role of parent during the teen years, the state refuses to play the important continuing role of parent during the next decade.

The services these vulnerable populations receive as children and adolescents often come to an end during the transition to adulthood, even if the need for them continues and even if current life circumstances present obvious difficulties.

In the special education system, by contrast, services extend into early adulthood and are tailored to individuals' needs. The federal Individuals with Disabilities Education Act (IDEA) requires secondary schools to begin developing individualized transition plans when students are fourteen. Each special education student must have a plan with long-term goals for education, vocational training, and general life skills, and that plan must specify the services needed to achieve these goals.

In some systems, reaching the age of majority brings drastic change. A stark example is the shift from the juvenile justice system to the adult criminal justice system. After reaching a state's age of majority (usually eighteen), youth who commit criminal offenses are no longer eligible for the juvenile justice system. Instead they move from the juvenile system, which views children as dependent and malleable and takes rehabilitation as at least its nominal goal, to the adult system, where the explicit goal is punishment.

In all these systems, the state assumes less responsibility for youth once they pass an age threshold beyond which they are no longer considered children. When they move across that arbitrary line and become adults, the systems that have been trying to meet their needs are no longer available. They either lose eligibility for assistance altogether or face a totally new set of eligibility requirements to enter systems with different missions. And when they *are* eligible for new services, adult-focused agencies rarely offer programs that address their specific developmental needs and rarely offer specialized training for staff toward this end. Continuing services for these vulnerable populations might not be necessary if government systems had prepared them fully for the transition to adulthood—and if the transition to well-paying jobs and early marriages were as smooth today as it was during the 1950s. No doubt some vulnerable youth still make that transition successfully, but for many others whose severe difficulties have kept them involved in these systems for years, success is highly unlikely.

That eligibility for assistance changes just as these youth begin the transition to adulthood is not the only problem with the eligibility criteria of these public programs. Each program is designed to respond to what is perceived to be a distinct need (such as disability or mental illness) or problem (such as crime), even though vulnerable young people do not fit neatly into such narrowly defined eligibility "boxes." Because public support systems for vulnerable youth have been designed around these categorical eligibility criteria, no one system is responsible for meeting the entire range of needs of the young people it serves, and each system uses its own eligibility criteria to engage in a process of gate-keeping that can deny youth access to services. For example, state child welfare and juvenile justice systems can be in conflict over which system should provide care for adolescents engaging in problematic behavior, and the way that conflict is resolved can have significant consequences for the kinds of services available to youth after reaching the age of majority.

Commonalities during the Transition to Adulthood

As these seven vulnerable groups struggle during the transition to adulthood to get work and to start families of their own, the particular profile of outcomes varies across the groups, but they share much in common.[7] One commonality is that males, the poor, and youth of color are over-represented in every group. Another is that youth in every group vary widely as to the seriousness and type of problem or need. A third commonality is population overlap—that is, that members of one group often belong to another group as well. A fourth is that members of every group have poor outcomes in many domains. And the final commonality is that in every group the factors that contribute to success are the same.

Over-Represented Groups

Vulnerable populations generally have a larger share of males, of youth from poor families, and of youth of color than does the general

population.[8] Young men are over-represented both because specific biological factors are relevant to certain disabilities and because higher rates of typically male behavior bring them into contact with a government system. For example, autism, a disability that leads to placement in special education, is more common among boys than girls.[9] And illegal behavior, which is far more common for males than females, brings contact with the juvenile and criminal justice systems.[10] Differences in behavior may also elicit reactions from within the service systems that lead to this over-representation. Teachers, social workers, and police, for example, may be more troubled by the disruptive behaviors more common among males than by the depressive symptoms more common for females.

Youth of color are also over-represented in each of the vulnerable populations. The criminal justice system incarcerates African American men at six times the rate of whites.[11] And youth with disabilities are twice as likely as youth in the general population to be African American.[12] The over-representation of minority group members is partly attributable to poverty, which is sometimes an eligibility factor (as with foster care) and sometimes a risk factor (as with poor mental health) for the problem targeted by the system. Poverty can also play a role in the decision-making process regarding entry to a system. A family's standing in the community and whether it has the resources to purchase private counseling, for example, may influence whether a school principal decides to allow a family to address its child's misbehavior or to turn the matter over to the police or social services.

It would be a serious mistake, however, to assume that all youth in these vulnerable populations are poor. Even the most advantaged families sometimes have children with serious problems. And these families' resources may help them to obtain public services when needed, as when middle-class parents obtain a private diagnosis and press the special education system to provide corresponding assistance. Even so, the rate of poverty is 50 percent higher among disabled youth than among other youth.[13]

Poverty is also important at the community level. Rates of crime and delinquency are high in poor neighborhoods, in part because of the absence of the strong ties among neighbors that could enable an effective response to anti-social behavior.[14] High crime rates in these areas enmesh more youth in the juvenile and criminal justice systems, and the resulting victimization and family disruption raise risks for mental health, family stability, and disability. Again, though, there are countervailing dynamics in resource-rich neighborhoods. For instance, because of the higher overall levels of safety and academic achievement in such neighborhoods, a youth's minor transgressions can result in arrests and struggling students are more likely to land in special education.

Diversity of the Populations

It is important to keep in mind that, although each vulnerable group is defined by a problem or need and a corresponding service system, its population is far from homogeneous. Instead, youth in each population vary greatly as to the seriousness and type of problem or need. The special education system, for example, covers youth with mental retardation as well as youth with emotional and behavioral problems. And this diversity in problems or needs may correspond to underlying population differences. For instance, childhood disadvantage and educational failure is more common among serious

and repeat offenders than among first-time offenders.[15] Both before and during the transition to adulthood, youth with different problems require different resources. Youth who are blind and youth with an orthopedic impairment require quite different services from the health system; likewise the mental health system must provide different services to those suffering from moderate depression and to those experiencing a serious thought disorder, such as schizophrenia.

Youth in these seven groups also differ in the age at which their vulnerability arises, a variation that has implications for how long they are involved with a particular system. Some youth enter foster care as infants; others, as teenagers. Usually, being in these vulnerable populations as young adults represents at least some continuity from adolescence, but exceptions exist. Some mental health problems, for example, typically appear in early adulthood, and young adults can become involved in the criminal justice system without having previously encountered the juvenile justice system.[16] Because research on the transition to adulthood is quite limited for most of these groups, much less is known about them as young adults than as children and adolescents.

Overlap among the Vulnerable Populations

Treating vulnerable youth as belonging to distinct groups is somewhat misleading, because the youth served by these different systems overlap to a large degree and in many different combinations. No good epidemiological data document how many youth are involved in more than one of these systems, but evidence shows that overlaps between specific pairs of systems are extensive. For instance, 35 percent of emotionally disturbed youth in special education are arrested as juveniles.[17]

One likely source of such overlaps is that the same risk factors, such as parental substance abuse, learning problems, and community disadvantage, dispose involvement in many of these systems. For instance, both incarcerated adolescents and foster youth typically have serious academic deficits, raising the likelihood of special education placement for both.[18]

Another source of overlap is the administrative links between the systems, with each sometimes referring youth to others. Special education and mental health professionals may refer youth to one another, and problems at school may lead administrators to call in justice personnel or child welfare. In some cases, one professional suspects a problem that falls into another professional's domain. In other cases, two different systems may provide services addressing the same problem, such as school assistance and outside counseling for an emotional disorder.

Yet another, and unfortunate, source of overlap is that involvement in one system may exacerbate other problems, thereby leading to contact with other systems. For instance, youth who come to the juvenile justice system with high rates of externalizing problems, such as violent behavior, often suffer as well from internalizing problems, such as anxiety and depression.[19] If the justice system removes a youth from friends and family to reside in a correctional facility, that experience could well exacerbate any internalizing problems and lead to contact with the mental health system. Similarly, the disruptions of moving into and out of hospitals, foster homes, and residential treatment facilities will disrupt learning and interfere with success at school, which has consequences not only for special education but also for delinquency.[20] In this vein, research has found

that removal from the home and multiple placements occasioned by spending time in foster care are also associated with increased criminal activity.[21]

Poor Outcomes in Many Domains
Regardless of the service system in which these youth find themselves, many experience poor outcomes across the major domains—education, employment, family formation—that mark the transition to adulthood.

Regardless of the service system in which these youth find themselves, many experience poor outcomes across the major domains that mark the transition to adulthood.

Members of all seven of these vulnerable groups fare poorly at completing high school and obtaining the postsecondary education critical to occupational and financial success in today's economy. One study finds that only 54 percent of youth discharged from foster care at age eighteen complete high school within 2.5 to 4 years, compared with 78 percent of same-age peers in the general population.[22] Limited education is particularly striking among young adults who have been incarcerated as either juveniles or adults, with studies reporting that fewer than 20 percent have diplomas or GEDs.[23] Similarly, fewer than 15 percent of homeless youth over age eighteen have high school diplomas.[24] Educational deficits are genuine but less dramatic for some other groups such as young adults who were in special education, youth with mental health problems, and youth with physical disabilities.[25] Even so, education is often severely limited among the members of these groups whose problems are more serious. For instance, young adults with multiple physical disabilities have only a one in twelve chance of completing a higher education.[26] Although data on rates of college attendance generally are more scarce, rates appear to be remarkably low for all vulnerable groups. By age twenty, less than 10 percent of former foster youth have attended college.[27]

One of the primary tasks of the transition to adulthood—to begin full-time employment with the aim of achieving financial independence—proves a greater challenge for all of these vulnerable groups than for the general population. Again, the differences are moderate for some groups, more stark for others. For instance, 57 percent of youth from special education have full-time employment three to five years after high school, compared with 69 percent for other youth.[28] But only about one-third of homeless youth are employed full-time.[29] As with education, consequences can be more extreme for youth with more serious problems: 39 percent of young adults aged eighteen to thirty with serious physical disabilities are in the labor force, compared with 72 percent of those with mild disabilities and 79 percent of the general population.[30]

The combination of limited education and employment has understandable consequences for the living circumstances of the vulnerable groups. Research on this topic for former foster youth, homeless youth, and young adults involved in the juvenile justice system shows that all are likely to live below the poverty level, to have trouble paying bills and other expenses, and to depend on public

assistance.[31] The nature of the problems that arise also depends on a group's particular challenges and life histories. For instance, former foster youth and homeless youth have high rates of homelessness and unstable living situations, and establishing an independent household is especially problematic for young adults with physical disabilities or mental retardation.[32]

Rates of marriage do not appear to differ much between the vulnerable groups and the general population.[33] Perhaps this similarity between the two groups should not be surprising given the low rates of marriage among all young adults today, a reflection of combined trends toward later marriage among the highly educated and toward lower lifetime marriage rates in some disadvantaged groups.[34]

A more distinctive feature of family formation for the vulnerable populations is high rates of parenthood, especially outside of marriage. For instance, about a third of female former foster youth are raising children on their own by age twenty-one.[35] Similarly, half of young women diagnosed with learning disabilities or emotional disturbances are mothers three to five years after they finish high school, compared with less than one-third of the general population.[36] More than a quarter of young women involved in the mental health system experience unplanned pregnancies, compared with less than 10 percent of the general population.[37] Taken together with the other difficulties of the vulnerable groups, these high rates of parenthood pose serious problems. A large share of women who had been in foster care, for example, reported that their children suffered from health, education, or behavioral problems, or had been removed from their homes.[38] Members of these vulnerable groups also engage in more high-risk sexual activity, as reflected in the number of partners and sexually transmitted diseases, and they are more often subjected to sexual victimization.[39]

Other impediments block the path toward adulthood. Some obstacles are simply continuations of earlier problems, such as criminal behavior by young adults who had been involved in the juvenile justice system and mental disorders among young adults with mental health problems as adolescents.[40] But most of these populations also face a wide variety of new problems. For instance, young adults formerly involved in the foster care, special education, and mental health systems have high rates of criminal behavior;[41] those formerly involved in the foster care and juvenile justice systems have elevated rates of mental health problems;[42] and almost all the vulnerable groups have high rates of substance use.[43]

Factors Contributing to Success

Despite their vulnerabilities, many youth in all of the populations achieve at least a basic level of self-sufficiency, and some go on to reach more substantial success. Those who succeed tend to be characterized by resilience—the ability to surmount difficulties and to recover quickly from stressful events or mishaps.[44] The resources that contribute to resilience come in many forms, from individuals' skills and personality, to supportive relationships with other people, to involvement in groups like churches and clubs. The more researchers can learn about these sources of resilience, the more they can strengthen social policy by showing how government assistance can enable people to do the most for themselves. A hallmark of policies based on resilience is an emphasis on youth taking an active role in creating their own success—a counter to the notion that social programs take away from individual responsibility.

Research has also begun to identify other factors that promote success in the transition to adulthood. One is success at school. Not only is school success a positive outcome in its own right, but it is a valuable resource that enhances success in many domains, particularly employment, which places an ever-increasing premium on education. Support from family and friends is a second common protective factor, as would be expected given all young adults' need for support from others during today's extended transition to adulthood. For example, research has found healthy interpersonal relationships valuable in helping juvenile offenders desist from crime.[45] Similarly, healthy interpersonal relationships characterize the successful youth who leave residential treatment facilities.[46] Certain personality traits, such as persistence and confidence, also enable some vulnerable youth to make a successful transition to adulthood.[47]

Four Policy Challenges

A review of current public policies directed toward vulnerable youth in transition reveals problems in four areas.[48] First, eligibility criteria exclude youth from services that might benefit them; second, funding for transition services is inadequate; third, lack of coordination across service systems hampers appropriate service delivery; and, finally, many service professionals lack training in developmental issues for young adults.

Eligibility criteria often prevent needy youth from using the services that *are* available. For instance, before recent changes in federal policy, transition services that were available to youth in foster care were quite limited for those who left care before aging out.[49] A youth who spends several years in foster care before being adopted at age fourteen may well benefit from transition services as much as a youth who ages out. Such inconsistency works against other goals of the child welfare system—in this case, although adoption is encouraged by public policy, it penalizes youths in terms of their long-term prospects. Similarly the juvenile justice system offers after-care and support only to youth placed in residential settings, not to those on parole.[50] Placement on parole may reflect a range of policies determined by the attitudes of judges or the local community, attitudes that may have little to do with a youth's need for assistance in making the transition to adulthood.

Overall service delivery is hampered by limited funding in relation to the actual need.[51] For example, although the federal government gives states $140 million a year to help prepare foster youth for the transition to adulthood, that total translates into very little per youth. Even if the states allocated all of that funding to services for the approximately 25,000 youth who exit foster care each year to legal emancipation, the share going to each former foster youth between eighteen and twenty-one would be less than $2,000. Because there are no age restrictions on the use of these funds and because states often target youth sixteen and older, the actual amount spent per youth is undoubtedly even less.

A third policy challenge is that the service systems operate independently and almost in isolation from each other. They rarely even communicate except regarding specific youth, and sometimes not even then. The lack of communication reflects narrow federal eligibility criteria that also make it hard for local government and private-sector service providers to aggregate funding across sources, leading to gaps in, and duplication

of, services. For instance, in many communities youth in the juvenile justice system have no way to obtain mental health services. Service delivery is also hampered because the child- and adult-serving systems operate independently of each other. Youth entering adulthood encounter entirely new systems, such as vocational rehabilitation, and typically there is little communication even between child and adult arms of the same systems.

The attitudes and training of service providers pose the final policy challenge. Even if the relevant agencies and departments were to work well together in a given community, young adults might still have trouble finding providers who are aware of their age-specific needs, much less trained to address them. Research has demonstrated, for example, that medical providers are ill-prepared (or even unwilling) to discuss issues of sexuality with adolescents with disabilities.[52] Another developmental issue facing medical personnel for patients of this age is the youths' increased rights to privacy on reaching the age of majority. The law provides young adults with important privacy rights, though their families usually remain important in their lives, and medical professionals typically do not know how to explore ways that families might provide support.

Policy Options
We believe that the United States needs a developmentally appropriate and socially inclusive system of support for vulnerable youth in transition to adulthood. In this section we touch on the broad theme of social inclusion and then turn to five policy options that can help create such a system. These options involve a mix of specific reforms in the public systems involved as well as broad policies that would pertain to all youth making the transition.

Vulnerable populations deserve special attention during the transition to adulthood not only because they have more trouble meeting life's challenges than their peers but because all young adults are facing especially big hurdles today. The public programs and entitlements that vulnerable youth receive during childhood and adolescence are the nation's explicit acknowledgment of their special needs, and similar supports should be available as they make their way into adulthood. Such supports should not, however, be viewed as perpetuating a helpless dependence, but as enabling them to shape their own future.

The fundamental principle of social inclusion is that a democratic society benefits when all its members participate in the full range of community affairs. Viewing vulnerable populations from the perspective of social inclusion shifts the focus from the personal difficulties or limitations of the populations to society's portrayal of and treatment of them. This broader perspective calls for identifying policies and practices that exclude or alienate certain groups from the larger community. It also entails themes of agency, rights, and power for vulnerable groups to act on their own behalf; of reciprocity among individuals, groups, and the state; and of affection and obligation among all parties. Social policies that follow from the concept of social inclusion enhance opportunities where they are lacking and remove barriers to the full participation of some groups.

From the social inclusion perspective, the reason for meeting the needs of vulnerable groups is not simply to improve their lives, but to help them to become fully contributing members of society and thereby to benefit the lives of all. Vulnerable youth have a good chance of making a successful transition to adulthood if society provides the supports that suit their circumstances. For the general population of youth, today's longer and more uncertain transition to adulthood requires increasing supports from their families and the higher education system. The vulnerable populations lack comparable supports that would enable them to participate more fully as citizens. More effective public policies for this group are thus a means for social inclusion.

The policies a society adopts send messages about the relationships between citizens and the state, about who counts and whose voice should be heard. The eligibility cutoffs that deprive these vulnerable populations of services as they make the transition to adulthood carry the message "You're on your own."[53] The services that *are* available to them usually apply to some category of deficiency, such as mental illness, and are likely to carry stigmas.[54] Gaining access to services should not require overcoming a tangle of bureaucratic webs, and the services available should be suited to young adults' developmental needs and competencies.

To reach the goal of a socially inclusive support system for vulnerable youth, we recommend five policy options. The first embraces steps that would help all youth, such as better curriculum and support services at community colleges, universal health care, and a higher minimum wage.[55] As youth in vulnerable populations move toward adulthood, they face the same difficulties as other youth, but with fewer resources and skills. Any policy steps that can reduce the difficulties that all youth face will be especially valuable to the vulnerable youth.

A second option would be to improve the existing systems of care for children and adolescents. Services and policies that better meet their needs as children and teens would prepare them more effectively for key life tasks of the transition. First and foremost, the systems of care must minimize the damage they do to those they serve. No doubt any damage they do is unintentional, and it is difficult to distinguish such damage from the very problems that bring youth into these systems in the first place. Even so, the systems sometimes interfere with, rather than aid, the development of those in their care, as when youth experience unstable placements in the child welfare system or become victims of violence in the juvenile justice system. All practitioners involved in social services have struggled with this daunting problem for decades, but it must be addressed.

A third option that would broadly benefit vulnerable youth would be to address the loss of access to programs and services at, or too soon after, the age of majority. Abundant evidence confirms that the difficulties these populations experience during childhood and adolescence have continuing consequences as they transition to adulthood. The heavy dependence of most of today's young adults on their families makes it clear that the need for public investment in the vulnerable populations does not end at age eighteen. Extending the age eligibility of youth-serving systems well into young adulthood would be consistent with normative transitions to adulthood nowadays. And because the life circumstances and developmental needs of early adulthood differ from those of adolescence, policies and practices must be tailored to this age period.

The fourth policy strategy would be to move from a set of independent systems to a single, integrated system. Integration is needed not only across service systems, but also between youth and adult systems. Integration is also needed at two levels—at the administrative level, to coordinate eligibility and financing, and at the service level, to ensure that clients receive a non-redundant and comprehensive set of services in an efficient manner. Integration would also have to bridge the differing cultures of current systems. For instance, many juvenile justice personnel see their mission as protecting the community rather than providing service to youth.[56]

Viewing vulnerable populations from the perspective of social inclusion shifts the focus from the personal difficulties or limitations of the populations to society's portrayal of and treatment of them.

The final policy option that would improve both child and adult service systems is to shift to a family focus. Such a focus would recognize the diversity of the clients served and increase the involvement of parties most prominent in youths' lives. Like other youth today, these vulnerable populations remain closely tied to and rather dependent on their families, even when those families are dysfunctional. For example, most youth leaving the foster care system continue to have contact with their families of origin.[57]

Because a system that better recognizes and then meets the needs of its clients may deliver more services, funding will pose a challenge. The critical questions are how much is society willing to invest in vulnerable populations during the transition to adulthood, and what would be the most effective use of such an investment? Fortunately, there is growing interest at the national and state level in developing policy directed toward better supporting vulnerable youth making the transition to adulthood.

Recent Federal Policy Developments

Washington's heightened interest in improving supports for vulnerable young adults is evident both in moves to expand the federal role in the lives of these youths and in efforts to improve coordination of the systems that serve them.

The Fostering Connections Act of 2008 provides a compelling example of a shift in U.S. social policy toward a socially inclusive approach to a vulnerable population of youth in transition. The law amends Title IV-E of the Social Security Act to allow states, at their option, to care for and support foster youth until the age of twenty-one provided that the youth are engaged in one of four activities—completing high school or an equivalency program, attending postsecondary or vocational school, participating in a vocational program, working for at least eighty hours a month—or are incapable of these activities because of a medical condition. Young people aged eighteen and older can be living independently in a supervised setting as well as placed in a foster home or group care setting.

The Fostering Connections Act marks a philosophical shift toward acknowledging continuing state responsibility to act *in loco parentis* for foster youth into early adulthood. The title of the law implies a shift from encouraging youth to be independent (the language used in earlier policy directed toward foster youth in transition) toward helping them make the connections they will

need to be successful adults. The law's provisions stress that state-supervised out-of-home care for young adults ought to differ in significant ways from care provided to minors. States must, for example, engage these young adults in activities that are developmentally appropriate (for example, higher education and employment) and must create more developmentally appropriate care settings for young adults (for example, supervised independent living arrangements).

The new federal law gives states entitlement funding to provide transition-age youth with basic necessities and case management services, thus providing a foundation on which states can build a range of supports. Although many states have policies, at least on paper, that call for providing independent living services through age twenty-one, the poor economic circumstances of youth who leave foster care and the resulting instability of their living arrangements arguably undermine efforts to engage these young people in services. The ability to use Title IV-E funds to stably house foster youth between eighteen and twenty-one may allow states to better engage youth in other services available from child welfare agencies. Giving state child welfare agencies IV-E funding to continue providing case management beyond age eighteen may also help these agencies play the coordinating role that is necessary to help young people navigate the various public systems charged with assisting them—postsecondary education, workforce development, health and mental health services, and housing.

It is too soon to know whether the Fostering Connections Act will lead to the improved adult outcomes for foster youth envisioned by its sponsors, particularly because it provides support only to age twenty-one. Moreover, foster youth make up only a small proportion of all vulnerable youth. However, the foster youth population exhibits all of the challenges that characterize vulnerable youth in transition. If the comprehensive array of support provided by the new law is shown to significantly improve the transition to adulthood for foster youth, states may be encouraged to provide more support to other populations of vulnerable youth.

Perhaps the most important example of federal efforts to improve coordination between the systems that serve vulnerable youth is the Shared Youth Vision Initiative.[58] It began as a cross-agency partnership formed in response to the 2003 White House Task Force Report on Disadvantaged Youth, which identified the need to integrate systems at the federal, state, and local levels to move vulnerable youth into adulthood. In 2004, the Department of Labor formed a Shared Youth Vision partnership with the Departments of Education, Health and Human Services, and Justice. Since its inception, the partnership has engaged thirty states in planning, and the states now have formally established Shared Youth Vision teams. Nine federal agencies (Defense, Education, Health and Human Services, Housing and Urban Development, Justice, Labor, Social Security Administration, Transportation, and the Corporation for National and Community Service) are involved, and the partnership provides technical assistance, capacity building, and peer-to-peer support. Planning grants have been awarded to sixteen pilot states to provide more intensive and targeted support in advancing the initiative's concepts and implementation.

The Shared Youth Vision effort has led to a wide array of promising state- and local-level collaborations between youth- and adult-serving systems. For example, in the Arizona collaboration, several state and local youth-serving agencies provide coordinated support to youth transitioning from the child welfare and juvenile justice systems in two counties. The goal is to strengthen partnerships with local educational entities and employers to prepare, employ, and retain young people transitioning from care into employment. Alabama's project serves youth in the child welfare and juvenile justice systems, as well as youth with disabilities, out-of-school youth and dropouts, and youth living in poverty. High-level professional staff, representing each of the several state agencies involved, meet regularly to address inter-agency frictions, budget cuts, and turf battles. The project targets eight counties that make up one of the state's administrative regions. Four Alabama Career (One-Stop) Centers in the region lead the initiative at the local level. Although the Shared Youth Vision initiative has supported a variety of state initiatives, the effectiveness of these efforts in improving outcomes for vulnerable youth has yet to be evaluated.

Moreover, although the initiative is a promising start in cross-system coordination and collaboration, the categorical nature of federal program eligibility and funding is likely to remain a serious obstacle to creating a socially inclusive and developmentally appropriate system of support for vulnerable youth in transition to adulthood. For example, youth served by the juvenile justice and child welfare systems are often housed in the same group care and therapeutic foster care placement settings, but juvenile justice youth who do not meet criteria for Title IV-E funding are not eligible for many transition services available to foster youth, thus complicating the task of providing services in the homes of many young people.

Creative use of waivers of federal funding requirements could offer opportunities for Shared Youth Vision pilot states to experiment with more flexible and comprehensive approaches to providing services to the broad population of vulnerable youth. For example, Title IV-E funding can be used only for room and board for those in child welfare. Waivers, however, could allow some of those funds to be used for mental health services. Similar federal waivers, in combination with rigorous evaluation research, have been used effectively in identifying promising approaches to moving parents from welfare to work, in reforming Medicaid, and in identifying strategies for moving children out of long-term foster care.

Researchers have not yet provided either comprehensive, representative descriptions of the populations or systematic information about how they fare during the transition to adulthood.

Research Needs

Another requirement for developing more effective support for vulnerable youth in transition is more and better research. With a few notable exceptions, such as the National Longitudinal Transition Studies in special education, data on these populations, especially during the transition to adulthood, are limited. Researchers have not yet provided either comprehensive, representative descriptions of the populations or systematic information about how they fare during the

transition to adulthood. And though promising directions for policy and practice are being identified, few interventions have been tested empirically. For the most part, our policy recommendations reflect common sense and matters of fairness and justice, rather than strong evidence. Certainly policies should be logical and ethical, but they must also be based on detailed and accurate analyses of the problems to be addressed and on empirical tests of how well alternative strategies work.

Top research priorities include identifying which youth are in greatest need and which would benefit most from transition programs. The two groups likely overlap in terms of race, gender, and many other characteristics, but whether and how they do is unknown. This issue is critical given the heterogeneity of the populations served and the shortage of funds overall. Quite likely some youth need much more help than others to succeed, and different youth need different types of help. The lack of knowledge about these differing needs is especially problematic because it makes it extremely difficult to target the limited resources available for such help.

Administrative data represent a potential resource to help identify the size of the vulnerable youth population, its involvement over time in various public systems, and important transition outcomes for the population. Developments in information technology are allowing states to develop databases that offer more accurate and more comprehensive information on individuals' needs for services and history of involvement with the systems. These data sources can be linked across systems to identify individuals who have been involved in multiple systems, perhaps signaling greater need for services. Linked administrative data can also help identify youths' trajectories through various systems, identifying potential gaps in services and opportunities to target interventions. Many outcomes of interest during the transition to adulthood, such as employment, college enrollment and degree completion, crime, and receipt of public assistance, can be monitored using administrative data.[59]

Such data also provide an opportunity to understand innovative practices as they occur. States and localities exercise considerable autonomy in operating systems for vulnerable youth, leading to variation in the programs and policies implemented. That variation provides a learning opportunity for researchers who can systematically describe these policy and program variations across jurisdictions.[60] Linking data on program and policies, system involvement, and outcomes can provide an opportunity to determine which programs and policies are linked to better outcomes.

Endnotes

1. Zeng-Yin Chen and Howard B. Kaplan, "School Failure in Early Adolescence and Status Attainment in Middle Adulthood: A Longitudinal Study," *Sociology of Education* 76 (2003): 110–27; Andrew Cherlin, *Marriage, Divorce, and Remarriage* (Harvard University Press, 1992); Alan C. Kerckhoff, Stephen W. Raudenbush, and Elizabeth Glennie, "Education, Cognitive Skill, and Labor Force Outcomes," *Sociology of Education* 74 (2001): 1–24; Sara McLanahan and Karen Booth, "Mother-Only Families: Problems, Prospects, and Policies," *Journal of Marriage and Family* 51 (1989): 557–80; Michael D. Newcomb and Peter M. Bentler, *Consequences of Adolescent Drug Use: Impact on the Lives of Young Adults* (Newbury Park, Calif.: Sage, 1989).

2. William T. Grant Foundation Commission on Work, Family, and Citizenship, *The Forgotten Half: Non-College Youth in America: An Interim Report on the School-to-Work Transition* (William T. Grant Foundation Commission on Work, Family, and Citizenship, 1988).

3. In this article we summarize and extend the volume on this topic titled *On Your Own without a Net: The Transition to Adulthood for Vulnerable Populations*, edited by D. Wayne Osgood and others (University of Chicago Press, 2005), which was sponsored by the MacArthur Foundation's Network on Transitions to Adulthood. The aims of that volume were to identify the challenges facing groups for whom the long process of becoming an adult is likely to be most difficult and to bring attention to the special policy issues concerning them that arise during this period.

4. Ibid.

5. Mark E. Courtney and Darcy Hughes Heuring, "The Transition to Adulthood for Youth 'Aging Out' of the Foster Care System," in *On Your Own without a Net*, edited by Osgood and others (see note 3), pp. 27–67; D. Wayne Osgood and Laine O'Neill Briddell, "Peer Effects in Juvenile Justice," in *Deviant by Design: Interventions and Policies That Aggregate Deviant Youth, and Strategies to Optimize Outcomes*, edited by K. Dodge, T. Dishion, and J. Lansford (New York: Guilford Press, 2006), pp. 141–61; Devah Pager, "The Mark of a Criminal Record," *American Journal of Sociology* 108 (2003): 937–75.

6. E. Michael Foster and Elizabeth J. Gifford, "Developmental and Administrative Transitions for Special Populations: Policies, Outcomes, and Research Challenges," in *On the Frontier of Adulthood: Theory, Research, and Public Policy*, edited by Richard A. Settersten Jr., Frank F. Furstenberg Jr., and Rubén G. Rumbaut (University of Chicago Press, 2005), pp. 501–33.

7. Osgood and others, eds., *On Your Own without a Net* (see note 3).

8. E. Michael Foster and others, "The Transition to Adulthood for Vulnerable Youth and Families: Common Themes and Future Directions," in *On Your Own without a Net*, edited by Osgood and others (see note 3), pp. 375–90.

9. Phyllis Levine and Mary Wagner, "Transition for Young Adults Who Received Special Education Services as Adolescents: A Time of Challenge and Change," in *On Your Own without a Net*, edited by Osgood and others (see note 3), pp. 202–58.

10. Terrie E. Moffitt and others, *Sex Differences in Antisocial Behaviour: Conduct Disorder, Delinquency, and Violence in the Dunedin Longitudinal Study* (Cambridge University Press, 2001); John T. Whitehead and Steven P. Lab, *Juvenile Justice: An Introduction*, 2nd ed. (Cincinnati, Ohio: Anderson Publishing, 1996).

11. Christopher Uggen and Sara Wakefield, "Young Adults Reentering the Community from the Criminal Justice System: The Challenge of Becoming an Adult," in *On Your Own without a Net*, edited by Osgood and others (see note 3), pp. 114–44.

12. Robert W. Blum, "Adolescents with Disabilities in Transition to Adulthood," in *On Your Own without a Net*, edited by Osgood and others (see note 3), pp. 323–48.

13. Levine and Wagner, "Transition for Young Adults Who Received Special Education Services as Adolescents" (see note 9).

14. Robert J. Sampson, Stephen W. Raudenbush, and Felton Earls, "Neighborhoods and Violent Crime: A Multilevel Study of Collective Efficacy," *Science* 277 (1997): 918–24.

15. Uggen and Wakefield, "Young Adults Reentering the Community from the Criminal Justice System: The Challenge of Becoming an Adult" (see note 11).

16. Phillip M. Lyons Jr. and Gary B. Melton, "Coping with Mental Health Problems in Young Adulthood: Diversity of Need and Uniformity of Programs," in *On Your Own without a Net*, edited by Osgood and others (see note 3), pp. 304–22; Elaine P. Eggleston and John H. Laub, "The Onset of Adult Offending: A Neglected Dimension of the Criminal Career," *Journal of Criminal Justice* 30 (2002): 603–22.

17. Levine and Wagner, "Transition for Young Adults Who Received Special Education Services as Adolescents" (see note 9).

18. He Len Chung, Michelle Little, and Laurence Steinberg, "The Transition to Adulthood for Adolescents in the Juvenile Justice System: A Developmental Perspective," in *On Your Own without a Net*, edited by Osgood and others (see note 3), pp. 68–91; Mark E. Courtney and others, *Midwest Evaluation of the Adult Functioning of Former Foster Youth: Outcomes at Age 21* (Chicago: Chapin Hall Center for Children at the University of Chicago, 2007).

19. Chung and others, "The Transition to Adulthood for Adolescents in the Juvenile Justice System" (see note 18).

20. Travis Hirschi, *Causes of Delinquency* (University of California Press, 1969).

21. Courtney and Hughes Heuring, "The Transition to Adulthood for Youth 'Aging Out' of the Foster Care System" (see note 5).

22. Ibid.

23. Chung and others, "The Transition to Adulthood for Adolescents in the Juvenile Justice System" (see note 18); Uggen and Wakefield, "Young Adults Reentering the Community from the Criminal Justice System" (see note 11).

24. John Hagan and Bill McCarthy, "Homeless Youth and the Perilous Passage to Adulthood," in *On Your Own without a Net*, edited by Osgood and others (see note 3), pp. 178–201.

25. Levine and Wagner, "Transition for Young Adults Who Received Special Education Services as Adolescents" (see note 9); Blum, "Adolescents with Disabilities in Transition to Adulthood" (see note 12).

26. Blum, "Adolescents with Disabilities in Transition to Adulthood" (see note 12).

27. Courtney and Hughes Heuring, "The Transition to Adulthood for Youth 'Aging Out' of the Foster Care System" (see note 5).

28. Levine and Wagner, "Transition for Young Adults Who Received Special Education Services as Adolescents" (see note 9).

29. Hagan and McCarthy, "Homeless Youth and the Perilous Passage to Adulthood" (see note 24).

30. Blum, "Adolescents with Disabilities in Transition to Adulthood" (see note 12).

31. Courtney and Hughes Heuring, "The Transition to Adulthood for Youth 'Aging Out' of the Foster Care System" (see note 5); Hagan and McCarthy, "Homeless Youth and the Perilous Passage to Adulthood" (see note 24); Chung and others, "The Transition to Adulthood for Adolescents in the Juvenile Justice System" (see note 18).

32. Courtney and Hughes Heuring, "The Transition to Adulthood for Youth 'Aging Out' of the Foster Care System" (see note 5); Hagan and McCarthy, "Homeless Youth and the Perilous Passage to Adulthood" (see note 24); Levine and Wagner, "Transition for Young Adults Who Received Special Education Services as Adolescents" (see note 9); Blum, "Adolescents with Disabilities in Transition to Adulthood" (see note 12).

33. Osgood and others, eds., *On Your Own without a Net* (see note 3).

34. Elizabeth Fussell and Frank F. Furstenberg Jr., "The Transition to Adulthood in the Twentieth Century: Race, Nativity, and Gender," in *On the Frontier of Adulthood: Theory, Research, and Public Policy*, edited by Richard A. Settersten Jr. and others (University of Chicago Press, 2005), pp. 29–75.

35. Courtney and Hughes Heuring, "The Transition to Adulthood for Youth 'Aging Out' of the Foster Care System" (see note 5).

36. Levine and Wagner, "Transition for Young Adults Who Received Special Education Services as Adolescents" (see note 9).

37. J. Heidi Gralinski-Baker and others, "Risks along the Road to Adulthood: Challenges Faced by Youth with Serious Mental Disorders," in *On Your Own without a Net*, edited by Osgood and others (see note 3), pp. 272–303.

38. Courtney and Hughes Heuring, "The Transition to Adulthood for Youth 'Aging Out' of the Foster Care System" (see note 5).

39. Ibid.; Hagan and McCarthy, "Homeless Youth and the Perilous Passage to Adulthood" (see note 24); Chung and others, "The Transition to Adulthood for Adolescents in the Juvenile Justice System" (see note 18).

40. Chung and others, "The Transition to Adulthood for Adolescents in the Juvenile Justice System" (see note 18); Gralinski-Baker and others, "Risks along the Road to Adulthood: Challenges Faced by Youth with Serious Mental Disorders" (see note 37).

41. Courtney and Hughes Heuring, "The Transition to Adulthood for Youth 'Aging Out' of the Foster Care System" (see note 5); Levine and Wagner, "Transition for Young Adults Who Received Special Education Services as Adolescents" (see note 9).

42. Courtney and Hughes Heuring, "The Transition to Adulthood for Youth 'Aging Out' of the Foster Care System" (see note 5); Chung and others, "The Transition to Adulthood for Adolescents in the Juvenile Justice System" (see note 18).

43. Osgood and others, eds., *On Your Own without a Net* (see note 3).

44. Stuart T. Hauser, "Understanding Resilient Outcomes: Adolescent Lives Across Time and Generations," *Journal of Research on Adolescence* 9 (1999): 1–24.

45. Chung and others, "The Transition to Adulthood for Adolescents in the Juvenile Justice System" (see note 18).

46. Gralinski-Baker and others, "Risks along the Road to Adulthood: Challenges Faced by Youth with Serious Mental Disorders" (see note 37).

47. Ibid.

48. Osgood and others, eds., *On Your Own without a Net* (see note 3).

49. Courtney and Hughes Heuring, "The Transition to Adulthood for Youth 'Aging Out' of the Foster Care System" (see note 5).

50. David M. Altschuler, "Policy and Program Perspectives on the Transition to Adulthood for Adolescents in the Juvenile Justice System," in *On Your Own without a Net*, edited by Osgood and others (see note 3), pp. 92–113.

51. Altschuler, "Policy and Program Perspectives on the Transition to Adulthood for Adolescents in the Juvenile Justice System" (see note 50);" Courtney and Hughes Heuring, "The Transition to Adulthood for Youth 'Aging Out' of the Foster Care System" (see note 5).

52. Blum, "Adolescents with Disabilities in Transition to Adulthood" (see note 12).

53. Thus the title of the volume on which this article is based, *On Your Own without a Net*, edited by Osgood and others (see note 3).

54. Lyons and Melton, "Coping with Mental Health Problems in Young Adulthood" (see note 16).

55. Richard A. Settersten Jr., "Social Policy and the Transition to Adulthood: Toward Stronger Institutions and Individual Capacities," in *On the Frontier of Adulthood: Theory, Research, and Public Policy*, edited by Richard A. Settersten Jr. and others (University of Chicago Press, 2005), pp. 534–60.

56. Altschuler, "Policy and Program Perspectives on the Transition to Adulthood for Adolescents in the Juvenile Justice System" (see note 50).

57. Courtney and Hughes Heuring, "The Transition to Adulthood for Youth 'Aging Out' of the Foster Care System" (see note 5).

58. Abt Associates, *Common Sense, Uncommon Commitment: A Progress Report on the Shared Youth Vision Partnership* (Washington: U.S. Department of Labor, 2009).

59. Foster and others, "The Transition to Adulthood for Vulnerable Youth and Families: Common Themes and Future Directions" (see note 8).

60. See, for example, A. Dworsky and J. Havlicek, *Review of State Policies and Programs to Support Young People Transitioning out of Foster Care* (Chicago: Chapin Hall at the University of Chicago, 2009).